To Carey Bob
from
Dad,
Christmas, 1931.

Thomas A. Edison.

THOMAS · A · EDISON
··· BENEFACTOR · OF · MANKIND ···

The Romantic Life Story of the
World's Greatest Inventor

BY
FRANCIS TREVELYAN MILLER, LL.D., Litt.D.
Author of "The World's Great Adventure," "Portrait Life of
Lincoln," "The World in the Air," etc., etc.

Illustrated

Edison   Printed in the U. S. A.

FOREWORD

THIS book is presented as the dramatic life story of the man who "transformed the world" — an inspiring romance of industry, perseverance, and epoch-making achievement. It has the distinguished privilege of being the first standard life of Thomas A. Edison with an historian's estimate of his *completed* labors as the "Benefactor of Mankind." To fix his historical position and establish the value of his life work for humanity, we have placed behind him the background of the times in which he moved and the world events which were taking place, thus allowing the reader to estimate how great a factor he was in human progress.

This book, therefore, portrays the foundations of modern civilization, with full credit given to the generations of scientists and inventors who preceded Thomas Edison and blazed the trail for his epochal achievements. This plan further allows us to establish his position not only as an inventor, but as one of the world's greatest scientists — a man of creative imagination and genius who made his discoveries in scientific research and then materialized them for practical service to all mankind.

The investigations herein recorded required twelve years of labor with world-wide research by an able staff of authorities, which awaited the end of Edison's remarkable career to bring them to a climax in this stirring and inspiring narrative now given to the world six weeks after his death.

We wish to acknowledge our indebtedness to the hundreds of authorities who have assisted in making this work

(3)

possible. The mass of materials, documents, and records, would make a library in themselves. Edison left behind him in his private archives probably more than 300,000 entries in his own handwriting, with instructions, as we note herein, for "one hundred years in the future." It has been our duty to assay the materials in public libraries, contemporary records in the public press, and straighten out contradictions as well as to settle disputes, even to the extent of dates, facts, and figures.

This service has been rendered by the coöperation of statistical organizations connected with the great industries which were founded on Edison's life work. These economists come to their first agreement in this book that the property values created in the United States alone by Edison's basic patents exceed $25,000,000,000. Researches in the Patent Office at Washington further fix the number of patents actually granted to Edison at 1099 — with foreign patents in thirty-four countries, applications and caveats, bringing the records of experimental inventions and patents up to an estimate of 3,000. This figure is confirmed by Edison's patent attorneys.

We are further indebted in our efforts to establish historical facts to the Edison Pioneers, whose records are given herein; to the Smithsonian Institution and the British Museum and the Electrical Institutes of the various countries; to the Edison Industries at West Orange, and the workers in the Edison Laboratories; to John V. Miller, brother-in-law and coworker with Edison for his valuable advice and access to records in the Edison home; to William H. Meadowcroft, for fifty-two years confidential secretary to Thomas A. Edison; to Arthur J. Walsh, vice president of Thomas A. Edison, Incorporated; to Frank A. Wardlaw, secretary of the Edison Pioneers;

to Joseph Wheelan, official photographer at the Edison Laboratories.

Acknowledgment is made to Charles Edison, son of Thomas Edison, and Mr. Walsh, for the rights to present in this book the historical sketches at the beginning of each chapter; also to Frank Kuchenmeister, the skilful artist who drew them; and to the King Features Syndicate and Thomas A. Edison, Incorporated, for permission to give them this historical record under copyrights from the valuable brochure and syndicate series by the eminent coworker of Edison, Arthur J. Palmer, with the editorship of William H. Meadowcroft.

To the Edison family we are deeply indebted for this permission to record for posterity and to make available for the schools of America, the official Edison Questionnaires in the Edison National Contest for Scholarship Awards. The original documents were delivered to us for this book.

We wish further to commend to our readers for authoritative information concerning the life and achievements of Thomas Edison the works of William H. Meadowcroft and those of Frank L. Dyer and the late Thomas Commerford Martin, which we commend as of the highest value to all students.

The historian is personally under obligations to the John C. Winston Company and to its Editorial Department; to Frederick A. Barber, and to his personal assistants Miss Ann Woodward and Miss Marion Stribling. With these comments this book is presented to the world which Thomas Edison served as the "Benefactor of Mankind."

— Francis Trevelyan Miller

CONTENTS

CONTENTS

CONTENTS

CHAPTER I

THE TALE OF TWO WORLDS—BEFORE AND AFTER EDISON

He has led no armies into battle. He has conquered no countries. He has enslaved no peoples. Yet he wields a power the magnitude of which no warrior has ever dreamed.*

The Famous "Spool of thread" Lamp

Carbonized cotton thread was the filament used in Edison's first electric lamp.

THE hands of the clock stopped at 3.27 A.M. — the clock in the famous Edison Laboratories at West Orange in New Jersey. Three minutes before — at 3.24 on the morning of October 18, 1931, the "Master" at his home not far away in Llewellyn Park had gone on his "Last Great Discovery." The distant glow in the night skies hung like a halo over the "World's Greatest City" which he had helped to create — New York.

Three days later — October 21, 1931 — the golden rays of the autumn sun flooded through the windows at "Glenmont." Strains of music — the melody of the "Little Gray Home in the West" melting into Beethoven's "Moonlight Sonata" and Wagner's "Song to the Evening Star" — floated through the Edison home. The "Grand Old Man" who had given his life to turn darkness into day, to give light and music and happiness to the peoples

*Tribute to Edison at his memorial services at "Glenmont," Llewellyn Park, West Orange, New Jersey; 3 P.M., October 21, 1931. Written by his associate, Arthur J. Palmer.

of the earth, lay at rest in a veritable paradise of flowers —
roses, orchids, and honeysuckles — a perfect tribute from
every civilized country in the world.

STORY OF THOMAS EDISON — A ROMANCE OF TWO WORLDS

Life was a grand adventure to Thomas Edison. He
lived in two worlds — the world as he found it and the
world which he helped to re-create. And what a contrast
from the bleak, cold day on the American "frontier" along
the snowbound shores of Lake Erie — eighty-four years
before — when he was born in obscurity in the little brick
house in the quaint village of Milan, Ohio, on February 11,
1847 — to the day he was proclaimed as the "Greatest
American since Washington and Lincoln."

His adventures rival in their actuality even the fan-
tastic tales of Jules Verne or the travels of Marco Polo, for,
while he was an explorer, he explored the world from the
laboratory. Where he stood, there everything *was* — waiting only for the intelligence of man to reveal it. Day by
day, he delved into its wonders and mysteries, to unlock
the secret doors to the natural laws which lie within our
reach like hidden treasures.

Take out of the world today the work of men like
Thomas Edison, and civilization would collapse. What
would life be without a Gutenberg and the printing press;
without Watt and the steam engine; without Fulton and
the steamboat; without Stephenson and the locomotive
and the railroads; without Whitney and the cotton gin,
or Howe and the sewing machine, or McCormick and the
reaper? Life would be reduced to drudgery. Civilization
is the creation of the inventor and the scientist.

What would happen if suddenly the telegraph invented
by Morse, the telephone invented by Bell, and all the

inventions since Benjamin Franklin were wiped out of existence without immediate new discoveries to take their places? Take away from the world all knowledge of electricity, destroy the power houses, put out all the electric lights, blot out all that Edison has given the world with all the wealth the inventors have created, and every nation in the world would fall. Poverty and distress, famine and panic and pestilence would sweep the earth. The human family — what survived of it — would be forced to rebuild itself from the ruins.

What Edison Means in Everyday Life

We shall in these pages follow Edison, step by step, through his adventurous career; watching him as he leaves his home, with courage and perseverance fighting his way against poverty and failures; working in his laboratory night and day; overcoming almost insurmountable obstacles; and giving the world some 3,000 inventions which to a large extent have reconstructed our everyday life. The wealth which has been created from his genius in property values exceeds $25,000,000,000 in the United States alone. It employs and gives livelihood to over one million, with wages reaching a billion dollars a year. This with the production from their labor mounts up to stupendous figures estimated around $50,000,000,000 — more money than the Pharaohs and Cæsars and all the kings and emperors have ever known.

Whatever we do or wherever we turn, we see the hand of Edison; we live and read and work by his light; we send our telegrams through his improvements which helped to develop the telegraph system; we talk over the telephone through the transmitter which he gave it. When we listen to the phonograph, it is Edison's genius which makes it speak;

when we watch tne world's events pass before our eyes over the screen in the motion pictures and hear them talk, it is but another of his "miracles"; when we listen to the radio, it is Edison again who helped give it voice. These are but a few of the wonders which he performed with the aid of many other inventors in making the world what it is today.

If Edison had lived in the "Dark Ages" he would have been charged with "Black Magic," put to trial, and executed as a "sorcerer." Even in early America he would have been accused of witchcraft. Imagine his making the dead speak from a disk, or flashing the human voice across continents and oceans! These, through natural laws which he discovered, are far greater "miracles" than those which sent "holy men" to torture and death. And yet, they are not even mysterious; they are the ordinary events in our daily life

Edison's Secret: His Unconquerable Youth

This, too, is the story of "Unconquerable Youth." Thomas Edison never grew old in spirit; while years made their inroads and shoulders stooped, he remained at all times the "eternal boy" we shall see as we follow him through. Like Alexander the Great, who, at 17 years of age, started on his conquest of the world, young Edison (two thousand years later) started out to conquer new worlds far beyond the most ambitious dreams of the ancient warriors. Alexander waged his warfare with the power of armies and the sword; Edison met his problems with the power of the mind. His victories are those of a "plain American boy" who leaves a rich heritage of inspiration, courage, and character to the youth of all nations and races.

EDISON'S BIRTHPLACE

In this little brick house at Milan, Ohio, Thomas A. Edison was born. At that time and for many years thereafter, the kerosene lamp was the only illuminant — till Edison himself invented the incandescent light.

THE EDISON HOME

In 1886 Edison bought the estate at Llewellyn Park, New Jersey, and this was his home for forty-five years.

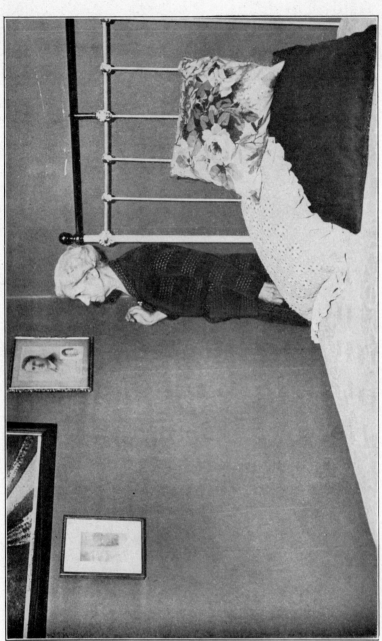

Photo by Wide World

THE BIRTHPLACE OF EDISON

A corner of the bedroom in the little house in Milan, Ohio, where Edison was born. Miss Marietta Wadsworth, first cousin of Edison, is seen looking at his picture.

At the age of twenty-four, Edison was perfecting new systems of communication which would place a driving force behind world progress; at thirty the talking machine and the electric light were on the way; at thirty-two he was a world-famous figure. When Lindbergh at twenty-five years of age won the hearts of the world, he immediately gained the intense admiration of Thomas Edison who became his stanch friend.

The great steps in human progress have been made by youth, or on foundations laid in youth. Hannibal crossed the Alps on his invasion of new kingdoms at twenty-six; Cæsar was a power in the Roman Empire at twenty-eight; Columbus was leading important expeditions at twenty-five; Nelson was commanding his forces at twenty-three; Joan of Arc had "saved France and joined the immortals" at nineteen.

And so we shall find Edison far on his road to great achievements in youth, fortified with the hardy stock of courageous pioneers behind him.

Hardy stock of courageous pioneers.

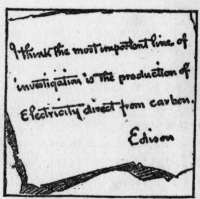

Edison's distinctive handwriting.

CHAPTER II

THE GREAT ROMANCE — FOUNDATIONS OF GENIUS

The first Thomas Edison and his son.

THE story of Thomas Alva Edison begins with the building of the American nation. His foundations were laid in the hardy stock of the pioneers — strong men who blazed the trails for civilization on the American continent.

He declared that "Genius is one per cent *inspiration* and ninety-nine per cent *perspiration*" — but even behind this is another great force: The heritage of a race of men who gave him his strength of character, fortitude, and endurance.

Great age was the heritage of these forefathers. His great-grandfather lived to 104 years; his grandfather 102 years; his father 92 years; and under the tremendous speed of modern times he lived 84 years, 8 months, 7 days, although he frequently said, "I have lived a thousand years in a single night."

The first Edison came to America from Holland about 1728; the pioneers on his mother's side had come to the New World earlier from England and Scotland. And so the sturdy character of the hardy Dutch was in him; the blood of the great "Empire Builders" — the English; and the fortitude of the "Noble Scot."

When Edison's maternal forebears came to America, it was a vast continent of savage men and savage beasts with little more than 5,000 colonists on the edge of the wilderness; when his paternal forefathers came, it had a population of 500,000 (1730); when he was born, it was the home of 20,000,000 people (1847); when he died, it was a great democracy of more than 120,000,000 people and the richest nation in the world (1931).

The First Edisons in America

It was a daring and adventurous voyage when these first pioneers came to the New World. Aboard little sailing vessels, they staked their lives against the hazards of stormy seas. Edison's maternal Argonauts (the Elliotts) arrived on the shores of New England during the Puritan migrations that followed the arrival of the Pilgrims at Plymouth Rock, 1620. We find them fighting through the Indian Wars and in the ranks of the American Revolution. They were Scots, intermarried with the English, imbued with the spirit of the Magna Charta. One of these adventurers, John (spelling the name Eliot), was an "Apostle to the Indians," learning their language and introducing Christianity into the savage race. He was learned in the Bible and Shakespeare, and his boyhood days were lived in England when Shakespeare was a familiar figure on the streets of London.

The first Edisons were Dutch, from the Zuider Zee, in the days when the windmill was the power behind human progress. The lure of the New World was in their blood, for it was the Dutch who had discovered the Island of Manhattan when the *Half-Moon* sailed into the harbor in 1609; it was a Dutchman, Peter Minuit, who purchased the island from the Indians for twenty-four dollars in 1624, and named it New Amsterdam, building the little village of brick houses which became New Netherlands. It was the picturesque Peter Stuyvesant, with his wooden leg, who had been forced to surrender the Dutch city to the English in 1664.

WHEN NEW YORK HAD 5,000 POPULATION

Little did the first Edison who stepped foot in New York (1728) realize that this village, with its population of 5,000, was to become the greatest city in the world, emblazoning the glory of his own grandson five generations in the future. This first Edison immigrant had landed and established his home across the bay from Staten Island, on the New Jersey coast, where Elizabethport now stands, and later moved inland a few miles to the village of Caldwell, where he settled and prospered. It is interesting to note that his descendant, a century and a half later, in these same Orange Mountains, near by, was to amaze the world with his inventions.

The "South Sea Bubble" had burst and adventurous men were seeking fortune on the Western Continent as the new land of opportunity. The first Edison dared the seas at a time when the famous pirates infested the shores of America; the notorious Captain Kidd had been seized and executed; while Edward Teach, who has won fame in history and fiction as "Blackbeard, the Pirate," had been killed, but their followers were still challenging ships at sea. Dutch slave ships were bringing their cargoes of Negroes from the coasts of Africa. The first great excitement he witnessed was when the Negro plot to burn New York was discovered, and fourteen slaves were burned at the stake and eighteen hanged, while the white conspirators were dangled at the end of a rope.

THOMAS EDISON I — AND THE AMERICAN REVOLUTION

The Edison family was firmly established among the "First Americans" when the American Revolution broke out. Among the stanchest of patriots in the fight for independence was one Thomas Edison, the great-grandfather of the Thomas Edison who was to make the name distinguished for posterity. He was a stalwart figure, standing over six feet tall, defying time even to his last days at one hundred and four years of age. We find him established as a bank official on Manhattan Island, a vigorous exponent of liberty, when the first shots were fired in the Revolution at the battles of Lexington and Bunker Hill, in 1775; his spirit was aroused by the Declaration of Independence, July 4, 1776; and he was indignant in his protest when the British took possession of New York City and held it until the close of the war. The execution of Nathan Hale as an American spy caused him to reserve his patriotic utterances for his family fireside, to avoid meeting a similar fate. The British were in New York and he must make the best of it.

Violent disputes arose in his home, however, when he discovered that his son, John Edison, was becoming deeply impressed by the dazzling brilliance of the British military officers in the streets of New York. The city had become the refuge of Loyalists, as the British called them, or Tories, according to the American viewpoint; they were flocking here from all parts of the colonies to find safety under the British flag. Young John Edison looked upon them as patriots to their own country, while his father declared that the American cause was just and righteous. He argued with his son the causes of the American Revolution; both were intrenched in their views, with the dogged firmness of their Dutch fathers. While the father did everything within his power for the cause of independence, the son spent much of his time with the Tory refugees and the British officers. The convictions of both were founded on what each believed to be principles and conscience, according to the ground on which they stood.

EDISON PIONEER SIGNS CONTINENTAL CURRENCY

Throughout the colonies, the American Revolution continued to rage: (1776) Washington retired across the Delaware, amid floating ice, in a blinding storm on Christmas night; the Battle of Trenton was fought; (1777) Cornwallis attempted to capture General Washington, and was routed at the Battle of Princeton; the Stars and Stripes were adopted as the flag for the new republic; Burgoyne advanced from Canada and captured Fort Ticonderoga, only to meet with disaster in the Battle of Bennington; the Battle of Brandywine was fought and the British forces occupied Philadelphia; Washington attempted to recapture the city in the Battle of Germantown; Burgoyne was forced to surrender at Saratoga. Then came the winter at Valley Forge, with its hardships and privations.

This first Thomas Edison, in 1778, was signing the Continental currency which was helping to finance the Revolution. The "Battle" of Valley Forge was fought; and Benjamin Franklin in France was negotiating the treaty which recognized American independence. On the sea, John Paul Jones, a Scot by birth, was winning historic victories. The Battle of Monmouth was fought; the British evacuated Philadelphia; Sir Henry Clinton was hemmed in at New York by Washington's army.

The first bank of the new nation was chartered in Philadelphia in 1780. Battles were raging on all the fronts: (1780) Charleston fell; the Battle of Camden was waged and the Battle of King's Mountain; Generals Rochambeau and LaFayette, with their French troops, came to the aid of the American army; Cornwallis waged his campaign in Virginia; Count de Grasse entered Chesapeake Bay with a French fleet; and at last came the surrender of Cornwallis at Yorktown ending the American Revolution on October 19, 1781.

TRAGIC BREAK IN THE EDISON FAMILY

The dispute between Thomas Edison, the first, and his son John, however, had created a tragic breach in the Edison family. When the Peace Treaty was signed, in Paris, and the British army evacuated New York, in 1783, the Tories found themselves in a difficult situation. Washington delivered his Farewell Address to his army and retired to Mount Vernon in Virginia. British statesmen at the Peace Conference had attempted but failed to secure "some practical consideration from the new nation for the claims of these people who were now left without a country." The new republic found it necessary to protect itself against all possible dissension within it ranks; moreover, many of the Tories were "animated by a feeling of bitter animosity" against the new nation.

What is known as the "Great Exile" resulted; it is estimated that from the Thirteen Colonies "between forty and fifty thousand people found refuge in British North America" in the exodus following the Revolution. Strange as is this coincidence in history, the refuge of many of them was Nova Scotia — the Acadia from which the French were driven into exile when the English took possession (seventy years before the American Revolution), and the historic event which Longfellow memorialized in the narrative poem, *Evangeline*, where he relates the burning of Grand-Pré after they deserted their homes:

"When on the falling tide the freighted vessels departed,
Bearing the nation, with all its household goods into exile,
Exile without an end, and without an example in story."

JOHN EDISON JOINS THE EXODUS

The Tory evacuation began in 1783. "Upwards of twelve thousand men, women, and children embarked at the City of New York for Nova Scotia and the Bahamas." As the ships sailed from the port, "neighbors were arrayed against neighbors and families were divided." The more violent of the anti-republicans were banished and prohibited from returning to their homes. Many of them took neither money nor household goods as they went into the wilderness to start life anew; some of these Royalists had been judges, officials, and landed proprietors in the colonies; they blamed their misfortune and disaster on the stubbornness of King George III, who, they declared, had forced them into the tragic situation. Of such is the aftermath of war.

John Edison was among these exiles. His patriot father's devotion to American Independence had been at the cost of his son. The ardent youth sailed away at the time that all the other members of the Edison family were celebrating the victory of their cause.

His father, Thomas Edison, the first, lived on through the birth of the nation, with increasing devotion to its steady development. The Constitution for the new republic was ratified by the Convention in Philadelphia, September 17, 1787. We can see this patriarchal Thomas Edison, great-grandfather of the inventor, as he reads its preamble with pride:

"We, the people of the United States, in order to form a more perfect Union, establish justice, insure domestic tranquillity, provide for the common defense, promote the general welfare, and secure the blessings of liberty to ourselves and our posterity, do ordain and establish this CONSTITUTION for the United States of America."

The first Edison arrived in America from Holland in 1728.

The great-grandfather of Edison helped to finance the Revolution.

CHAPTER III

EDISON PIONEERS ON THE TRAILS IN CANADA

Dangers of the trail in the early days of the Edison family.

THE trail now leads to Canada. Here, in the "Land of Evangeline," and along the Canadian frontier, John Edison cast his future in the development of the Great Dominion. Love and courtship went on in the forest primeval, until he was happily married and housed in a thatch-roofed cottage in the quaint little village of Digby, a seaport in Nova Scotia. Here a son was born in 1804 — Samuel Edison, who was to grow up into stalwart manhood and become the father of the world's great inventor.

Here, too, begins another tale of love in Acadia, for, over the trail in Ontario, Samuel Edison was to meet and marry the girl who became the mother of Thomas Edison. And here, in Ontario, the boy Thomas was to begin his career as telegraph operator at Stratford Junction, from which he rose to world fame. Thus Canada and the whole British Empire join hands with the United States in honoring Thomas Edison.

John Edison had settled down in Nova Scotia as an ardent Canadian. Under the laws of the Canadian Government, he had become entitled to a grant of six hundred acres of land in Upper Canada. When the boy Samuel was seven years old, the family decided to take possession of the property.

The wagon train, drawn by oxen, started on the long, slow journey through forests and over the plains, camping on the trail at night, cooking their food over camp fires, until, at last, they reached the northern shores of Lake Huron and set up their home in the frontier town of Bayfield in 1811. Along the way they had fished and hunted and traded with the Indians. Soon, the nomadic family was moving on from Bayfield to Vienna, Ontario, along the northern bank of Lake Erie. Here, John Edison settled down and remained for the rest of his life.

Edison's Memory of His Grandfather

He was a familiar figure on the streets of the village, where his famous grandson, at five years of age, visited him. "It was the only time I ever saw my grandfather," he said in later years. "I remember him perfectly — he was 102 years of age. His head was covered with snow-white hair as shaggy as a lion's mane. He walked with a heavy cane and resented my efforts to assist him. He would sit for hours under a great tree in front of the house and nod to every passer-by as he chewed tobacco incessantly. I stood at a distance and looked at him with great admiration. He seemed to me to be as old as Methuselah. That year he died. He had one ambition, and that was to live to be 104, so that he could equal and even beat the record of my great-grandfather, with whom he had the violent dispute in the American Revolution — but he was beaten by two years."

Thus, the man of iron, who had lived through the American Revolution, who had followed eagerly the news from the battles across the seas in the Napoleonic Wars, cheering vociferously when he heard of the fall of Napoleon at Waterloo and his exile to St. Helena, went out like a warrior himself on the frontiers of Canada.

Samuel Edison, father of the future Thomas Alva, was now a young man in Vienna — a native-born Canadian. The town on Lake Erie was a center of activity. Immigrants were flocking into the country as an aftermath of the War of 1812. Soldiers who had fought in the army of Napoleon were crossing the seas to take up their homes in the New Dominions. Scots from the Highlands were coming in great numbers. The first steamboat crossed the Atlantic in 1819, and soon Samuel Cunard, a native Nova Scotian, was to establish the line that has become famous in the world's maritime history. The Erie Canal was opened in 1825, and the first passenger railroad on the Western Continent, a horse-drawn, rail car known as the "Baltimore and Ohio," was begun in 1828.

MARRIAGE OF SAMUEL EDISON AND NANCY ELLIOTT

These events created wide interest in Vienna. The young Samuel discussed them with the village school-teacher, Nancy Elliott, who was one of the most brilliant young girls on the frontier. They found a bond of common interest in the events of the day, which found its culmination in romance and marriage in 1828 — Samuel was then twenty-four years of age and Nancy was but eighteen. This is an historic union, because it was to give a new genius to the world.

The charming and highly intelligent young bride had come to Canada from Chenango County, New York, where she was born in 1810. She was the daughter of Reverend John Elliott, an early Baptist minister, and her grandfather was an old Revolutionary soldier of Scottish descent,

Captain Ebenezer Elliott, who had fought seven years through the war and then settled down at Stonington, Connecticut.

Grandmother Elliott was a Scotch Quakeress, Mercy Peckham, whom the Captain had met in Connecticut and married. The Elliott family had migrated to New York State, where Nancy was born, and then on to Vienna. Here, the old soldier lived, drawing his pension at Buffalo, and here he died when over a hundred years old. Thus, Nancy Elliott was to bequeath longevity to her son along with the Edison record of endurance. She was a product of culture; two of her brothers became Baptist ministers, following in the footsteps of their father and two uncles.

Epoch-making events were now stirring Canada. It was in the throes of a crisis, into which Samuel Edison was being swept. He was the young keeper of a hotel in Vienna when the Canadian Rebellion was brewing. The French migration to the "New Land" threatened to overwhelm the English and much bitter rivalry was developing. Riots were breaking out along the frontier, and secret organizations were being formed under such names as the "Sons of Liberty" and the "Patriots," with Mackenzie and Papineau as their fiery leaders. So great did the agitation become that an attempt was made to set up a republic.

Samuel Edison in Canadian Rebellion

Strange as it may seem, when the Canadian Rebellion was raging in 1837 — on the accession of Queen Victoria to the throne of Great Britain — we see the ardent Samuel Edison a captain in the ranks of Mackenzie's insurgents. Six feet tall, a man of strong physique, he led his men into the conflict, fighting for the cause which his father, John Edison, had so violently opposed during the American Revolution and which had caused his banishment fifty-four years before.

The Edisons again were divided. Old John, at this time eighty-seven years of age, was living in Vienna and stood for the cause of the British Crown more ardently than ever. The son, Samuel, was fired with the old spirit of his grandfather, Thomas, back in the States. These incidents prove the strong individuality and adamant convictions of the Edison mind. They were men of iron will and determination.

The coincidence which now took place has seldom been paralleled in history. The "cause" of John Edison this time was victorious — and the "cause" of Samuel Edison, the son, met with defeat. Canada arose from the Rebellion, stronger than ever, with a uniting of the Provinces under a Federal Union. It entered upon a new era in its Constitutional history which was to develop into the Great Dominion as it stands today. Mackenzie fled to the United States, along with many of his followers, and was held for some months as a prisoner by the American Government for creating disturbances along the border which threatened to involve the two countries in war.

THE PERILOUS FLIGHT THROUGH THE WILDERNESS

Samuel Edison found himself, as his father had before him, a man without a country. Exile to Bermuda was facing the more violent of the insurgents. Without waiting for official orders, Samuel, with his wife, decided to seek refuge in the United States. Secretly and hurriedly, they started on the journey — one hundred eighty-two miles toward safety.

This flight — with little food or sleep — was through the wildest country, infested by unfriendly Indians and fraught with constant danger. Sleeping wherever they could find shelter under the forests, and living on herbs or whatever game they could shoot in the woodlands, with here and there a "bite" with a pioneer in a frontier cabin, they continued their perilous flight through heavy storms.

It has been compared to the perilous journey of Daniel Boone, who traveled a hundred sixty miles through the forests in four days, eating but one meal, after his escape from the Shawnees. Family tradition even states that the strong Samuel Edison carried his wife, Nancy, in his arms, fording rivers and threading dangerous spots in the forest. How much of the journey was made afoot, and how many miles were traveled on horseback or in wagon, has not been recorded.

It was with a feeling of intense relief that they found themselves, at last, safely across the border, in the United States. Wandering through the various towns along the shores of Lake Erie, seeking a spot for a new home, for a period of nearly two years, they finally came to the thriving little hamlet of Milan, Ohio, in 1842, where the event took place — five years later — that was to establish the name of Edison throughout the world.

The romance of the village school-teacher and Samuel Edison.

Fiery leaders in the days of high hats and tail coats.

CHAPTER IV

THE RED BRICK HOUSE IN THE CANAL VILLAGE—A NEW WORLD SHRINE

Boyhood days along the canal; the young road-builder at work.

THERE is a little red brick house on the hill, overlooking the beautiful valley, in the charming village of Milan, Ohio. It stands as a landmark in the dawn of a new age in human progress.

On the front door is the old iron knocker placed there by Samuel Edison. On the lawn a black-cherry tree, which he planted about the time the boy of destiny was born, still blossoms profusely. Within the house is a room, measuring eight by nine feet. Here Thomas Alva Edison came into the world on the bleak, cold day of February 11, 1847. The event took place in the month of the birthdays of Washington and Lincoln, and the red brick house is to the age of invention what Mount Vernon and the log cabin are to the hearts of the people.

This is the home which Samuel and Nancy Edison established when they came from the frontiers of Canada. It was on the far northern border of the plains which Lincoln traveled—a northern outpost to the Western prairies. The mothers of Lincoln and Edison both bore the same name—Nancy; and both died without any

Photo by Underwood

PRESIDENT HOOVER AND THE THREE CRONIES

A notable group gathered at Fort Myers, Florida, to honor the inventor on his 82nd birthday. From left to right are the President; Henry Ford; Edison; and Harvey Firestone.

From the Laboratory
of
Thomas A. Edison,

Orange, N.J. June 24th. 1916.

Mr. Joseph Metzger,
266 South Second St.,
Brooklyn, N. Y.

Dear Sir:

Your favor of the 21st instant has been received, and I beg to say in reply that Mr. Kahan misunderstood me. I stated to him that I believe in the existence of a Supreme Intelligence pervading the Universe.

Yours very truly,

Thos A Edison

Photo by Wide World

EDISON'S RELIGIOUS BELIEF
A signed statement by Mr. Edison clearing up a misunderstanding.

realization that their sons would take their places among the world's great men.

Let us visit the Edison home in Milan on this historic day. The quaint little one-storied house, standing on the bluff overlooking the canal, was the home of peace and contentment. The happy family lived on the one floor, with rooms finished in the attic. A log was burning in the fireplace.

SCENE IN THE EDISON HOME

Samuel Edison, bearded according to the custom of the times, his face weatherbeaten by his outdoor life, his heavy homespun clothes of the frontier hanging upon his six-foot frame, stood looking at the new arrival. Beside him were the two other children who had come to the Edison home — the elder boy bearing the name of William Pitt, after the great English statesman, and little sister Tannie Edison, who looked with pride on the new baby brother.

Nancy Edison held him in her arms — a fragile child with a well-shaped head and large gray eyes — the "very image of his mother." He was just another baby in the family; now they had two boys and a daughter. The children looked upon him with curiosity. William Pitt, who was clever with his pencil, sat down and tried to draw a picture of him, while Tannie, who spent much time in writing, went off to write a story about him. Father Edison strode out of the house and went down to the village to tell the neighbors about it.

"It's a boy!" he said. "Looks just like his mother, and I hope he has her good disposition and common sense. We have named him Thomas Alva — Thomas after his great-grandfather in the American Revolution, and Alva

3

after old Captain Alva Bradley. He is my best friend and he ought to feel honored. We are going to call him 'Al' for short, as we do the Captain. I hope the boy does him credit." Captain Bradley was the owner of vessels plying the trade along the Great Lakes.

Thomas Alva was somewhat of a late arrival in the Edison household; his father was forty-three years old and his mother was thirty-seven when the boy was born — nearly twenty years after their marriage. His grandfather, John, back in Canada, was then in his ninety-seventh year.

On the Village Streets of Milan

Samuel Edison stood high in the community as a man of honesty, integrity, and unimpeachable character; his word was "as good as a Government bond." The days as a hotelkeeper back in Ontario were gone forever. He had set up a workshop in Milan where he was making hand-wrought shingles; the demand for his durable product was large in the region and he employed several men.

Milan was a flourishing town on the Huron River, not far from the lake, and a ship canal connected it with the head of navigation at Lockwood Landing. Shipbuilding was one of the chief industries. Twenty vessels a day would come up the canal to load their cargoes of wheat. The grain was brought in in four- and six-horse wagon loads from the surrounding country. It looked at this time as though it might some day be "as big as Chicago," for the Western Reserve was a vast wheat field. Six hundred wagons a day came over the rough roads to the towpath canal. So flourishing became the port that the line of oxen- and horse-drawn wagons extended from one to two miles.

This was the scene in which little Thomas Alva found

himself, sitting as a child in front of the red brick house, looking down at the canal and watching what seemed to him to be an endless procession of oxen and horses and wagons that must reach to the end of the world.

He was not considered a strong child and his unusually large head caused the town doctor to warn, "He might have brain trouble." He did have — but it was the kind of brain trouble that makes human progress. The lad had an enormous bump of inquisitiveness. His endless questions caused the villagers to shake their heads. "I don't know," they would answer. "Why don't you know?" he would ask. Unable to satisfy his penetrating curiosity, they decided that the boy must be "mentally unbalanced, and likely to be a lifelong burden on his parents."

Events began to take place in his life when he was a lad of three years of age. The gold rush to California was creating excitement. Milan was on the trail that led to great fortune across the continent. Young Al stood for hours and watched the covered wagons on their way to the far-off gold fields. As they camped in front of his home, he fired at them a barrage of questions: "Where did you come from? — Where are you going? — What for? — Why?" The Easterners looked on with amazement.

"This was my first impression of a great world beyond," he told a friend in later years. "I had a great longing to climb into those prairie schooners — just to see where they were going. Gold didn't mean a thing on earth to me — in fact it hasn't meant much to me all my life. But I did want to know where those wagons went when they disappeared down the road." The boy had no slightest suspicion then of the splendid trail he was destined to follow.

STORIES TOLD ABOUT "AL" IN MILAN

The spirit of adventure was aroused within him and he wandered away down to the canal where the lumber gangs were loading timber on vessels to sail out to the Great Lakes. These rough, strong-armed men from the forests fascinated him. They sang as they carried the heavy logs on their shoulders; they were the boisterous songs of the wilderness, most of which should not be repeated; they were for men only. Young Al, being a man at five years of age, learned them all by heart. He would stand on the logs and sing these songs of the wilderness at the top of his voice. Instinct, however, taught him to shout them with the lumberjacks and not attempt to do it at home. This is an early indication not only of memory, which was to build up a vast mental storehouse of information, but of fine discretion.

He was a handsome lad with sensitively intelligent features. His mass of hair, however, was unruly; it refused to lie down, it refused to part, neither would it curl. When standing silent and thinking, he was always running his hands through it; his father decided to "cure him of the habit" and cut it short, much to the dismay of his proud mother. His high forehead was now more prominent than ever, accentuated by a scowl when listening to talk he could not understand. His brows would contract, his lips tighten, and with determination he would walk off quickly. Slipping out of the house, he would make a bee line for the canal, sliding down the bluff, and hurrying down the towpath as if his life depended upon it. The shipbuilding yards were his destination. There he would pick up every tool he could find and examine it, plying the workmen with questions.

The sawmills were his next strategic invasion. Dragging away the loose planks, he started to build plank bridges over the mill stream. Frequently he had narrow escapes — he fell into the canal. The world came very near losing one of its future great men; when he was rescued, he showed no fright. His continuous search for knowledge got him into difficulties and danger. To satisfy his curiosity, he tumbled into one of the grain elevators and was barely saved from being smothered to death. Attempting to shorten a strap, he held it in his fingers and persuaded another boy to strike it with an ax — the result was that he lost the top of a finger.

Nothing seemed to escape the penetrating mind and keen eyes of this boy. Observing a goose sitting on her eggs, and noting the result, he decided to try it himself. His father found him in the barn sitting on a nest of eggs which he had collected for the experiment.

"What are you doing?" demanded his father.

"I'm hatching out chickens!" answered little Al.

"Well, I'll tell you now, son, it can't be done that way," replied the father.

"Why not? If the hens can do it, why can't I?"

This irrepressible urge for investigation led him frequently to attempt the impossible. He decided to investigate a bumblebees' nest near the orchard fence. Walking up to it cautiously, he peered into it. There seemed to be "nobody at home;" so he took a stick and began to prod into its mysteries. At that moment an obstreperous ram, spying an excellent target in the seat of the boy's trousers as he leaned over at the bumblebees' nest, made a charge like the "Light Brigade" — and Al was over the fence, with ram left behind and the bumblebees following. That night, according to tradition, he was "much in need of arnica."

Patience and industry in this lad were indefatigable. He was always working; he tried everything that was in sight. He went into the store and inspected the goods; he went to the village square and looked up at the huge elms and maple trees to "see what they were doing"; he sat on a stone and laboriously copied the signs over the stores, showing great skill in accurate drawing and draftsmanship. One day, however, his curiosity led him to investigate the secrets of fire. He proceeded to build a fire in the barn so that he might closely observe its progress. The flames spread more rapidly than he had calculated and he barely escaped with his life, but the barn was totally destroyed. Father Edison, deciding that this exceeded even the boundaries of inquisitiveness, took him to the village square where he publicly spanked his son as a warning to other youths.

LEARNING THE GRIM MYSTERY OF DEATH

The grim mystery of death now came within his realization. With one of his playmates, a son of the wealthiest man in the town, he went to the "Old Swimming Hole" in the creek. The lads jumped in. Suddenly young Al called to his comrade — there was no answer. He looked — and saw only bubbles rising on the surface of the water. The boy had disappeared! He called again and waited; then paddled near to the mysterious spot which seemed to be deep and dark. Here he stayed till nightfall and gazed in wonderment. Puzzled and lonely, he walked off in silence and went home. Two hours passed. When the missing boy failed to return, a search was started for him. He had last been seen with little Al Edison and they came to the Edison home to make anxious inquiry.

"I don't know where he's gone," said the lad, grief

stricken. "He went down into the deep hole in the creek
and didn't come back!" The lad told all the circumstances
in detail as if stunned by this revelation of death. The
creek was dragged and the body recovered.

EDISON ANECDOTES INDICATE CHARACTER

These and many other stories are told by the folks in
Milan — tales of the first seven years of Thomas Edison's
life in the little red brick house on the hill. They have
become traditions such as surround the lives of all men
who rise to heights of fame. Like the curiosity of Isaac
Newton when he saw the apple fall from the tree and discovered the law of gravitation, these human adventures of
the mind give indications of the unfolding imagination.
The commonplace frequently is the doorway to great discoveries. These Edison anecdotes are more than folklore
— they are penetrating insights into the formulation of
character. Every story told about Thomas Edison's childhood is a direct guidepost to his future achievements.

In later years he was asked, "What is the chief
ingredient for success of a man's career?" His reply was
"Imagination, plus ambition and the will to work." Even
in those early days of Edison, in the little canal village of
Milan, he began to exibit these "characteristics of success."

Milan today is a new world shrine to these first seven
years of Edison's childhood. It will be Mecca for generations as long as the little red brick house stands. When
the railroad came, it failed to pass through Milan and left
it in its picturesque seclusion on the banks of the Huron
River, with its old Main Street shaded by towering trees.
The canal days are gone and there is hardly a trace of the
ditch.

"The irony of fate," exclaims an historian, "that

one should be born in a village who was destined to create an entire revolution in the mode of rapid transit; that a child born in a house on a bluff overlooking the canal should be endowed with wonderful perceptions of chained lightning," and that modern progress should leave it in its seclusion — a New World shrine.

Listening to the songs of the lumberjacks.

Chased by a ram.

CHAPTER V

BOYHOOD DAYS OF THOMAS EDISON ON AMERICAN "FRONTIER."

Watching the covered wagons go by.

GREAT events were awakening the "frontier" in the boyhood days of Thomas Edison. The railroad had come — the great "Iron Horse" that was to push forward civilization until the vast resources of a continent were within the reach of the people. Great cities were to rise along the paths of the iron rails; frontier towns were to become huge industrial centers. The bell of the locomotive was everywhere ringing the death knell of the old era.

The Edison family foresaw these conditions, and little Al, seven years old, listened with amazement as he heard them discussed by his mother and father. Samuel Edison came home indignant, because the "wise men" of Milan refused to allow the extension of the railroad into the village. "It will ruin the town," they declared. "It will destroy our business on the canal. Milan will be as big as Chicago if they will let us alone."

But this decision proved to be the decline and fall of Milan. The time to "move on" had arrived. The Edison family bade "good-by" to the little red brick house in Milan and moved on to the activities that were taking place in

Michigan, where we find them reëstablished in their new home in Port Huron, in 1854. Samuel Edison had decided to start "right." Through the frugality of Mother Edison, they had saved money in Milan and felt that they should give the children the advantage of it in the new home. The little "eight by nine foot" room where Al had been born now gave way to a "mansion."

THE EDISON HOME IN PORT HURON IN MICHIGAN

The Edison home was a large colonial house, through which young Al roamed with bewilderment. Surrounding it were ten acres overlooking the wide expanse of the St. Clair River as it flowed out from Lake Huron. This colossal estate, as it appeared to young Al, was once an old Government fort reservation, and he imagined that he could see the blockhouses, with the Indians stealing up from their canoes in the river during the night to attack it — he could even see the flashes from the muskets.

Port Huron was in its pristine glory — throbbing with enterprise and prosperity as a great lumber center. Its wealth, large for those days, was invested in sawmills, shipping, and allied industries. Samuel Edison entered vigorously into the life of the community; he became a dealer in grain and feed; he was active in the lumber industry in the Saginaw district; he helped finance wheat crops and lumber camps in the forests; he conducted market gardening on his seven acres, and here we shall find young Al starting on his business career at eight years of age.

"EDISON TOWER" — AND ITS YOUNG GATEKEEPER

Father Edison conceived a startling enterprise. He erected a huge wooden observation tower over a hundred feet high. The summit was reached by winding stairs, with an observation platform which commanded a magnificent view over the river, hills, and forests. It was called by the villagers, "Edison's Tower of Babel," as it stood on the highest point of the Edison acres, near the old colonial house. Samuel built it largely with his own hands and the assistance of some of the neighbors, while little Al worked industriously on what he considered his first great venture. It loomed larger to his boyish eyes then did in later years the leaning tower of Pisa or the tower of the Empire State Building. He would stand on its summit with an old telescope and "sweep the skyline like a Columbus discovering a new world."

The Edison tower was a landmark along the frontier. Al distributed handbills announcing that it was "open to the public" for one of the most beautiful views in the world, overlooking Lake Huron and the St. Clair River. The entrance admission at first was twenty-five cents, and Al was a sort of gatekeeper. The receipts for the first two months were three dollars. Then came the day when the railroad company began to advertise excursions and the highest receipts were reached when six hundred came to see the lake, picnic in the grove, and stand on the top of "the highest tower in America," according to the reports of the region.

The sensation subsided, however, and the business at the tower began to decline. When the wind blew strong, the Edison tower rocked, much to the consternation of those who were climbing its rickety stairs. Less adventurous people, when they felt the structure shake and tremble under their feet, became frightened and turned back — even after paying their money. The price was reduced to ten cents, including the "look through the telescope," but visitors to the tower slowly grew fewer and fewer, until its sole occupant on many days was Al, as he stood on the top and surveyed the skyline.

SIX HUNDRED DOLLARS IN A YEAR AS MARKET GARDENER

The next enterprise in which we find Al engaged is market gardening. The Edison acres were growing vegetables, for which the boy decided to develop a market. Loading an old wagon with onions, lettuce, peas, cabbage, potatoes, turnips, beets, and carrots, Al sat on the seat driving the family horse through the streets with the "best vegetables ever grown." With him was a chore boy, Michael Oates, a little Dutch lad who became his business partner.

The young merchants peddled from house to house in the city, and even went to near-by neighboring towns. They added apples, cherries, pears, plums, and grapes to their line, buying from other farmers, until this developed finally into a vegetable store. The profits one year were six hundred dollars. This money was turned over to the safe-keeping of Mother Edison.

THE FIRST EDISON LABORATORY IN MOTHER'S CELLAR

But in the head of young Al there were bigger ideas; he was absorbed in the wonders of chemistry and used all his spare time to read everything he could find on the subject, spending all his spare money for such books as could be obtained in the town. There were strange things going on in the cellar of the Edison home. Al had taken possession of it and began "buying out" the drug stores to start his experiments.

Two hundred bottles were lined up on crude wooden shelves, which he had built, each bearing the label, "Poison" — a warning so that no one would disturb them. With an elementary textbook on physics in his hand, he made his tests, believing nothing until he had tried it and seen it work. This characteristic followed him throughout his life — he must prove everything.

His "man Friday" was young Michael Oates, on whom he tried his first experiments. Al saw no reason why a man should be unable to fly: "If birds can fly, why can't men?" Wings were all right if you had them; otherwise it was necessary to find some other means. Michael was persuaded to make the test.

Al looked over his bottles marked "Poison" and decided that if sufficient gases could be generated in Michael to blow him up and make him lighter than air, but one result could happen — he would rise like a balloon. He came to the conclusion that the only chemical he possessed with these gaseous elements was Seidlitz powder, and mixing a large dose he persuaded his "man Friday" to swallow it — for the sake of science.

The results were disastrous: Michael began to suffer pains in the stomach which made him writhe until his groans attracted the folks upstairs. Rushing into the cellar, they found the chore boy deathly pale and sick, while Al was seeking new chemicals from his shelves to counteract the damage he had done, on the general principle that if you "don't succeed at first, try, try again." Father Edison, however, appeared with a switch kept for emergency purposes behind the old Seth Thomas "grandfather" clock. Michael did not rise, but Al did, as the switch was vigorously applied!

Mother Edison, who always was sympathetic with his rising genius, ordered the removal of the laboratory, with its two hundred bottles. Al pleaded with her not to clean up what they called the "mess in the cellar," and promised to do big things if she would only give him a chance.

A compromise was reached; he agreed to make no further experiments on his friends and to keep the laboratory under lock and key, so that no one could be placed in danger. He was further given a copy of Parker's *School Philosophy*, a textbook in elementary physics, which he promised to follow in future tests.

There is a story, however, told in Port Huron, but unauthenticated, that he did make one more human experiment; namely, giving a fright to a Negro servant to see if she would turn pale (as did Michael Oates) and remain white!

Thus, we find the future Thomas Edison in his first laboratory, in Port Huron — when he was between ten and eleven years of age. It was a happy family, with never a discord except on such occasions as created by Al in his adventurous moods. Mother Edison was encouraging the children in the development of whatever talents they might show. The older brother, William Pitt, showed genius with his pencil and there was talk about sending him abroad to study art with the Masters, but this was apparently abandoned, for we find him in later years the manager of the local street railway lines at Port Huron, starting on an electrical career, in which he became keenly interested. The sister, Tannie, showed a high order of literary ability and was constantly writing. Al, too, had a talent for sketching, and whenever a problem arose, he reached for a piece of paper and began to work it out in clever drawings.

A Scene with the Edison Family

The life in the Edison home is described by old residents in Port Huron. It was one of the finest types of the American home. Samuel Edison was one of the best liked men in the community. He was a man of tremendous energy.

Nancy Edison was the ideal mother. With their three children, she would gather about the table and talk over their problems with them. Whatever interested the children was of vital importance to the parents. They even discussed the news of the day.

This was the time when Daniel Webster was "thundering" in the United States Senate; Jefferson Davis and Stephen A. Douglas were defending States' Rights, while Lincoln was coming to the front on the floor of the House. Japan had been opened by Commodore Perry; the Crimean War and the Great Mutiny in India were attracting attention.

But matters of even greater interest were the extension of the railroads, the discovery of petroleum, and the development of the great West. Little Al was fascinated by the laying of the first Atlantic cable under the ocean to connect the Western and Eastern hemispheres.

The boy Thomas Edison was acquiring the knowledge that was to make him, too, a great figure in human progress.

Once upon a time Edison was "the vegetable boy."

The gaseous mixture that failed to supply the power to fly.

CHAPTER VI

SCHOOL DAYS—EDUCATION OF YOUNG EDISON BY HIS SCHOOL-TEACHER MOTHER

The schoolmistress feared that there was no future for young Edison.

"MY mother was the making of me." The whole secret of Thomas Edison's education is told in these seven words. It is one of the most notable examples in history of what a mother can do for her son by patient guidance and loving comradeship. His longest period in school was no more than three months. Like Theodore Roosevelt, he was not considered a strong boy.

The boy Edison was not an easy lad to rear; he had the determination of his grandfathers in him. His father could not quite fathom him—he considered that he must be either stupid or a genius. The willow switch was a dismal failure in attempts to discipline him; he required encouragement and refused to be challenged. No one but his mother seemed to understand him, and it is under her loving influence that we see him develop.

The first and only attempt to send young Al to school met with disaster in Port Huron. The country schools at this time were confined largely to "readin', writin', and 'rithmetic, taught to the tune of a hickory stick." They had turned out many great men — such as Thomas Jeffer-

ENJOYING LIFE AT EIGHTY-FOUR

A happy snapshot of Mrs. Edison reading messages of congratulation to the world-renowned inventor on his eighty-fourth birthday.   The picture was taken at the Edison winter home in Fort Myers, Florida.

AT WORK IN HIS LABORATORY

Here the persistent inventor carried through the most exciting and most exhaustive series of experiments ever undertaken by an American physicist. The photo shows him as he looked in 1918.

son and Andrew Jackson — but they were unable to penetrate the mind of the Edison boy. He sat and drew pictures on his slate; he looked about and listened to everybody else; he asked "impossible questions," but refused to reveal what *he* knew, even under the threat of punishment. The children called him the "dunce," and he generally stood at the foot of his class.

WHEN THE SCHOOL-TEACHER CALLED HIM "ADDLED"

It was during one of these sieges that the inspector visited the school and the teacher told him his troubles.

"That Edison boy is 'addled,'" reported the teacher. "He is not worth while keeping in school any longer."

"I am never going to step my foot in a school again as long as I live," declared young Al when he returned home and told his mother. "The teacher says that I am 'addled.'"

Mother Edison was aroused to indignation. "I have been a school-teacher myself and that is no way to treat a boy." Taking him by the hand, she brought him back to the school and faced the teacher with the accusations.

"You don't know what you are talking about," she exclaimed. "He has more brains than you, and that is what is the trouble. I will take him home and teach him myself, and show you what can be done with him."

The Edisons marched doggedly home — mother and child — and the education of Thomas Edison began. By the time he had reached nine years of age, he had read, with his mother's help, Gibbon's *Decline and Fall of the Roman Empire*, Hume's *History of England*, Sears' *History of the World*, Burton's *Anatomy of Melancholy*, and the *Dictionary of Sciences*.

4

At eleven years of age, he had even made an attack on Newton's *Principia* and was an "authority among the boys" on the Bible, Shakespeare, and American history. He knew all about the wisdom of Plato; why Socrates took the poisoned cup; and how Demosthenes learned to be a great orator by putting pebbles in his mouth to keep himself from stammering. Blind Homer and the tales of the Odyssey were intimate events in his life. Moreover, he could run up and down the list of the world's great inventors and their inventions, as if they were lined up in front of him.

Perhaps most significant was the story of Galileo, who shook the scientific world of his time by the simple device of dropping a one-pound and a five-pound weight from the leaning tower of Pisa. When they both struck earth at the same time, a new method of discovering truth was born. It was the method of discovering truth by experiment, rather than by examining authorities. It was the method by which Edison revolutionized the world.

Laying Solid Foundations for the Future

And back of all this was Mother Edison, who, through the four years since her son was accused of being "addled," had stayed with him like a sentry on duty, pouring into him all the knowledge of her own school-teacher days on the Canadian frontier.

The elementary foundations had not been forgotten. She taught him geography as a fascinating journey through the world in which he lived, with mental travels over the continents and through the nations, sailing the rivers, climbing the mountains, and exploring to the ends of the earth.

The rudiments and advantages of correct English she taught him also, and the accuracy of mathematics. Already she had guided his hand into a penmanship that was almost like steel-plate engraving. Nothing that she considered of value to him as a foundation in his life had been neglected. It was in mathematics that he found his most serious difficulty, as his mind was too imaginative for figures. This followed him throughout his life.

"I can always hire some mathematicians, but they can't hire me," he once remarked in self-defense.

And, with all this, Mother Edison trained him in the standards of ethics — the value of honesty, integrity, truth, and industry — instilling into him a love of country and humanity.

THE BOOKS YOUNG EDISON READ

Father Edison developed intense pride in his son's progress. No Edison, as we have seen, could be challenged, and he, too, had accepted the country school-teacher's proclamation as a declaration of war. He offered the boy a small sum of money for every book he could master. The boy started out to read every book in the Port Huron Library. His father, however, placed a taboo on fiction, but his mother, realizing the imagination of the boy, again came to his defense and led him through the classics.

His first favorite author was Scott, with the Waverley novels, the tales of his mother's ancestral country, living in his imagination in the days of *Ivanhoe* and *Rob Roy* and *The Heart of Midlothian*.

His youthful mind was inspired by *Robinson Crusoe*, and he had a burning ambition to duplicate the feats of the wonderful man who with a few bits of rope and timbers from a wreck on a desolate island made for himself the things that he needed. Then there was *Pilgrim's Progress*, in which he followed Pilgrim on his long struggle to overcome every temptation and every obstacle on the path to the Beautiful City.

Dickens was then a popular author of the day — living and writing at this time — and young Al reveled in *Oliver Twist*, the little foundling from the workhouse who rose to good fortune. *David Copperfield* and *Dombey and Son* were the "new books" at the public library.

His Great Admiration for Victor Hugo

Victor Hugo's great novels were being translated into English and appearing on the shelves, for he, too, was living and working at this time. The insatiable Al was amazed by the adventures of the *Hunchback of Notre Dame* and his love for the gypsy sorceress who is hanged as a witch and whose death he avenges. He became so enthusiastic over Hugo that we find him waiting for his new books in years to come, entranced by the life of Jean Valjean and the vagabond gamin in *Les Misérables* when it appeared in the library some four years later. In truth, he became such a devotee of the "new French author" that his friends nicknamed him — Victor Hugo Edison.

Mother Edison would sit for hours and read with him — sometimes high up in the observation tower, or on the front porch in summer, and before the open fire on winter nights. Leaving these diversions, they would return to books on chemistry and science. He was eager to learn about electricity and no less enthusiastic in devouring books on chemistry, a subject that became the passion of his life.

Father Edison and the other Edison children frequently sat in the circle and listened to the mother's flow of knowledge. The boy Al possessed her wonderful gift and, with his marvelous memory, he never needed to be told anything twice. They read together *The Penny Encyclopedia* and he became a walking encyclopedia himself.

At times they would sit and play checkers and backgammon, but Al's vigorous mind was always wandering away from the game on new conquests in the fields of information.

MOTHER EDISON'S LOVE FOR ALL CHILDREN

An old neighbor in Port Huron has described these scenes at the Edison home: "When, at certain times of the day, I passed the old homestead, surrounded by its luxurious garden and fragrant orchards in summer, I found Mrs. Edison and her son on the front porch. She seemed to set certain times of the day for them to be together and study. The front porch was a sort of schoolroom — with one pupil. The older children went to the public school. The boy looked and acted like his mother. Everybody noticed their comradeship. He was a good-natured little fellow and as sharp as steel. He listened to every word she said and seemed to think she was a fountain of wisdom. Children passing the house looked upon her as a friend. She loved them all as if they were her own, and used to come down to the gate with her hands full of doughnuts and apples to give to the children as they passed on their way to school."

THOMAS EDISON'S TRIBUTE TO HIS MOTHER

"I discovered early in life," Thomas Edison once told a friend, "what a good thing a mother was. When she came out as my strong defender, when the school-teacher called me 'addled,' I determined right then that I would be worthy of her and show her that her confidence was not misplaced. She was so true, so sure of me. I felt that I had someone to live for, someone I must not disappoint. She was always kind and sympathetic and never seemed to misunderstand or misjudge me.

"The good effects of her early training I can never

lose," he continued. "If it had not been for her appreciation and her faith in me at a critical time in my experience, I should very likely never have become an inventor. You see, she believed that many of the boys who turned out badly by the time they grew to manhood would have become valuable citizens if they had been handled in the right way when they were young. Her years of experience as a school-teacher taught her many things about human nature and especially about boys. I was always a careless boy, and with a mother of different character I should have probably turned out badly. But her firmness, her sweetness, her goodness, were potent powers to keep me in the right path. The memory of her will always be a blessing to me."

Edison's mother directed her son's education.

The street was an open school for the boy.

CHAPTER VII

HE STARTS ON HIS GREAT CAREER — TWELVE YEARS OF AGE

The first big exciting moment in Edison's career.

I NEED more money," declared young Edison at twelve years of age to his family. "I am going to do things and I must have more money. There is no reason why I cannot get a regular job and work during the time I am not studying."

"What do you want to do?" inquired Mother Edison.

"I want to be a newsboy on the trains of the Grand Trunk Railway," he said. "I can sell magazines and newspapers and make money, and at the same time I can read them all free of charge! While off duty in Detroit, I can read books in the free library."

Mother Edison protested that he was too young to become a breadwinner, while Father Edison declared that he was able to take care of his son. The boy's arguments, however, were according to the Edison tradition; he had made up his mind and intended to earn his own way in the world. His mother tried to dissuade him with visions of the dangers — he might fall from the train — there might be smash-ups — it would keep him out too late at night.

Historian's Note: The anecdotes and personal reminiscences in this chapter were told directly by Thomas Edison to friends, each of whom gives his own version. It was The Author's privilege to hear him relate many of them.

Again, a compromise was reached and young Edison applied for the concession "to sell newspapers, books, magazines, fruits, and candy on the trains of the Grand Trunk Railway running between Port Huron and Detroit." It was a monopoly, and all the profits were to go to him; he made the arrangements and drove the bargain himself.

EDISON'S FIRST JOB — NEWSBOY AND CANDY BUTCHER

During the interval while waiting for the concession to be granted, he "tried out his hand" by selling newspapers on the streets in Port Huron, putting into practice his own modernized version of the old maxim, "Everything comes to him who hustles while he waits." Then the great day came when he boarded the train on his first job in 1859. The hours required him to rise at six o'clock in the morning and he seldom got to bed before eleven o'clock at night — a seventeen-hour day. The train left Port Huron about 7.00 A.M. and arrived in Detroit at 10 A.M. Young Al generally hurried off to the Detroit Public Library, and caught his train on the return trip which brought him back to Port Huron about 9.30 P.M.

It was an accommodation train, made up of three cars — a combination baggage and smoking car and two ordinary passenger cars, one of which was "reserved for ladies." The baggage car, which was headquarters for the "candy butcher," was divided into three compartments — one for mail, one for trunks and packages, and one for smoking. The young merchant kept his papers, magazines, and books with his stock of goods in the smoking car.

His chief complaint was that he had "too much waste time on his hands." Then, another of his ingenious ideas struck him; he would remove his first laboratory from his mother's cellar and set it up in the baggage car. Whether or not to transfer the two hundred bottles marked "Poison," or to set up a new laboratory, was quite a problem. His final decision was to maintain two laboratories; with the profits from his sales on the train he began to purchase chemicals at the large pharmacies in Detroit and bring them into the smoking car. The transition was cautious but sure, and soon the Grand Trunk Railway found itself creating a new institution.

THE WORLD'S FIRST LABORATORY ON WHEELS

Tarry here a moment over this picture: A lad, twelve years of age, with thick, tousled brown hair and baggy clothes, leaning over the chemicals in this crude moving laboratory with textbook in hand, mixing his chemicals and trying to prove the simple formulas in elementary chemistry. Its results in years to come were to be as epoch-making as that day, nearly one hundred years before, when the boy Isaac Watts, watching the vapor rising from the kettle in his mother's kitchen, discovered the power of steam.

But even these "industries" were not sufficient to absorb the energy of little Al Edison. He must expand — something must be happening off the train while he was on it. So he opened two stores in Port Huron — one for the expansion of his "periodical business" and the other for the development of his "vegetable business." Two boys were taken as partners on a profit-sharing basis. The periodical store, with newsboys selling on the streets and delivering at homes, was doing a good business until the young owner discovered that the boy in charge was not making correct reports. He caught him "holding back profits" and was so disturbed by this revelation of dishonesty that he ordered the store closed abruptly. The vegetable store prospered, with its supply of garden produce, butter, and berries in season, and the wagon still delivering "direct to the customer."

Al acted as buyer in the open markets in Detroit and could be seen every day bargaining for produce in the streets, taking advantage of sales, and lugging two large baskets which he carried to the baggage car and brought to Port Huron to reënforce the supply from the home farmers.

"I just commandeered that baggage car as if I owned it," he explained in later years. "To this day I cannot explain why they never asked me to pay freight. I suppose it was because I was so small and my industry impressed them. It took nerve, at least, to do a free freight business on a United States mail car. There never was a complaint and I kept this up for a long time. At the stations along the line I bought butter from the farmers and was quite a dealer in blackberries during the season. My purchases were made at a low wholesale price and I gave the wives of the trainmen and engineers the benefit of a discount. This may partially explain why no complaint ever came from the railroad."

The business as "candy butcher" and newsboy on the train also increased. When an express train was put on the line, he secured that concession, too, and installed a newsboy. Then an immigrant train, with seven to ten coaches, was put on the Grand Trunk and he employed another boy to sell "bread, tobacco, and stick candy" to the Norwegians bound for Iowa and Minnesota. There was little news trade on this train, as the passengers were unable to read English. The earnings of this young "merchant prince" (rivaling in its embryonic instinct the early enterprise of John Wanamaker or Marshall Field) mounted as high as ten dollars a day, approaching events which were to carry them up to twenty dollars a day.

How Edison Started His "Twenty-Hour Day"

His family was now convinced that he was fully able to make his own way in the world; his mother insisted that he retain the profits for his chemical laboratory, while he insisted that she should take one dollar a day for board during the few hours he was at home. He wanted things on a business basis. His father insisted, however, that the dead line on his bedtime should be eleven-thirty at night. The boy merchant found this impossible, with his many duties, especially as he had acquired many books on elementary science which demanded his attention; moreover, he was becoming deeply interested in telegraphy and was spending much time with the operators.

It was his custom to take home all unsold stock of newspapers and he noted that his father generally was waiting for them with considerable eagerness, taking full advantage of this free library which was brought home every night. Samuel Edison was soon lost in the events of the day, and this gave his son the opportunity to "steal a few more hours."

Young Al had started a "new telegraph company." He strung a line of common stovepipe wire from his home to that of a neighboring boy. For insulators, they had hung bottles on nails driven into trees or on flimsy poles. Old rags were wound about the magnet wire and bits of spring brass were used for telegraph keys. In his effort to obtain current at minimum cost, he experimented with cats as a possible source of static electricity. While he succeeded in making their hair stand on end, the cats resented their new duties and left their bleeding marks on the young inventor's hands as they fled. It was finally found necessary to resort to batteries, and the two boys were soon exchanging messages.

Young Al Wins Victory Over His Father

"I told you that you must be in bed by eleven-thirty at night," ordered Samuel Edison. This was a challenge to his son which must be met. The budding genius devised a scheme to overcome it. On the next night he left this stock of papers with his chum. Father Edison was waiting as usual and seemed much disturbed. Young Al then sprang his strategy — he could get the news for his father over the "private wire." The scheme, for a moment, perplexed his father, but finally with a twinkle in his eyes he exclaimed, "All right, let's try it!"

The lad sat down and clicked the password to his chum. Immediately, the "news" began to come over the wire. Al wrote it out in longhand and handed it to his father to read. The scheme worked perfectly — Father Edison was still reading at one o'clock in the morning! And the novelty so appealed to him that it was continued for several nights. Edison, junior, had won his victory; he had found a way to get good practice every night and stay up until the early hours of the morning. When this schedule was firmly established, he brought the papers home again each night, but Father Edison never again entered a protest. The boys continued this midnight practice, becoming fairly adept in the first principles of electric telegraphy, until a stray cow wandered through the orchard and pulled the line down.

The day's routine as "candy butcher" and news dealer on the Grand Trunk lines continued, with hours crowded in at the Detroit Library and continuous experiments in the laboratory in the baggage car. He had come into possession of a translation of a work on "Qualitative Analysis" by a German professor, Karl Fresenius. With his increasing collection of test tubes, jars, and batteries, he worked out these problems as the laboratory on wheels rolled along.

MEMORIES OF THE EARLY NEWSBOY DAYS

Memories of these days from 1859 to 1860, just before the outbreak of the Civil War, have been related by some of the boys who worked for young Edison. "Most of the boys tried to get jobs with Al when there was no school on Saturdays," records one of them. "I was one of his several candy butchers on the trains. He told me very clearly what my duties were and then left the business entirely to me. I seldom saw him except to make reports, as he was too busy to talk. He was a quiet lad, completely preoccupied with what he was doing. He wore a cheap suit of clothes until it was worn out and then he would buy another. He never by any chance blacked his boots. His mother always kept him supplied with clean shirts, but he did not look as if he often combed his hair. He never seemed to care anything about money for himself. When I handed him the profits, he would simply put them into his pocket and walk off and buy more chemicals. One day I asked him to count it, but he said: 'Oh, never mind, I guess it's right!'

"Our young boss was a generous fellow and would take us to dinner and pay for it himself. I believe that I was one of the few persons that could make him laugh, though no one enjoyed a good story better than he, but he was always studying and never seemed to listen to what we boys were saying. He always carried a book in his pocket and seemed to be thinking about something. We boys were deeply impressed by his honesty and integrity. I don't believe a better young fellow ever lived."

THOMAS EDISON'S OWN STORY OF HIS BOYHOOD

Thomas Edison, to his last days, whenever he met any of his "old boys," would sit and relive his boyhood: "I well remember the week before Christmas when my train jumped the track near Utica," he related. "We had four old Michigan Central cars with rotten sills and they collapsed in the ditch. My supply of candies, figs, dates, raisins, were strewn all over the track. I hated to see them go to waste, so I attempted to eat them on the spot. The result was that our family doctor had the time of his life."

"I had a great time studying the passengers," continued Edison. "There were all sorts of people — good, bad, and indifferent. It was a wonderful education in human nature that has been of value to me throughout my life. I remember a day in 1860, just before the Civil War broke out. Two fine-looking young Southerners, with a colored servant, boarded our train in Detroit. They bought tickets for Port Huron. I was going through the train with the evening papers when I came to the seat occupied by these young aristocrats." This is the conversation that ensued:

"Boy, what have you got?" asked one of the men.

"Papers!" replied Al.

"All right," exclaimed the passenger as he took them and threw them out of the window. Then, turning to the colored servant, he said: "Nicodemus, pay this boy!"

Nicodemus opened a satchel and paid young Edison. By this time the passengers were all watching the strange transaction. Al went back to the baggage car and filled his arms with magazines and illustrated papers. Taking them back, the strange customer seized them and threw them out of the window also, exclaiming:

"Get your money from Nicodemus!"

The boy merchant quietly returned to his stock and came back with all his old novels and whatever he had been unable to sell. He was a little fellow and the pile reached above his head as he tugged down the aisle. The passengers rocked with laughter.

"Novels — all the latest novels!" exclaimed young Al.

The passenger promptly took them and threw them out of the window — and again Nicodemus settled. The mysteries of this strange character aroused the boy's curiosity and he decided to test him to the limit. Returning to the apparently inexhaustible supply in the car ahead, he staggered out with his entire stock as a "candy butcher" — molasses candy, popcorn balls, cracked hickory nuts. All went out of the window.

"I felt like Alexander the Great," explained Edison in relating the anecdote. "I had one more chance. I had sold all I owned. Finally, I put a rope on my trunk, which was about the size of a carpenter's chest, and started to pull this through the passenger car. It was almost too much for my strength, but at last I got it in front of those men. I pulled off my coat, shoes, and hat and laid them on the chest."

"What have you got?" demanded the customer.

"Everything, sir, that I can spare that is for sale."

"Nicodemus, pay the boy!" ordered the amazing passenger. "Then take them all out of the door in the rear of the car and throw them overboard."

"What's the bill?" asked the man like a thoroughbred gentleman.

"Twenty-seven dollars," replied young Al. The bill was promptly paid and the man left the train at Port Huron.

"I found these men were from the South," explained Edison later, "and I have always retained a soft spot in my heart for Southern gentlemen ever since."

A Wild Night Ride on the Runaway Engine

These boyhood days of Thomas Edison are as classic as the adventures of Mark Twain's "Tom Sawyer." We

find him fascinated by the mechanism of the steam locomotive and riding with the engineer in the cab whenever
he could get a chance. His wondering eyes examined into
its intricacies — fire box, boiler, valves, and levers. One
day on a level stretch of track the engineer turned the
throttle over to Al and allowed him to pilot the train.
Suddenly the boiler "primed" and a deluge flooded the
young driver. He turned and found the engineer asleep,
so he stuck to his post.

"This was the first big exciting moment in my life,"
explained Edison in relating it. "I reduced the speed to
twelve miles an hour. I knew that if the water ran low the
boiler was likely to explode. When I had gone about twenty
miles, a volcano of black, damp mud blew out of the stack
and covered the engine and myself. I started to awaken
the engineer, when it stopped. When we approached the
next station, I climbed out on the cowcatcher and opened
the oil cup on the steam chest to pour oil in, when there
was a tremendous noise. The steam rushed out with such
force that it nearly knocked me off the engine. I succeeded
in closing the oil cup and got back to the cab. Just before I
reached the junction there was another outpour of black
mud and the whole engine was a sight. Finally, I brought
the train of seven cars safely to its destination. There was
a roar of laughter as we pulled into the yard. The engineer,
upon being awakened, admitted that he had been to an
all-night dance of the trainmen's fraternal organization on
the night before."

He Carries Message Through Midnight Forests

Young Edison's reputation as a boy who always carried
the "Message to Garcia" was known throughout the
Michigan country. The captain of one of the largest

steamboats on the Great Lakes had died suddenly, and Al was called on to carry a message to another captain who lived fourteen miles away. He was offered fifteen dollars to go and fetch him; but he stood out for twenty-five dollars so that he could get another lad to accompany him. With these terms agreed upon, he started out at night with his hired corporal. It was pitch black and raining in torrents. The path was through dense forest — a wild country with its bear, deer, and wild animals. Every stump in the dense forest looked like a bear. His comrade suggested that they seek safety in a tree and wait for daylight.

"Bears can climb trees," exclaimed Al indignantly. "And this message has got to be delivered tonight!"

Then one of the lanterns went out — then the other. The lads plodded on until finally the faint gleam of dawn appeared; the captain's house was in sight and the message was delivered.

"In my whole life I never spent such a night of horror as this," explained Thomas Edison to his friends. "I thought if I ever got out of that scrape alive I would know more about the habits of animals and everything else. I got a good lesson: 'Be prepared for all kinds of mischance when you undertake an enterprise.'"

These experiences followed Edison through his life, and he frequently moralized on them. Here is one of his stories:

"I was riding home one night on the wagon with one of my boys — just before midnight. We had to pass a soldiers' graveyard where three hundred men were buried who had died from a cholera epidemic which took place at Fort Gratiot, near by, some years before. We used to shut our eyes and run the horse full speed past this graveyard. If the horse stepped on a twig, my heart would give

5

a violent jump. It is a wonder that I haven't died of heart disease long ago. I finally became immune until all fear of graveyards passed from my system. I got to be without fear — like Sam Houston, the pioneer and founder of Texas; Houston lived some distance from the town and generally went home late at night. The path led through a dark cypress swamp over a corduroy road. His friends decided to test his alleged fearlessness. A man with a sheet over his head jumped from behind a tree and confronted Houston, suddenly. Sam stood still a moment, peering at the white figure, and then shouted in stentorian tones:

"'If you are a man, you can't hurt me. If you are a ghost, you don't want to hurt me. And if you are the devil — come home with me, *I married your sister!*'"

"How I Got My First Black Eye" — Edison

A night could be spent in relating these stories of Thomas Edison's newsboy days. "I once got a black eye fighting over the Prince of Wales," he related. "It was in 1860 when Prince Edward, later King Edward, came to Canada. There were great preparations over the border, opposite Port Huron, in the town of Sarnia. We all went over to witness the event. British flags draped the town and carpets were laid on the crosswalks for the Prince to walk on. Floral arches were erected and we all gathered about the grand stand where the Prince was to be greeted by the mayor. I began to cheer — but I cheered the wrong man — it was the Duke of Newcastle.

"When the Prince finally arrived, I looked upon the youth and he didn't seem any different to me from any of the other boys. The Canadian lads took offense at this remark and a general fight was started. My father was born in Canada and I had great love for the country, but

I was born in the States and thought it was my duty to defend them. We Yankee boys got badly licked that historic day and I got a black eye that I took home with me as a memento." This anecdote is especially interesting in conjunction with events that were later to occur when Thomas Edison was to receive from King Edward the Gold Albert Medal awarded by the Royal Society of Arts in recognition of his life achievements.

Distant rumblings of tragic events were now reverberating through the United States. Thomas Edison was fourteen years of age. As he passed through the trains, selling his newspapers, there were excited discussions among the passengers over the day's news. At the railroad stations everybody was waiting to hear the last word, while in the streets crowds gathered.

The candies didn't go to waste.

A cheer that started a fight.

CHAPTER VIII

HIS ADVENTURES IN TRAGIC DAYS OF THE CIVIL WAR

"WAR! War! All about the big war!" The voice of Al Edison rang through the train and the railroad stations along the route of the Grank Trunk system in Michigan in 1861. What had been feared, now happened — and the country found itself in the throes of the most tragic fratricidal war in the world's history.

The world's first railroad newspaper was written, printed, and published by Edison when he was only fifteen.

The young news merchant — now fourteen years old — found the demand for his newspapers increasing with amazing rapidity. There was a rush for his supply on the trains and at every station, until he was nearly mobbed. The fall of Fort Sumter on April 13, 1861 — the first bloodshed on the streets of Baltimore on April 19, 1861 — the battle of Bull Run on July 21, 1861 — all proved mints to young Thomas Edison. The news of every engagement caused great excitement. Every battle fought during the next few months was a battle won for him — it produced profits to be used in his "laboratory on wheels."

The winter of 1861–62 made him an "important man" in the towns along his route where he had built up a "monopoly of the news trade" with his newsboys working for him. It was an April day in 1862 when he saw the dense crowds standing before the bulletin boards in Detroit reading the announcement of the terrible bloodshed at the battle of Shiloh, or Pittsburg Landing, in which the great General Johnston was killed. He conceived a brilliant idea and rushed to the telegraph operator in the Detroit depot to put it into immediate action.

"I will give you *Harper's Weekly*, and any other papers you want, for three months, if you will agree to telegraph this news to all the station agents ahead and tell them to put it on the bulletin board," offered young Edison.

"It's a bargain," replied the telegraph operator.

Great Idea Sells 1000 Papers a Day

The boy hurriedly copied the headlines, with the request to the agents, and the news was hot on the wire. He then decided that this stroke of business genius should sell at least one thousand newspapers. Hurrying over to the office of the *Detroit Free Press*, he announced:

"I want to see the editor on important business — important to me, anyway."

He was admitted to the inner sanctum immediately, where two men were eagerly scanning the latest telegraph despatches from the battle fronts.

"I want a thousand papers," demanded young Edison. "I have only got money for three hundred and I want credit."

"You can't have it," explained the first spokesman. "You will have to pay cash." The boy news merchant then told them what he had done. The second man looked at him with admiration and patted him on the shoulder.

"You have got a great idea, my boy," he exclaimed. "Go, get the papers — we will give you credit." This man, he afterwards learned, was the astute journalist, Wilbur F. Storey, who subsequently founded the *Chicago Times* and became celebrated in the newspaper world.

The tug-of-war now started. The thousand papers were lugged to the train by Edison and two boys — and they were on their journey. Between the stations they were vigorously engaged in folding the newspapers so that they could be quickly handed out to the customers. Let Edison tell the story himself at this point:

CROWDS WAIT FOR NEWS FROM BATTLE FRONTS

"The first station was Utica — a small town where I generally sold two papers. I saw a crowd ahead on the platform that was so large I thought it was an excursion. There was a rush for me the moment I landed. Then I realized that the telegraph was a great invention. I sold thirty-five newspapers in the next minute.

"We next pulled in to Mount Clemens, a town of about one thousand population. I usually sold six to eight papers there. I decided that if the demand at this station warranted it, I would raise the price from five to ten cents. The crowd was there and I raised the price. So it went all along the route — crowds everywhere. In order to gain time in arriving at Port Huron, it was my practice to jump from the train at a point about a quarter of a mile from the station, where the train slackened speed. I had drawn several loads of sand to this point to make the jump with safety and had become quite an expert. My faithful young assistant, Michael Oates, the Dutch boy, met me with the horse and wagon at this sand pile. I shoved my entire stock of newspapers off the moving train and made the jump."

The faithful Michael was waiting. Piling the newspapers on the wagon, they approached the outskirts of the town, where they were met by a large waiting crowd. They stopped in front of a church where a prayer meeting was just closing and the congregation came rushing out. As one observer said: "The deacons must have forgotten to pass the plate at that meeting" — for everybody had the coins in their hands. Young Edison stood up in the wagon and shouted:

"Twenty-five cents apiece, gentlemen! I haven't enough to go around!"

Almost a riot resulted — he sold out. And when he got home, he counted out the largest day's receipts he ever had in the newspaper business. As he said himself: "I had made what to me was an immense sum of money."

NEWSPAPER PUBLISHER AND EDITOR

This brilliant coup, however, had been preceded by another event. When young Edison observed the increasing demand for news, he decided to go into the newspaper publishing business himself. He found a small second-hand press in Detroit and purchased it for a few dollars; then he bought some type — and these were lugged onto the baggage car. The Scotch conductor at first protested, but finally was persuaded that it would be a great thing for the Grand Trunk to have the first newspaper in the world printed on a moving train. The "laboratory on wheels" now found itself expanded into a diminutive newspaper plant.

"World's First Traveling Newspaper Plant"

The young editor's foresight convinced him that it would not do to attempt to compete with the war news in the Detroit dailies, so he decided to put out a sheet that would give all the news ("that's fit to print") from the small towns along the railroad. The telegraph operators at the stations were pressed into service as newspaper reporters to chronicle the local items. Occasionally, they would catch some country news on the wires and write it down for the traveling newspaper when the train came in.

The first issue of *The Weekly Herald* appeared — at three cents a copy, or eight cents for a month's subscription, "published by A. Edison," who was, as one chronicler records, "editor, reporter, compositor, make-up man, pressman, devil, advertising manager, circulation manager, and news agent." The circulation reached four hundred copies a month — "the largest circulation of any newspaper in the world printed on a train" — it being the only one!

The Weekly Herald really created wide interest, especially when the famous English engineer, Stephenson, on a journey to America, happened to be traveling on the Edison train one day and purchased a copy from him as the newsboy-editor came through the car. The ingeniousness of the scheme appealed to the famous Britisher and he was interested at once.

"I extend my compliments, young man," he exclaimed. "Your newspaper is as good as many I have seen edited by men twice your age. I want you to run me off an edition of one thousand copies."

This "special edition for England" almost swamped the capacity of the Edison laboratory-printing plant. The copies were sent all over the world, and even the *London Times*, the greatest newspaper of the day, extended its compliments and quoted from its columns. There was danger for a moment that the world would lose its future great inventor by turning him into, perhaps, an equally famous newspaper editor. But Fate was to intervene, as we shall see in the events that followed.

There is today, as far as known, but one copy in existence of Edison's *Weekly Herald*, and this is treasured at the Edison home, hanging on the wall of the inventor's den at Glenmont, Llewellyn Park, in West Orange, New Jersey. It is preserved under glass and is in excellent condition. Collectors would pay large sums of money for copies of this historic newspaper if they could be obtained. Search has been made throughout the country to secure them for museums and such "treasure houses" as the Smithsonian Institution at Washington and the British Museum.

It is through the courtesy of the Edison family that we are able to reproduce herewith for permanent historical record the complete contents of this now famous newspaper. The issue in the Edison home is dated February 3, 1862 — a few days before Thomas A. Edison reached his fifteenth birthday. It is a single sheet, about the size of a handkerchief, printed in three columns on both sides and unfolded. The top circulation of this newspaper, other than the special English edition ordered by Stephenson, was eight hundred copies — five hundred copies to regular subscribers and three hundred copies sold on the train. All the work was done by Edison, and the profits reached forty-five dollars a month.

We present herewith an official transcript of the complete contents of this priceless treasure:

THE WEEKLY HERALD.
Published by A. Edison.
TERMS.
The Weekly Eight Cents per Month.

Local Intelegence.

Premiums:—We believe that the Grand Trunk Railway, give premiums, every six months to their Engineers, who use the least Wood and Oil, running the usual journey. Now we have rode with Mr. E. L. Northrop, one of their Engineers, and we do not believe you could fall in with another Engineer, more careful, or attentive to his Engine, being the most steady driver that we have ever rode behind (and we consider ourselves some judge haveing been Railway riding for over two years constantly,) always kind, and obligeing, and ever at his post. His Engine we understand does not cost one fourth for repairs what the other Engines do. We would respectfully recommend him to the kindest consideration of the G. T. R. Offices.

The more to do the more done:—We have observed along the line of railway at the different stations where there is only one Porter, such as at Utica, where he is fully engaged, from morning until late at night, that he has everything clean, and in first class order, even the platforms the snow does not lie for a week after it has fallen, but is swept off before it is almost down, at others stations where there is two Porters things are visa a versa.

J. S. P. Hathaway runs a daily Stage from the station to New Baltimore in connection with all Passenger Trains.

Professor ——— (name unreadable) has returned to Canada after entertaining delighted audiences at New Baltimore for the past two weeks listening to his comical lectures, etc.

Did'nt succeed:—A Gentleman by the name of Watkins, agent for the Hayitan government, recently tried to swindle the Grand Trunk Railway company of sixty-seven dollars the price of a valise he claimed to have lost at Sarnia, and he was well night successful in the undertaking.

But by the indominatable perseverance and energy of Mr. W. Smith, detective of the company, the case was cleared up in a very different style. It seems that the would be gentleman while crossing the river on the ferry boat, took the check off of his valise, and carried the valise in his hand, not forgetting to put the check in his pocket, the baggageman missed the baggage after leaving Port Huron, while looking over his book to see if he had every thing with him, but to his great surprise found he had lost one piece, he telegraphed back stateing so, but no baggage could be found. It was therefore given into the hands of Mr. Smith, to look after, in the meantime Mr. Watkins, wrote a letter to Mr. Tubman Agent at Detroit, asking to be satisfied for the loss he had sustained in consequence, and referring Mr. Tubman to Mr. W. A. Howard, Esq., of Detroit, and the Hon. Messrs. Brown and Wilson of Toronto for reference. We hardly know how such men are taken in with such traveling villians, but such is the case, meantime Mr. Smith, cleared up the whole mystery by finding the lost valice in his possession and the Haytian agent offered to pay ten dollars for the trouble he had put the company to, and to have the matter hushed up.

Not so, we feel that the villian should have his name posted up in the various R. R. in the country, and then he will be able to travel in his true colors.

We have noticed of late, the large quantitys of men, taken by Leftenant Donohue, 14 regt. over the G. T. R. to their rendezvous at Ypsalanta and on inquiring find that he has recruited more men than any other man in the regiment. If his energy and perseverance in the field when he meets the enemy, is as good as it was in his recruiting on the line of the Grand Trunk R. he will make a mark that the enemy won't soon forget.

Heavy Shipments at Baltimore—we were delayid the other day at New Baltimore Station, waiting for a friend, and while waiting, took upon ourselves to have a peep at things generly; we saw in the freight house of the GTR. 400 bls of flour and 150 hogs, waiting for shipment to Portland.

Birth.
At Detroit Junction G. T. R. Refreshment Rooms on the 29th inst., the wife of A. Little of a daughter.

We expect to enlarge our paper in a few weeks.

In a few weeks each subscriber will have his name printed on his paper.

Reason Justice and Equity, never had weight enough on the face of the earth to govern the councils of men.

Notice.
A very large business is done at M. V. Milords Waggon and carriage shop, New Baltimore Station.   All orders promptly attended to.   Particular attention paid to repairing.

Ridgeway Station.
A daily Stage leaves the above Station for St Clair, every day, Fare 75 cents.

A Daily stage leaves the above named place for Utica and Romeo, Fare $1.00.

Rose & Burrel, proprietors.

Oppisition Line.
A Daily Stage leaves Ridgeway Station for Burkes Cor. Armada Cor. and Romeo.

A Daily stage leaves Ridgeway Station on arrival of all passenger trains from Detroit for Memphis.

R. Quick, proprietor.

Utica Station.
A daily Stage leaves the above named Station, on arrival of Accommadation Train from Detroit for Utica, Disco, Washington and Romeo.

S. A. Frink, driver. Mr. Frink is one of the oldest and most careful drivers in the State. (Ed.)

Mt. Clemens.

A daily stage leaves the above named station, for Romeo, on arrival of the morning train from Detroit, our stage arrives at Romeo two hours before any other stage.

Hicks & Halsy, prop.

THE NEWS.

Cassius M. Clay will enter the army on his return home.

The thousandth birthday of the Empire of Russia will be celebrated at Novgorod in august.

"Let me collect myself," as the man said when he was blown up by a powder mill.

GRAND TRUNK RAILROAD.
(With woodcut of Railway Train)

CHANGE OF TIME.
Going West.
Express, leaves Port Huron, 7.05 P. M.
Mixed for Detroit, leaves Pt. Huron at 7.40 A. M.
Going East.
Express leaves Detroit, for Toronto, at 6.15 A. M.
Mixed for Pt. Huron leaves at 4.00 P. M.
Two Freight Trains each way.

C. R. Christie, Supt.

STAGES.

New Baltimore Station.

A tri-weekly stage leaves the above named station on every day for New Baltimore, Algonac, Swan Creek, and Newport.

S. Graves, proprietor.

MAIL EXPRESS.

Daily Express leaves New Baltimore Station every morning on arrival of the train from Detroit. For Baltimore, Algonac, Swan Creek and Newport.

Curtis & Bennett, proprietors.

PT. HURON STATION

An omnibus leaves the station for Pt. Huron on the arrival of all trains.

LOST LOST LOST.

A small parcel of cloth was lost on the cars. The finder will be liberally rewarded.

MARKETS.

New Baltimore.

Butter at 10 to 12 cents per lb.
Eggs at 12 cents per dozen.
Lard at 7 to 9 cents per lb.
Dressed hogs at 3.00 to 3.25 per 100 lbs.
Mutton at 4 to 5 cents per lb.
Flour at 4.50 to 4.75 per 100 lbs.
Beans at 1.00 to 1.20 per bush.
Potatoes at 30 to 35 cts. per bushel.
Corn at 30 to 35 cts. per bush.
Turkeys at 50 to 65 cts. each.
Chickens at 10 to 12 cts. each.
Geese at 25 to 35 cents each.
Ducks at 30 cents per pair.

ADVERTISEMENTS.

Railway Exchange.
At Baltimore Station.

The above named Hotel is now open for the reception of Travelers. The Bar will be supplied with the best of Liquors, and every attention will be paid to the comfort of the Guests.

S. Graves, proprietor.

Splendid Portable Copying
Presses for Sale at
Mt. Clemens, Orders Taken,
By The Newsagent on the Mixed.

Ridgeway Refreshment Rooms:—I would inform my friends that I have opened a Refreshment Room for the accommodation of the traveling public.

R. Allen, proprietor.

To the Railroad Men.
Railway men send in your orders for Butter, Eggs, Lard, Cheese, Turkeys, Chickens and Geese.

W. C. Hulch, New Baltimore Station.

*   *   *   *   *

ARREST MICHAEL OATES — SEARCH FOR EDISON

These were great days but they were soon to end with two narrowly averted tragedies. Michael Oates — Edison's "Man Friday" — got arrested and. Al himself went into secret hiding. It all happened at Fort Gratiot where soldiers were quartered on their way to the battle fronts in the South. The two "magnates" were on their way home one dark night when they heard the call of the sentries.

Edison, in a moment of mental relaxation, imitated the call. The second sentry, thinking it was the terminal sentry who called, repeated it to the third — and so on. This brought the corporal of the guard to the outpost. Young Michael was captured, taken to the fort, and locked up in the guard house. Al was ordered to halt, but disappeared down the road in the darkness, reached his home, and rushed into the cellar.

Again let Edison tell his own story: "There were two barrels of potatoes in the dark cellar. I hurriedly poured the remnants of one into the other, sat down quickly, and pulled the empty barrel over my head, bottom up. The soldiers arrived, wakened my father, and the search began with candles and lanterns."

"I am absolutely certain that I saw him run into this cellar," exclaimed the corporal. "I can't see how he could get out. Is there a secret hiding place anywhere around here?"

"No, sir!" replied Father Edison, emphatically. "There is not!"

"Most extraordinary," muttered the corporal as he left.

"And I was mighty glad when they left," explained Edison in relating his experiences. "I certainly was cramped — and the potatoes I had dumped out of that barrel were rotten and violently offensive."

Next morning, Michael Oates, after a bad night in the guard house, was severely reprimanded and released. He and Al Edison decided right there never to interfere again with military discipline — they would let the Civil War go on without them.

Train Lurches — Baggage Car in Flames

The second tragedy, which followed quickly, was not so easily averted — it resulted in changing young Edison's entire life. It was in 1862; George Pullman, who was then working out plans for his "palatial drawing room and sleeping cars," had met young Edison and predicted his genius; he had presented the boy with an outfit of wooden apparatus for his "rolling laboratory." The traveling-printing office and the laboratory were flourishing when they met with disaster.

Edison was working in the baggage car on the next edition of *The Weekly Herald* — while one of his newsboys

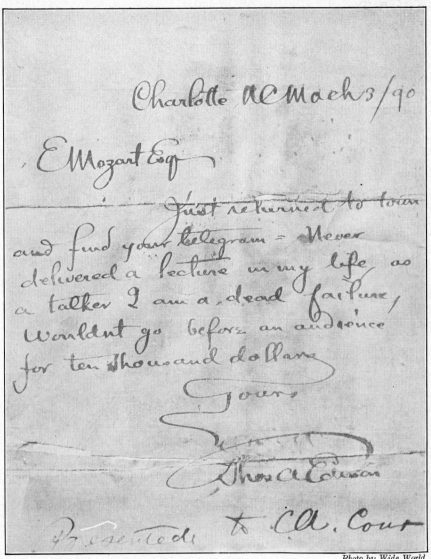

"NOT FOR TEN THOUSAND DOLLARS!"
Edison was an inventor, and he knew it. He was not a lecturer—and he knew that
also, as is evident from this letter.

TWO FAMOUS SCIENTISTS
Thomas Edison with Charles P. Steinmetz discussing an electrical problem.

FRIENDS AND CO-WORKERS
For half a century John Ott worked with Edison.   They are seated beside the first phonograph which they had perfected many years before.   They died on the same day.

was selling papers through the passenger cars. The train was going on high speed when it reached a stretch of badly laid track. *There was a sudden lurch!* The baggage car trembled, and a stick of phosphorus in the laboratory was thrown heavily to the floor. It burst into flame with intense white heat. Young Edison pulled down his coat and began fighting the fire as it spread through the baggage car.

It looked for the moment like a seething furnace when, attracted by the thick smoke that rolled through the train, the conductor appeared. He was a dour Scot by the name of Alexander Stevenson. With his mouth firm, he glared at Edison and then grabbing pails of water extinguished the growing conflagration. Walking up to the young scientist, he let out a flood of eloquence and soundly boxed the boy's ears.

This blow has been said to be the cause of Edison's deafness throughout the remainder of his life. But Edison himself ·has said that it was only the beginning. The real tragedy he told in his own words: "The blow at this time by Stevenson may have started it, but it was finished one day when I was standing on the station platform at Smith's Creek. I was trying to climb into the freight car with both arms full of papers when the conductor, attempting to help me, took me by the ears and lifted me up into the train. I felt something snap inside my head and my deafness started from that time and has ever since progressed." He referred to it later, as we shall see, as "a blessing" because it shut out the noise of the world and allowed him to concentrate.

Stranded Amidst Ruins — A Real Tragedy

The last disaster at the time of the fire came a few minutes later. As the train pulled into Mount Clemens

6

station, Conductor Stevenson, "an elderly man with iron-gray hair, a rubicund face, and an accent that would have been strong even in the Heart of Midlothian," completely lost his temper.   Without further ceremonies, he grabbed the bottles from the shelves and threw them out of the baggage car door; he picked up the printing press and type and threw that out of the door; he took up everything else he could lay his hands on and threw it out of the door — including young Thomas Edison.

And there, on the station platform at Mt. Clemens, he left Edison — with the first laboratory on wheels and first newspaper ever printed on a train in the world's history — stranded amidst the ruins.

The fire in the baggage car.

A dour Scot extinguished the conflagration.

CHAPTER IX

THE COURAGE OF YOUTH—ON THE ROAD TO SUCCESS

The wrathful conductor "dumps" the young inventor and his "gadgets" out of the train.

THE catastrophe, which befell Thomas Edison at fifteen years of age, caused the first crisis in his life. It was his first real test of courage, the forerunner of fires, accidents, and challenges, which he was forced to meet and to master throughout the years. The road ahead led to almost impregnable walls.

It must have seemed to him that the world had come to an end, but there is no record of his ever having admitted defeat. With the first "laboratory on wheels" in ruins at the railroad station at Mt. Clemens in Michigan, we find him gathering up the wreckage and taking it back to his home in Port Huron, where he started all over again in his mother's cellar. He came home, not as a prodigal son, but as a general in forced retreat, who must re-form his lines for his next advance.

The family made but one demand: "It must be agreed that no dangerous chemicals will be brought into the house. Moreover, the cellar must be abandoned and you must set up your laboratory in a room near the roof. We would rather have you over us than under us — then, if things go wrong, you can only blow up the top of the house!"

The famous printing plant was re-assembled and "business went on as usual" as if the Scotch cyclone had never struck it.   The next issue of *The Weekly Herald* came out on time and Edison stuck to his job as the news monopolist on the trains.   There was a peace treaty with the irate conductor and they became firm friends.

The old Scot had deep affection for the boy: "You're a bright lad," he said with a deep Highland accent.   "You will make your way in the world.   I well know you had no intent of doing any damage to anything or anybody.   But a train on fire is a dangerous thing, my lad.   It jeopardized the lives of my passengers and I had to act with severity. Now, go on and sell your papers — but don't bring any of those damned explosions into my train!"   It should be said that Alexander Stevenson, after long and faithful service, retired to a little cottage in a village near St. Johns, Michigan, where he sat with august dignity on the bench as Justice of the Peace and administered the law according to his own conscience.

So the new chemical laboratory "near the roof" was in full blast.   Test tubes were reinstalled, new supplies of chemicals put in stock, crude telegraph instruments set up, with a profusion of wire and tools collected from every possible source.   Young Edison was becoming deeply interested in the possibilities of electricity.   His experiences while riding on locomotives and in the railroad shops were turning him toward mechanics and invention.

Irate Subscriber Is End of a "Great Editor"

There was to be an abrupt ending to his success as a publisher.   A friend on the *Detroit Free Press* had given him some type for his rehabilitated printing office.   He thought he saw genius in the lad in the journalistic fields and advised him to expand *The Weekly Herald* into a policy which would give him a wider scope for activity. Al took in a partner — the "printers' devil" of the *Port Huron Commercial.* This lad believed in "sensations" and convinced his young proprietor that the newspaper should become "more personal" and create discussion of the community. Always willing to expand, he agreed to merge *The Weekly Herald* into a new publication to be called *Paul Pry* — the very name of which was indicative of its policy.

The new publication did command immediate attention and the community chuckled and argued over the jibes and thrusts that appeared in its columns. It was, in fact, too successful — even to the extent that after a few weeks an indignant subscriber appeared at the office and asked for the editor-in-chief.

"Where's Al Edison?" he demanded, with rage in his eyes, as his towering six feet and broad shoulders leaned over the "printers' devil."

"The editor is out — he is out selling his papers," replied the shivering partner.

The enraged subscriber started out on the trail of his quarry. Scouring the town, he asked everybody in sight if Al Edison had been seen "anywhere around." Al, however, refusing to heed warnings, walked into his foe an hour later on the street running along the St. Clair River.

"So you're the fellow who printed that piece in the paper about me, are you?" shouted the provoked subscriber in fury. Whereupon he grabbed the boy editor by the neck and the seat of his trousers and heaved him into the river. Thrashing about in the water, the stupefied publisher swam to shore wet and bedraggled, but otherwise undisturbed, and this was the end of *Paul Pry*, for young Edison decided that journalism was a precarious occupation and ordered the paper discontinued. There is no known copy of this publication in existence at the present time; if such a copy could be found it would be worth a considerable sum of money to the collectors.

EDISON'S TRIBUTE TO THE POWER OF THE PRESS

Edison, in relating these incidents during his life, once remarked: "This was the end of my career in journalism; probably it worked out fortunately for both the public and myself. It taught me one thing, however, and that is sympathy for all journalists. From that moment, I have had the deepest affection for newspaper men, for I know what they are up against. It is a great profession and I have found them my stanchest friends. People in the public eye belong to the community, and the public has a right to know what they are doing. It is the newspaper's business to keep the public informed, and everybody should coöperate with them to the fullest possible extent. This world of ours today is founded on correct information and we owe a great debt to the newspapers."

On other occasions he is quoted as saying: "I have come to the conclusion that the greatest factor in our progress has been the newspaper press. When one wants to do a thing the newspapers take it up. Everybody reads the newspapers, everybody knows the situation, and we all act together. . . . To let the world know through type who and what and where you are, and what you have that this great world wants, is the secret of success. The printing press is the mightiest machine to that end."

"DON'T WORRY — GOD WILL TAKE CARE OF HIM"

The energies of the irrepressible lad, after his "retirement as an editor," were concentrated on his job as a "candy butcher" and news merchant, with his interests rapidly developing in science and invention. His hours away from home continued to be from daylight to midnight. The family began to consider him as a man who knew his own business. Father Edison had settled down to the conviction that he was "master of himself — and anyway, he is an Edison and knows what he is doing."

"Al is all right!" exclaimed Father Edison. "Nothing will happen to him — don't worry — God is taking care of him!" Mother Edison *knew* that he *knew* what he was about; whatever happened, she placed implicit faith in him.

It was a morning in August, 1862; young Edison stood on the platform of the station at Mt. Clemens — the very station where, a few months before, he had been so tempestuously ejected from the baggage car. The "mixed" train, on which he was newsboy, was shunting the way-freight at the station. He stood talking with the station agent, who was also the telegraph operator — a sympathetic man with deep interest in the boy. His name was J. U. Mackenzie; he had a little son, two and a half years old, named Jimmie, who played around the station platform.

Jumps in Front of Train to Save Baby

While Al was talking with Mackenzie, he suddenly looked up and saw little Jimmie stepping out on the gravelled track directly in front of a box-car that was approaching at considerable speed. Edison's eyes caught the situation in an instant. Dropping his papers and his glazed cap, he made a dash for the child without a second to spare.

The car rushed upon him with such speed that it struck Al's ear, as he grabbed the child in his arms and leaped to safety. There was no brakeman on the box car as it roared by. The two boys lay apparently lifeless by the side of the

track.   Train hands picked them up and carried them to
the platform.   They were severely cut about the face and
hands by the gravel ballast on which they had fallen.
Mackenzie was so overcome that "he could only gasp out
incoherent words of gratitude," and Al, gathering up his
scattered papers, boarded his train and went on.

Mackenzie has left historic record of this scene: "It
was nine-thirty on a lovely summer morning," he testified.
"Tommy Sutherland, the train baggage man, who was an
eyewitness, told me that had Al been a second later he
would have lost a foot or been killed, as the wheel of the
car struck the heel of his boot.   I was in the ticket office,
and, hearing a shriek, ran out in time to see the train hands
carrying the two boys to the platform.   They had both
landed face-down in sharp, fresh gravel ballast, with such
force that, when rescued, their appearance was somewhat
alarming.   Examination, however, proved the injuries to
be only skin-deep.   The box car had been shunted with
terrific momentum because it contained ten tons of heavy
material assigned to the Jackson State Prison."

The Reward — It Changes Whole Course of His Life

"It is difficult for me to tell you how I felt," said
Mackenzie.   "I had witnessed the scene, a few weeks
before, when Al had been thrown from the baggage car with
his laboratory and boxed on the ear.   I saw how brave he
was at that time in his own troubles.   Now, he had saved
the life of my own son!   All the station agents and operators
along the line loved Al.   I began to rack my brain to see
how I could repay him for what he had done.   As I had no
money, I could not give him a reward."

When the train bearing Al rolled into the Mt. Clemens
station the next day, Mackenzie was waiting to meet the

newsboy: "Al," he said, "we all want you to know how grateful we are for what you have done. I'd like to do something for you; it isn't much, but it's all I can do. I will make you a telegraph operator and do everything I can to get you a job on the line."

This was a moment of important decision. Al stood in deep thought and then said he would be only too glad to accept the offer if it wouldn't be too much trouble for Mackenzie. Here was a chance to learn thoroughly the art in which he had earlier dabbled at home. Four days a week — for three months, young Edison dropped off the train when it stopped at Mt. Clemens twice a day to sit beside Mackenzie and take the instruction that was to direct him along the line of a great career. He absorbed the knowledge of the Morse code "like a wet sponge," as Mackenzie said. To give him more time at the telegraph instrument, Sutherland, the baggage man, offered to bring the evening papers as far as Mt. Clemens, where Al could pick them up and go on.

Two weeks passed on this daily routine, when the lad appeared with a set of telegraph instruments that he had made with his own hands. It was found that while he was on the Detroit end of the run, he had been going to the gun shop of Fisher & Long and asked for the use of a bench and some tools for a few days; his friend, J. A. Roys, who had sold him his first printing press, had vouched for him to the gun-shop proprietor: "He is a smart youngster and I prophesy great things for him!" exclaimed Roys.

The value of loyal friendships was making itself evident in the mind of young Thomas Edison. This discovery, too, was to play an important part in his future life. Three friendships already were landmarks in his progress as a boy: Storey and "the thousand papers"; Roys and the printing press; Mackenzie and the telegraph key.

Mackenzie was amazed at the perfection of the instrument and the speed which Edison developed with it. The hours of instruction, snatched from long and busy days, continued for twelve weeks — until the day when Mackenzie told Al that he was "a full-fledged telegraph operator and could graduate and take his first job."

"By this time," said Mackenzie, "he knew as much about telegraphy as I did."

BIDS FAREWELL TO NEWSBOY LIFE FOREVER

Al had staked everything on a career as a "telegraph man." He had bidden "farewell forever" to the life of a newsboy, a "candy butcher," and an embryo merchant, devoting eighteen hours a day to the mastery of telegraphy. His income was shut off and he was falling back on his savings.

His first venture was to put up a telegraph line from the station to the village at Port Huron; the distance was about a mile, and he established his office in a drug store. As telegraphy was a comparatively new medium of communication, confined largely to railroads, there were but few private messages to be sent by the residents of Port Huron; business was necessarily small and the income exceedingly limited.

Moreover, there was competition. The established telegraph office at Port Huron was in the jewelry store of a man named Walker, whose brother-in-law acted as operator. This brother-in-law was offered a job by the Army in the Military Telegraph Corps in these days of the Civil War, where the pay was high. He informed Walker that he was going into the Army and that the Edison boy could fill the position of operator at Port Huron. Mackenzie also endorsed him.

FIRST PAID JOB AS TELEGRAPH OPERATOR — PORT HURON

We find young Edison installed on his first paid job as a telegraph operator in Port Huron, in 1862–63. He put himself into the job with his usual vigor, staying on duty both day and night and sleeping near the telegraph instrument.

"Most of the business was done during the day," said Edison in explaining these hours, "but I stayed on at night because the press reports came over the wires until three o'clock in the morning and I would cut in and copy it as well as I could to become more rapidly proficient. The goal of the rural telegraph operator was to be able to take press."

Walker protested because young Edison also used his jewelry shop at night for a chemical laboratory; he began to lug in all sorts of bottles from the drug store and conduct experiments between messages; there were jars and wires scattered all over the place. He also annoyed Walker by making too free use of the watchmaker's tools on the little table in the front window. The business of the office seldom amounted to more than fifty to seventy-five dollars a month and Walker seemed to think that twenty dollars a month for young Al was "too high pay."

Then came what Edison considered his first "regular job" on the telegraph line, in 1863, at the age of sixteen years. He was given the "night wire" as a railway operator at Stratford Junction, in Canada, on the line of the Grand Trunk railroad. The wages were twenty-five dollars a month. This demonstrates again that Edison placed little value on money, for he had been in business where he had made almost that sum in a day. His object was to grow — to get somewhere in the world — and let the money take care of itself, according to the value of the services he could perform.

Here, he began to "burn the candle at both ends" — a telegraph operator at night and an experimenter and inventor during the day. The hours on duty were from seven P. M. to seven A. M. It was here at Stratford Junction that his inventive genius began to show itself in his attempts to improve the science of telegraphy (which had been invented by Morse in 1835, twenty-eight years before). Its operation consisted largely of signals and symbols used by the railway operators: the symbol "23" indicated a message of death or accident and is said to be the beginning of the slang expression: "bad luck, or 'hoodoo' — 23"; the symbol "73" was a telegraphers' symbol for "good wishes," or "good luck."

"I tried to get the telegraph men to explain to me the principle on which it worked," said Edison in later years.

"PULL HIS TAIL IN EDINBURGH — BARKS IN LONDON"

Young Edison's habit of always asking questions was increasing, not decreasing. He cross-questioned the telegraph men to explain the principle that made the telegraph work. They seemed to know little about it and to care less; to them it was only a job; they had a certain amount of work to do and they did it, without looking into the why's or wherefore's. But an old Scotch line repairer who operated the railroad wires for the Montreal Telegraph Company gave Edison this definition:

"If you had a dog like a Dachshund, long enough to reach from Edinburgh to London — if you pulled his tail in Edinburgh he would bark in London — that is the telegraph!"

"I could understand that," remarked Edison afterwards, "but I never could get it through me what went through the dog or over the wire!"

The old adage that "Necessity is the mother of invention" was proved true at the very beginning of the career of the youth who was to become the world's greatest inventor. Edison's very first invention was the product of necessity: his long hours on duty at Stratford Junction, which were from seven o'clock P. M. to seven o'clock A. M. The orders required that the operator send, every hour, after nine o'clock, the signal "6" to the office of the train despatcher. This "six-ing" was to prove that the operator was awake. Edison, however, proved that this was only "circumstantial evidence." The report came through from Edison's station always on the dot — never a minute before and never a minute after — but there was something mystifying about this exactness, as attempts to "get" him over his own wire frequently failed.

Edison's First Invention — and Its Results

One night, the train despatcher decided to investigate the conditions at Stratford; he opened the key and called for fifteen minutes; then, becoming alarmed that something terrible had occurred, he darted out and secured a hand car and hastened to the junction. Rushing to the station window and peering in as if he expected to find the operator murdered, he saw — young Edison sleeping soundly in his chair, thoroughly at peace with the world. Still believing that the boy might be dead, he reached out to shake him, when he saw a curious bit of mechanism on the table near the telegraph instrument.

It was a device which hooked the telegraph instrument with the clock. The inspector decided to wait and see what happened, believing it was an alarm that would arouse the sleeper. The hand of the clock finally reached the moment of the signal — but no alarm went off. The young operator kept on slumbering, and, to the astonishment of the inspector, the mechanism performed his duty for him!

"I could hardly believe my eyes," exclaimed the inspector afterwards. "When the hand of the clock struck the hour, the instrument 'got busy' and one lever threw open the key while the other sent the signal over the wire!"

What happened the moment after, however, is a different story: The inspector took one look at the sleeping lad, grabbed him by the collar, gave him a vigorous shaking-up — and fired him. Edison's first invention had worked perfectly, but he had neglected to take proper precautions for protecting himself. It is sufficient to say that this first invention was never patented, either by him or the telegraph company, but it was sufficient to prove the mechanical genius of the boy, which was to develop amazing proportions in the years to come.

"Fired" — His Second Job Is in Sarnia

The young operator's next job was at Sarnia, in Canada, and here circumstances set in against him before he had time to invent any new contrivance while under such close observation. Here is his own version of the historic episode:

"The job at Sarnia just suited me, as I could have the whole day to myself. I taught the night yardman my call so I could get half an hour's sleep now and then between trains. One night, I got an order to hold a freight train and replied immediately that I would do it. I rushed out to find the signalman, but before I could find him and get the signal set, the train roared past my station. I ran to the telegraph office and sent the report over the wire. The only reply I got was: 'Hell!'"

"I knew by instinct," explained Edison, "that the despatcher, on the strength of my message that I would hold the train, had permitted another train to leave the last station in the opposite direction. My mind was filled with visions of a head-on collision. There was a lower station near the junction, where the day operator slept. I started for it on foot. The night was dark and I fell into a culvert and was knocked senseless."

Two trains were rushing at each other at that moment. Suddenly, the engineers, peering alertly from their cabin windows, saw each other's headlight just ahead on the single track — pulled the levers — and brought their trains to a jolting stop but a few feet from each other. A disastrous accident had been prevented by a moment's quick action.

Investigation was made to fix the blame; the despatcher tried to throw the responsibility on the young telegraph operator. Edison was summoned to the General Manager's Office in Toronto on charges preferred against him for neglect of duty. He was not guilty, and he knew he was not guilty, but he also knew that he was to be made "the goat."

"Young man," exclaimed W. J. Spicer, the General Manager, noted for his severity, "this offense of yours is a serious one and I think I shall make an example of you. I can send you to the penitentiary for five years and ——"

The young telegraph operator could see that a delicate situation faced him; he realized that he was to become the victim of injustice and he would have to take quick action.

"Just at this moment," stated Edison when telling the facts about this incident, "two English gentlemen came in and Mr. Spicer rose to greet them. They engaged him in conversation and I seized the chance to slip quietly out the door. I headed for the freight depot, where I found a freight train about to start for Sarnia. I knew the conductor and

persuaded him to run me back to my station. He agreed.
I stayed on that freight train right through, but my pulse
didn't get down to normal while I was in Canada. I boarded
the ferry boat between Sarnia and Port Huron — and found
myself, at last, safe over the Canadian border, in the
United States."

While the boy slumbered the clock was on duty.   The trains stopped but a few feet apart.

Photo by Underwood

THE TRIBUTE OF A NATION

On behalf of the United States Congress, the "wizard of finance" (Andrew W. Mellon, Secretary of the Treasury) presents to the "wizard of electricity" (Thomas A. Edison) the Congressional Medal of Honor.

Photo by International News

RECEIVING THE JOHN SCOTT MEDAL

Presented by Supreme Court Justice Owen J. Roberts to Mr. Edison for his services to humanity. The Fund and Medal Award was established in 1816, by John Scott, chemist, of Edinburgh, Scotland.

Henry Ford talking to Thomas A. Edison

Edison's Menlo Park laboratory a shrine

Old village post office

Schoolhouse of Edison's days

Old tollhouse shoe shop

Old Lincoln courthouse

Sally Jordan's boarding house, where Edison's
men lived at Menlo Park

PHOTOGRAPHS FROM THE RECORDS OF HENRY FORD

Menlo Park Laboratory of Thomas Edison, reconstructed in its original form and preserved as an historic shrine at Dearborn, Michigan, stands among these old historic buildings.

CHAPTER X

EXPLORING THE MIDDLE WEST—IN SEARCH OF OPPORTUNITY

The veteran operators, who at first ridiculed the young telegrapher, are astonished at his marvelous speed.

FIVE years of wandering now began — a youth sixteen years of age trying to find his place in the world. Working his way from city to city, up and down the Mississippi Valley, he reached New Orleans determined to go to South America.

This period of "wanderlust" in Edison's life — 1863-68 — would have broken the spirit of most youths, with its hunger and discouragements, but it only put "mettle" into young Edison. As an itinerant telegraph operator he worked the "night wires" wherever he could get a job.

Sometimes with money, and sometimes penniless, he traveled on. All the time he was becoming more proficient as an operator, gaining speed, making experiments, and even being discharged for introducing "improvements and inventions." He was determined to be "master of his trade."

These wanderings began when he left Canada,—after the averted head-on collision. He was determined to live down that tragic experience, which threatened to shake his faith in human nature.

The Civil War was creating a great demand for telegraph operators; more than fifteen hundred of them were
on duty at the front in the Federal armies alone. General
Grant, in his memoirs, paid tribute to them in these words:
"Nothing could be more complete than the organization
and discipline of this body of brave and intelligent men."

Young Edison decided that there must be a great
demand for civilian operators along the railroad stations of
the war zone. He had never been away from home, but
felt that this was the time for him to make the break and
to go out on "his own." His father was in his sixtieth year,
and his mother was nearing fifty-four years of age. The
home-leaving was hard for the old folks, but they realized
that from now on he must "live his own life."

Edison Leaves Home and Starts "Wanderings"

After a short time around Port Huron, Detroit, Adrian,
Michigan, and then Toledo, Ohio, he bade "good-by" to
his family and left the old home — never again to return
to it except on brief visits.

We find the "roving telegraph operator" going on to
Fort Wayne, Indiana, and then to Indianapolis — he appears in Cincinnati, Memphis, and Louisville — then north-
ward again to Detroit and back to Louisville — southward
to New Orleans — and again to Louisville and to Cincinnati — and then once more walking into the old home at
Port Huron for a few weeks, only to leave for what was to
prove to be his "Grand Invasion of the East."

This is a story of Vagabondia with some of the most
romantic personalities in the development of the country.
Telegraph operators in these days were an adventurous
crew — hale, hearty, and filled with the spirit of good
comradeship. Young Edison found himself in a new world

among them, but they took him into their midst, as one of their own brothers. To them, he was the "Wolverene," the "Kid from Michigan," and the "Boy with the Big Ideas." His frank, homely honesty gained their immediate respect and admiration.

"When I arrived in Toledo I felt like a globe-trotter," said Edison in narrating these adventures. "I secured a day job over at Fort Wayne, but did not like it as I had become a 'night owl.' So, two months later, in the fall of 1864, I moved on to Indianapolis." It is interesting to note that upon his arrival in Indianapolis he dropped his boyhood name of "Al," and appeared from this time on as "T. A. Edison." "I was assigned to duty at the Union Station," he said, "at seventy-five dollars a month, for the Western Union Telegraph Company, whose service I now entered for the first time."

Here he was put on the night press wire. Finding that he "broke" frequently, he began to devise a mechanism to increase speed and accuracy. And, as remarkable as it may seem, the instrument he created at this time gave him the idea which in later years was to work out into the phonograph. His inventive genius was under way, and every minute of the night while at work he was seeking methods by which the utility of the telegraph could be expanded to its fullest powers.

"The urge to move on now carried me to Cincinnati, in February, 1865," he explained. "Here I found employment with the Western Union, at sixty dollars a month — fifteen less than in my former job."

"Plug Operator" Becomes "First-Class Man"

Because of his youth and inexperience, Edison was first rated at Cincinnati as a "plug," or inferior operator. This goaded his pride and he seized every opportunity to show that he was one of the best of them. Then came the big day when he was jumped from "plug" to "first-class man." He could look every telegrapher square in the eye and tell him to "shoot your copy as fast as lightning — it can't come too fast for me."

"Here, also," continued Edison, "I made the acquaintance of Milt (Milton F.) Adams, one of the most brilliant and friendly men I ever knew. It was he who, four years later, was to persuade me to 'go East.' Then there was Hank Bogardus — we called him 'Bogie.' Good fellow, Hank — fine operator, too. . . He came out to see me more than forty years afterwards, and borrowed five dollars. He went away and returned in three or four days, looking like a tramp and with a breath like a whiff from a charnel house. This time he wanted ten dollars. 'No,' I said, 'you get only five — that breath, Bogie, is going to cost you five dollars.' He ended his days in a freight car by death from exposure."

There were many picturesque characters on the telegraph wires in Cincinnati at this time; George Ellsworth, who was telegrapher to the famous Southern guerrilla Morgan when he made his raid into Ohio, and who escaped by swimming the Ohio River on an army mule; he finally became a bad "gun man" in the Panhandle of Texas, where he was killed. It was Ellsworth who urged Edison to invent a secret method of sending dispatches so that an intermediate operator could not tap the wire, claiming he could sell it to the Government for a large sum of money. Edison succeeded in making this instrument, which had in it the germ of the quadruplex, which he later developed, for sending four messages over one wire simultaneously.

First Exciting Experiences in Cincinnati

"Another interesting character whose friendship I made at this time was Stanton," said Edison. "I went down to the train to see him off to the cattle country in the West, and never expected to see him again. Six months afterwards, while working press wire in Cincinnati, about two A. M., there was flung into the middle of the operating room a large tin box. It made a report like a pistol and we all jumped up, startled. In walked Stanton."

"Gentlemen," exclaimed Stanton, "I have just returned from a pleasure trip to the land beyond the Mississippi. All my wealth is contained in my metallic traveling case and you are welcome to it."

The case was opened and it contained a solitary paper collar. Stanton had a woolen comforter around his neck, with his coat buttoned closely. The night was intensely warm. He opened his coat and revealed the fact that he had nothing over his bare chest.

"Gentlemen," ejaculated Stanton, "you see before you an operator who has reached the limit of impecuniosity!"

It was while Edison was in Cincinnati that the Civil War came to an end. Immense crowds gathered in the streets.

The night of April 14, 1865, was memorable in Edison's mind, not only because of the event that took place, but also because of the remarkable manner in which he received the news. He was at work in the telegraph office when he saw an excited throng outside the window, and sent a messenger boy to find out the cause. The boy came running back with a look of panic on his face. "Lincoln's shot!" he shouted.

Edison looked surprised and the operators glanced at one another in amazement. One of the men picked up the files of the press stuff which they had taken over the wire. There it was — the telegraph operator had worked so mechanically that he had handled the greatest news of the day without the slightest realization of its significance.

Youth That Looked Like Napoleon

Milt Adams has described Edison in these days: "I well recall him when he drifted in to take a job. He was a youth of about eighteen years, decidedly unprepossessing in dress, and rather uncouth in manner. . . His nose was very prominent, giving a Napoleonic look to his face. . . As an operator he had no superiors, and very few equals.

Edison stopped long enough in Cincinnati to eliminate the rats.

Most of the time he was 'monkeying' with batteries and circuits. He arranged in the cellar what he called his 'rat paralyzer,' a very simple contrivance, consisting of two plates insulated from each other and connected with a main battery. They were so placed that when a rat passed over, the fore feet on the one plate and the hind feet on the other completed the circuit and the rat departed this life electrocuted."

"Whenever we could get a breathing spell — and our capital was sufficient," continued Adams, "Edison and I would go to the theater. It was new then and he was deeply impressed by tragedy. Edison enjoyed 'Othello' greatly. He would sit thrilled before such actors as Forrest and John McCullough and then go back to the office and work all night as a 'lightning-slinger.' He was now getting eighty dollars a month, and added to this by copying plays for the theater, because he wrote a hand that looked like steel plate."

The two friends parted — Adams went North and Edison went South. His next stopping place was Memphis, Tennessee.

MEMPHIS VS. ST. LOUIS — EDISON WINS CHAMPIONSHIP

It was down in Memphis that they decided to "show this smart young Michigander a thing or two." The rival city of St. Louis held the championship with an operator who was chain lightning. Young Edison was put on his wire with orders to "blow the kid up." He started about fifty words behind. Then St Louis sped up until the receiver fairly "spit fire."

As the Memphis "gang" gathered around the new operator, they were amazed to see the "jay" was taking top speed and writing it out with his beautiful copperplate hand. Reaching over and opening the key, Edison shot back this message:

"St. Louis — get — a — hustle — on."

Cheers went up in the Memphis office that "shook the rafters." St. Louis had been "rawhiding" Memphis for a long time — at last they had found one of their own men, a newcomer, who could "rawhide St. Louis's electric cyclone." T. A. Edison was declared the "Champion of the Mississippi Valley." An old Tennesseean describes him on that day: "He wore a hickory shirt, a pair of butternut pants, tucked into the tops of his boots, which looked too large for him, and which evidently were guiltless of blacking." This was the new champion. "We took him out and gave him a dinner, but never were able to get 'the look of the slick operator into him.'"

WHEN ANDREW CARNEGIE WAS A TELEGRAPH OPERATOR

There were fast men on the wires in these days: Andrew Carnegie was starting out in life as an operator in the Civil War and the canny little Scot was said to be "streaked lightning." The youth who became Sir William Van Horne was a "speed man." George Kennan, who became one of the world's greatest war correspondents, was a crack operator in Cincinnati just before Edison arrived. Then there were such men as "Dick" Duncan in Pittsburgh; the Bunnells in Buffalo; and the Weir brothers in Cincinnati, probably the "greatest experts that telegraphy has ever produced."

Many stories are told of their speed. It was said of L. C. Weir, who later became president of the Adams Express Company: "He could take down two streams of press reports from two separate instruments at the same time, copying one with each hand on manifold sheets (using both his right and left hands with equal skill) and at the same time carry on a general conversation."

Honor among these operators had a strict code. The crime of all crimes was "tapping wires," or "listening in" on messages for the purpose of stealing quotations from the New York Stock Market and "beating the board." When a man was caught at this game it went hard with him; he was lucky if he didn't get a ride out of town on a rail.

Edison was assigned to catch one of these "double-crossers" whom he hated like vermin.

"Set a trap," was the order. "If he's innocent it won't hurt him — but if he's guilty it will *break his back!*"

Again we find Edison making inventions and improvements on existing apparatus which resulted in his being requested to "move on."

EDISON MOVES ON TO NASHVILLE AND LOUISVILLE

"The superintendent would not even give me a pass to Nashville," explained Edison, "so I had to pay my fare. I had so little money left that I nearly starved at Decatur, Alabama, and had to stay three days before going on north to Nashville. I went to the telegraph office, got money enough to buy a little solid food and secured a pass to Nashville. . . I arrived at Louisville on a bitterly cold day, with ice on the gutters. I was wearing a linen duster and it was not much to look at, but I got a position at once working on a press wire.

"The close of the Civil War," stated Edison, "had left everything in a desperate condition. Disorganization reigned supreme. The operators were coming in like derelicts from the war at all hours. One came in one night, drunk, and kicked over the stove; he piled every operator's table on top and tore the switchboard from the wall, smashing the batteries. Then he left the place, well satisfied with his destruction. Another one started to throw pistol cartridges into the flames on the fire grate. These would explode and I was twice hit by the bullets.

THE NIGHT THAT A POLICEMAN SHOT AT EDISON

"The Southern cities were wide open at this time. At night I would go with a companion for midnight lunch and find the faro bank running briskly. There were over twenty keno rooms running. One of them that I visited was in a Baptist Church — the man with the wheel being in the pulpit and the gamblers in the pews."

Among the famous men of the time whom Edison met in Louisville was the celebrated poet and journalist, George D. Prentiss, the editor of the *Courier-Journal;* he was the father of the humorous paragraphs in American journalism. The celebrated Colonel Henry W. Watterson was one of its "giant figures." Then there was Tyler, on the Associated Press, a Harvard man. Edison listened to them as they argued on the immortality of the soul. The young telegraph operator would listen to these discussions and then go out and buy books at auctions and secondhand stores. He bid in twenty unbound volumes of the *North American Review* for two dollars and had them bound and "dressed" at the telegraph office. About three o'clock one morning he was walking home at a rapid pace with ten of these volumes over his shoulder. Bullets began to fly about him. Then, suddenly, a policeman came rushing up.

"Why don't you stop when I shout for you to halt?" demanded the officer.

"I didn't hear you," explained Edison. "I am slightly deaf."

"Open that package and show me what you have got. Where did you get it?" commanded the policeman, seizing him as a suspicious character.

Edison slowly opened the package — as if a burglar caught with the booty — and there it was — books! A look of disgust passed over the policeman's face.

"It's lucky for you, boy, that I am not a better shot," he exclaimed. "You're lucky that I didn't kill you."

WORKS HIS WAY FROM DETROIT TO NEW ORLEANS

Edison again "moved on" — this time back north as far as Detroit, only to return soon to Louisville, where he became imbued with the lure to go to South America. Again he threw up his job and worked his way with a couple of telegraphers to New Orleans to catch a steamer for Brazil. There was a great riot in New Orleans upon their arrival, and mobs were roaming the streets. The steamer was seized by the Government, so the "Three Musketeers" started out to find another vessel.

"Why do you want to go to South America?" asked an old Spaniard from whom they were seeking advice.

"We hear there is great wealth down there," answered one of the telegraph operators.

"You had better stay right here in the United States," declared the Spaniard emphatically. "This is the land of opportunity — which can't be equaled anywhere on the face of the earth."

Young Edison's spirit of adventure was crushed right there; his two companions went on to Vera Cruz and died of yellow fever, but he returned to Louisville and again lost himself in the pages of books and more books — treatises on end — and continuous experiments, while "keeping on the job."

ON THE ROAD "BACK HOME" — AND ON TO THE "EAST"

"One night while conducting experiments," stated Edison, "I spilled a bottle of sulphuric acid. The acid ran out, went through to the manager's room below and ate up his desk and all the carpet. The next morning I was summoned before him and told that what the company wanted was operators, not experimenters. I was at liberty to take my pay and get out."

His wanderings led back to Cincinnati. Again he went on night duty — renting a room, purchasing an oil stove and a cot, with a foot lathe and some tools — and was soon engaged daytimes in his experiments. But the "wanderlust" was leaving him and he wanted to settle down where he could permanently build a laboratory and start out as an inventor. His thoughts led him back to Port Huron to see his family and the old house where he had his first laboratory in the cellar. The family greeted him with delight, and, while there was no "fatted calf," his mother prepared a regular Thanksgiving Dinner in his honor.

Then, one day, he sat down and wrote a letter to Boston; it was to his old friend, Milt Adams, asking if there was any chance for him in the East.

"Come along," came back the reply. "There is a big chance for you here and I will get you a job!"

The big day when Edison was jumped from "plug" to "first-class man."

A messenger boy brought the tragic news of Lincoln's assassination.

CHAPTER XI

"EASTWARD, HO!"—THE STRIKE FOR FAME AND FORTUNE

EDISON'S VOTE RECORDER

A time-saving device invented by Edison for recording votes in Congress, but Congress didn't want to save time and so rejected it.

EDISON reversed Horace Greeley's advice: "Go West, young man!" He decided to "Go East." "I blew in on a terrific blizzard," he explained in relating the incident of the journey — four days snow-bound on the train from Michigan, with the thermometer twenty-eight degrees below zero.

This was in 1868 — as Edison was approaching his twenty-first birthday. His adventures in the Middle West had given him a fund of knowledge, but little money. The journey to Boston was made on a "pass" which he negotiated with the Grand Trunk railroad back home in Port Huron, Michigan, for services rendered. When one of the two submarine cables which crossed the river, connecting the United States and Canada, was lost in a storm, young Edison had set up a device which made the remaining cable do the work formerly done by the two cables.

"We ran into the blizzard shortly after leaving Toronto," Edison reported. "Our train got snowed under in a cut, where we passengers were imprisoned for twenty-four hours. We got some fence-rail splints and made snowshoes, starting out through the blinding storm to find food. Finally, we reached a roadside inn, where the passengers on snowshoes found a refuge. We arrived in Montreal four days late. Among our comrades was a soldier who was returning from a furlough and feared court-martial, so I, with some of the other passengers, went to the military headquarters with him to testify in his favor."

On Way to Boston through Terrific Blizzard

"Here, in Montreal, I met with a happy surprise," exclaimed Edison. "I found my old friend, Stanton, who had 'reached the limit of impecuniosity,' in Cincinnati, without a shirt to his back, and was now on the job in Canada. He took me to his boarding house, where the board was one dollar and a half a week. Nobody got enough to eat and the bedclothes were too short and too thin, so we got little sleep with the thermometer at twenty-eight degrees below zero. When we woke up in the morning, the wash water in the room was frozen solid."

"There is one advantage to this boarding house," explained Stanton, "the usual live-stock accompaniment found in operators' boarding houses is absent. I presume that the intense cold has caused them to hibernate."

Edison's entrance into Boston, in 1868, was not exactly a historic event in a city so rich in its traditions, its battle of Bunker Hill, and its famous old elm where Washington had taken command of the army, at Cambridge. He reported immediately to his old comrade, Milton Adams, of the Cincinnati days, and was taken over to the Western Union, where he was introduced to the manager, George F. Millikan.

"When are you ready to go to work?" asked Millikan.

"Now," replied the young operator from the West.

That night Edison started on his first job in the East. The stranger, poorly clad, but always "at home" when he bent over his telegraph instrument, aroused the curiosity of the night men. Having heard from Adams that the boy had "speed," they entered into a conspiracy to "put up a job on the jay from the Woolly West" — to see if he could live up to his reputation.

FIRST JOB IN BOSTON — PLOT TO "SALT HIM"

A plot was "cooked up" with one of the fastest senders in New York to "salt the new man." The stranger was now given the "freeze out"; he was assigned to the New York No. 1 wire, given a pen and told to "go to work." There he waited for an hour — to test his patience — when he was ordered to a special table to take an important dispatch for the *Boston Herald*.

As the new operator sat down unsuspiciously at the table, the conspirators watched from a safe distance. The New York man started slowly; then he increased his speed; then he opened up "all he had in him," until the instrument hummed. The conspirators looked bewildered, as "the jay from the West" took his punishment with ease. Nothing that the New York "speed king" could deliver was too fast for young Edison.

This seemed to puzzle the sending operator on the other end of the wire in New York. It looked as if he were falling into his own trap and he resorted to all the tricks of the trade, slurring over his words, running them together, and sticking the signals. Edison was not in the least discomfited. He had been up against the same plots in the West, when he sent the "lightning-slinger" from St. Louis to his Waterloo. Here, again, he resorted to his old strategy, quietly opening the key, and flashed back to New York:

"Say — young man — change off — and send with your other foot."

Young Edison had won his first victory in the East — the Boston operators were now his friends — and the New York "speed king" was so broken up that night that he turned this job on that wire over to another man to finish.

LIVING IN A HALL ROOM WITH FARADAY'S WORKS

Edison found himself perfectly "at home" in Boston; he kept on the job at night and opened his first workshop, where he became busily engaged during the day under lock and key. What he was working on — nobody knew. It was a "state secret." It was apparent he had decided to take up science and invention where he had left off in his childhood home when he began his wanderings down the Mississippi River Valley. He did not regret his days of "wanderlust," but he remarked to his friend, Adams:

"Adams, I have got so much to do — life is so short — *I am going to hustle!*"

He began to develop again his insatiable desire for knowledge regarding the electrical forces. One day he picked up a secondhand set of Faraday's works and brought them home at four o'clock in the morning, sitting down and reading steadily until breakfast. "I think I must have tried about everything in those books," said Edison later. "His explanations were simple. He used no mathematics. He was the master experimenter. I don't think there were many copies of Faraday's works sold in those days. The only people who did anything in electricity were the telegraphers and the opticians, making simple school apparatus to demonstrate the principles."

"I was his constant companion in Boston," said Adams. "We lived in a hall bedroom, which helped to reduce our expenses. We got our meals at a boarding house about a mile away, where it was cheap. Edison was always working — eighteen to twenty hours a day. The morning he came home with Faraday's works, he rushed in as excited as if he had come from a fire. I couldn't break him away. I never saw a man devour anything so fast in my life. Then he rushed off to get a bite to eat and disappeared in his workshop for the day. We did not see him again until he showed up at the telegraph office for his night work."

Nights on Duty — War of the Cockroaches

The Western Union office was on the ground floor, not far from Boston Commons. It was the typical telegraph office of the times — "any old hole-in-a-wall which was in a central location." The Boston office had been used as a restaurant, which had left behind swarms of cockroaches. Most of the operators brought their midnight lunches with them, and promptly at the stroke of the hour, an old Irish vendor, called the "cake man," appeared. This was the signal for the cockroaches to march forth; they came in battalions, like armies — making their raids on sandwiches, apple pie, and whatever they could loot.

Edison's inventive genius was called upon to stop this invasion; he had succeeded in eliminating the rats in Cincinnati and there seemed to be no reason why he should not get the cockroaches out of Boston. Surely, the man who was destined to become "the world's great inventor" could master a problem like this.

He said nothing — but when he reported for duty the next night, there was a look of determination on his face. He had laid out a plan that might be conceived by some

8

future Napoleon in the annihilation of armies. It did not differ in principle from the electrically charged, barbed-wire barricades erected in the World War.

Armed with a roll of tin foil, he cut it into strips and stretched them around the table. Then he connected these strips with two heavy batteries and awaited the results. It required but a single cockroach to cross the dead line and to make the circuit complete.

"We awaited the slaughter with morbid interest," said one of the old operators in later years. "One big fellow came up to the post at the southeast corner of the room and stopped for a moment. Then he brushed his nose with his fore legs and started. He reached the first ribbon in safety, but as soon as his fore-creepers struck the opposite or parallel ribbon, over he went, as dead as a free message. From that time until after lunch the check boys were kept busy carrying out the dead." At midnight the cordon of defunct beetles around the table looked like a miniature Great Wall of China. The ingenuity of this device caused a Boston newspaper to interview Edison and write a half-column story, but the night manager protested against the publicity and "electrocutions were discontinued by request."

EXPLOSION OF THE MYSTERIOUS BOX

Frequently, when Edison left his workshop and reported for duty at the telegraph office, he brought with him mysterious packages. One night he laid something concealed in a metal case on the mantel back of the stove, muttering, "I don't believe it's any good." There it stayed for several weeks, until one chilly night a fire was started in the stove. A few minutes later there was a loud explosion — the front of the stove blew out. The operators rushed from the room, while Edison stood running his hands through his hair, and exclaimed, "Well, it *was* good, after all!" He had made some guncotton from a formula of his own.

There are many stories that have come out of the old Boston days which indicate the unfolding inventive genius of the young operator. It was the bad habit of many of the operators to carry away the tin dipper that hung on a nail on the wall over the tank filled with ice water for drinking. Edison decided to do something that would cure this bad habit. He connected the nail with a wire, at the other end of which were 190 cells of Fuller battery. Then he placed a sign below the dipper: "Please return this dipper." It is needless to say that this request was heeded. The dipper was never taken down, but there were a dozen wrenched arms in the office in less than an hour.

HUMOROUS ANECDOTES OF OLD BOSTON DAYS

"I remember once when Edison bought a new suit of clothes," stated one of the old operators. "It was not often he spent much money on these luxuries, but that time he got a thirty-dollar suit. The next Sunday he was experimenting in his workshop with a bottle of sulphuric acid. Suddenly the bottle exploded and the new suit was ruined.

" 'That's what I get for putting so much money in a suit!' was Edison's only comment.

Edison, himself, liked to relate the stories of these early days, especially those that recalled their financial straits. He was spending his entire income on chemicals and experiments and was chronically "dead broke."

"Adams and myself were together most of the time. We browsed around the secondhand book stores and he always took a great interest in whatever I was doing. Our finances were always strained, and when Adams was laid off, I let him sleep in my hall bedroom. I remember one morning after breakfast we saw a large crowd in front of two small gents' furnishing stores on Tremont Row. They were looking at a sign which read: 'Three Hundred Pairs of Stockings Received This Day — Five Cents a Pair — No Connection with the Store Next Door.' Then the store next door put up a sign in which it reduced the price to three cents a pair. The competitive war went on until the prices had fallen to the point where the last sign read: 'Three Pairs for One Cent!'

"I can't stand this any longer — give me a cent!" shouted Adams to Edison.

Edison pulled the cent out of his pocket and Adams pushed his way through the crowds into the store: "Give me three pairs!" he called out. The girl took down a box and handed it to him, but Adams was wary and opened it — it contained three pairs of baby socks. He demanded "men's size," but the proprietor indignantly informed him: "Well, sir, we do not permit one to pick sizes for that money!"

WHY THE INSULATOR SHOT AT HIS HEAD

What was to come out of the workshop was not yet revealed, but it was known that Edison was working on an "important invention" and also on some chemical formulas. The application of one of his formulas gave him a narrow escape from injury which might have cost him his life. There was some trouble on the New York wire No. 1, by operators constantly interrupting, or "breaking," to have words repeated which they had failed to get. New York claimed that Boston was one of the worst offenders.

It happened that the office boy was "down" on one of the operators and he asked Edison how to fix a key so that it would not "break," even if the circuit breaker was open, and also so that it could not be easily detected. Edison suggested that if he took a penful of ink and splashed it on the platinum points, it might produce the results; he figured that the chemical element in the ink was sufficiently thick to hold up when the operator tried to "break," while at the same time the current could still go through the ink.

The next night, the first test came. The operator was rapidly taking a long press report over the wire, but, when suddenly compelled to open his key, found that he couldn't — it had jammed. The office boy had done his "dirty work" a few moments before, when the operator had turned his head. Suddenly, there was a crash — a glass insulator was thrown with great violence at Edison's head — just missing him. The angered operator believed the inventor had been tinkering with his instrument.

"It would certainly have killed me if it had not missed," remarked Edison. "That operator had a violent temper."

ACCIDENT THAT MIGHT HAVE MADE HIM BLIND

It was at this time that Edison met with an accident which threatened his eyesight and might have made him blind for life. He was already deaf from his experiences as a train newsboy back in Michigan — and now he found himself facing even a greater danger. He himself told the story later:

"I was experimenting with a large induction coil," he said, "when I accidentally got hold of both electrodes. It clenched my hands on them so tightly that I couldn't let go. My only chance to get free was to back off so that the battery wires in my hands would pull the cells off the

shelf and break the circuit. I shut my eyes and pulled —
but the nitric acid splashed all over my face and ran down
my back.

"I rushed to the sink and climbed in, splashing water
over my head to dilute the acid and stop the pain. I thought
I was being burned alive. When I finally looked at myself
in the glass I was a ghastly black and yellow — my skin
was thoroughly oxidized. It was two weeks before I could
go out on the street. My face looked dreadful. My eyes,
fortunately, had been closed when the accident took place,
or I would have been blinded. The damaged skin peeled
off and new skin began to grow without leaving scars."

We shall see him meeting with a similar accident in
years to come — when exploding chloride of sulphur flew
into his eyes in his Menlo Park laboratory. His life was
one of constant danger, for he was always dealing with
powerful elements which he was trying to master.

During this experimental period, Edison became interested in the wonderful properties of nitroglycerin and
decided to undertake to make the compound. He produced
what he considered "a very small quantity" with such
success that it startled him with its "terrible and unexpected
results."

"The fact dawned upon us that we had a very large
white elephant on our hands," he confessed. "So at six
o'clock in the morning, I put the explosive into a sarsapa-
rilla bottle, tied a string to it, wrapped it in a paper, and
gently let it down into the sewer at the corner of State and
Washington streets."

EDISON DELIVERS HIS FIRST LECTURE

One day a request arrived at the Western Union from
the principal of a "select school," asking them to send one

of their experts to describe and exhibit the Morse telegraph to her "children." This job was awarded to Edison — with "special remuneration from the school." It is said, however, that when the appointed time came, Adams was unable to find Edison, and a search revealed him on the top of a house erecting a telegraph wire. Hurrying through the streets at the last minute, they arrived at the school with "a couple of sounders, a battery, and some wire" — to find to their horror and amazement an assembly of fashionably attired young ladies — they had expected to be greeted by boys.

"When Edison saw them, I thought he would faint," said Adams.

"Ladies and Gentlemen," Edison is accredited with stammering, "Mr. Adams will now lecture to you on the wonders of electricity."

There is a conflict of authorities over just what actually happened, but somehow they blundered through and were enthusiastically applauded by the "girls of the first families of Boston." The young women sat spellbound over the ill-kempt genius and he completely won the hearts of Beacon Hill and Commonwealth Avenue. Adams did the talking and Edison was the "wizard," who did the demonstrating.

"At any rate we got the money," explained Edison afterward. "I got out of this scrape and vowed never to 'lecture' again. But the 'lecture' had its compensations. Whenever I was walking on the streets after that and happened to meet these elegant young ladies, they bowed and smiled as if I were a long-lost friend. The other operators, knowing nothing about the episode, were much mystified over my large and exclusive acquaintance in Boston."

Edison soon found himself engaged on the construction of many private lines for business houses in Boston. He devised an alphabetical dial instrument which anyone could learn within a few minutes; this proved to be the forerunner of dials used in modern telephony. These instruments were made at Hamblet's shop, an inventor who was engaged in experimenting on electric clocks, which have since come into general use.

First Patented Invention of Thomas Edison

The first workshop in Boston finally produced its results. Thomas Edison appeared with his first patented invention — his name was recorded for the first time in the Patent Office in Washington, the office to which in the years to follow he was to "make a beaten path on the road to fame and fortune."

This first invention was a "Vote Recorder" — patent application signed October 11, 1868 — patent granted June 1, 1869 — No. 90,646. Its purpose was to facilitate counting the votes in the National House of Representatives at Washington. His experiences on the press wires had impressed him with the fact that there always was great confusion on the floors of Congress during the balloting.

Edison's "Vote Recorder" was a simple and practical electrical instrument, which could be placed on the Clerk's desk and attached by wire to the desk of every member in the legislative hall. All the senator or congressman had to do, when a question came up for vote, was to move a simple switch on his desk, either to the right or to the left, and it would register his vote on the machine at the Clerk's desk. It was an ingenious little device; the paper on which the vote was recorded was chemically prepared;

when the member moved the switch it closed the circuit — and an iron roller immediately passed over the paper under which was the type signifying the member's name. The contact of the type with the chemical paper turned it dark brown and practically printed the name on the roll of paper. There was an indicator that registered instantly the number of votes "for" and "against" — the machine counted the votes — insured accuracy — and gave a permanent record.

The secret of the mysterious little workshop in Boston was revealed. Edison had conceived this idea and taken it over to a maker of electrical apparatus on Court Street, one Charles Williams, where he had worked it out. The capital required was Edison's entire earnings as a telegraph operator and $100 which had been furnished by a fellow operator named Roberts. The Patent Attorney was Carroll D. Wright, later Director of the Eleventh Census and for twenty years United States Commissioner of Labor. Thomas Edison's days as a telegraph operator were now ended. He "threw up" his job at the Western Union and cast his lot with the world of inventors.

"Attacks Washington" with Vote-Recording Machine

With more borrowed money, he made his first trip to Washington. His arrival at the National Capital was unheralded and he had difficulty in securing sufficient influence to exhibit his "revolutionary Vote Recorder" before the proper committee. Finally, the day came when the young inventor stood before the chairman of the committee and several of the congressmen. The machine worked perfectly.

"Young man," exclaimed the chairman, "if there is one invention on earth that we don't want down here, it is this. One of the greatest weapons in the hands of a minority, to prevent bad legislation, is 'filibustering' on votes — and this instrument would prevent it."

This statement was the death knell of the "Vote Recorder." Edison realized its truth — he had failed to take into consideration political strategy and the maneuvers of the practical politicians. "Filibustering," and the changing of votes, is one of the most powerful weapons on the floor of Congress. Enormous time is wasted in each session for the deliberate purpose of gaining positions of advantage.

Young Inventor Takes Vow — and Returns to Boston

"Right there," declared Edison, "I made myself a pledge — I would never again waste any time in inventing anything that is not of general usefulness to the people, or that the people do not want and will not buy."

The young inventor returned to Boston, deeply disappointed, but in no way discouraged. He returned to his workshop and came out with a new "Stock Ticker," and we find him engaged in a ticker service at Boston with some forty subscribers, in a room over the Gold Exchange, in 1868. The first ticker had been invented by a man named Callahan in the preceding year, and had been introduced into service in New York. When Edison witnessed its immediate success, he set about to invent an improved ticker, which was to carry him to his first successful achievement.

"I advise you to go to New York," said his friend, Millikan, his former boss in the Western Union. "I have full faith in you and know you will 'make good.'" Edison had stopped over in New York on his way to Washington, but otherwise was an entire stranger in the great city.

Two Pals Part — Each to Go His Way

It is here that we meet the parting of the ways of two firm friends. "Good-by, Edison," said Milt Adams, grasping his friend's hand, "I have got sixty cents — and I am going to San Francisco."

How Adams worked his way across the continent is not known, but he disappeared and was next heard from on the Pacific, where he was leading a telegraphers' strike, standing under a big torch at night and selling patent medicines on the street; then he went to Peru, where, with a man who had a grizzly bear, he appeared in the bull ring. The bull killed the grizzly in five minutes and the adventure died right there.

Crossing the Andes, the adventuresome Adams installed himself in a market-report bureau in Buenos Aires — then he owned a restaurant in Pernambuco, Brazil. He was next heard from on the other side of the Atlantic, where, in the Transvaal, in Africa, he was running a panorama called, "Paradise Lost," in the Kaffir kraals. He appeared soon as editor of a newspaper in the Transvaal, and finally on the streets of London, where he was attempting to raise money for a railroad in Cape Colony. Years pass — until, one day, Adams comes back to meet his old friend, Edison, as we shall see as the life story progresses.

Edison, too, leaves Boston — on the night boat for New York.

CHAPTER XII

THE RISE FROM POVERTY TO INDEPENDENCE

Young Edison's first " big money." He wanted it all in bills, and he hadn't pockets enough.

WHEN the night boat from Boston sailed down through Hell Gate, the sun was rising over the City of New York. This morning in 1869 was the dawning of a new day for Thomas Edison as he stood on the deck, leaning over the steamer rail and gazing at the ships from all parts of the world in the harbor. What the future held for him, even he could not realize. The morning sunlight glistened on the scene before his eyes like the magical Kingdom of Cathay.

As he stepped down the gangplank, it was like another young Columbus starting out to conquer a new world. Here he was — twenty-two years old — in debt — penniless and without a friend in the great city. The last dollar he possessed had been paid for the boat trip when he left Boston. Like the first Americans who had thrown overboard the tea in Boston Harbor, he had thrown overboard everything he possessed on earth to make the new venture. Even his books and instruments and few belongings had been left behind as security for his debts. No one could have been poorer in worldly possessions — starvation stared him in the face. Benjamin Franklin, walking into

Philadelphia from Boston, with a loaf of bread under his arm, presents no more awe-inspiring picture than Thomas Edison entering New York "dead broke."

But there were some things that could not be taken away from him — his courage, his perseverance, his experience, and the knowledge and character which he had gained in his boyhood days "back home." These were now his entire capital.

EDISON'S FIRST DAY IN NEW YORK — PENNILESS

"My first thought after leaving the boat," he said in describing this historic day, "was to find some way to get breakfast. I was without sufficient money to obtain it. The journey to Washington with my 'Vote Recorder,' and my experiences with the statesmen at the National Capital, had put me heavily in debt. The funds I had borrowed to develop the 'stock ticker' and the 'Duplex' telegraph instrument were gone. Everything I possessed, and everything I had earned since twelve years of age, had been 'invested in acquiring experience and knowledge.' "

Hungry, he passed the coffeehouses and looked in as he walked along the street, until finally he came to a warehouse where a tea taster was inspecting a cargo just arrived from Ceylon.

"I wonder, sir," said Edison, "if you could give me a cup of tea?" This cup of tea was granted — his first breakfast in New York.

His first day was spent largely in visiting the telegraph offices to find the operators with whom he had "conversed" in stolen moments over the wires from Boston. Finally he walked into a good-natured operator who had heard all about him: "I am out of a job myself," he said, "but I will be glad to loan you a dollar." This was Edison's first friend in New York — and his first dollar. That night he walked into the gas-lighted restaurant across the way from Washington Market and ordered his supper.

"I had to make my dollar go a long way," he explained later, "so I ordered apple dumplings and coffee. It seemed to me that I had never eaten anything so good in all my life. I found the coffeehouse was famous for its food and was known through the country as 'Smith & McNell's.'"

Three Days on One Dollar — Sleeps in Battery Room

Then he had an idea — he would look up that "speed king" who had tried to "salt" him from this end of the New York wire No. 1. Jerry Borst was found at his telegraph instrument down in Printing House Square.

"He was the most silent man I had ever met," stated Edison. "He listened, stroked his beard and said nothing, but he took me over about midnight to an all-night lunch house in a basement — Oliver's — and pointed out the celebrated newspaper men there." It was here that they gathered for midnight lunch — such great men as Horace Greeley of the *New York Tribune;* Henry Raymond of the *New York Times;* Charles A. Dana of the *New York Sun,* and James Gordon Bennett of the *New York Herald;* Joseph Pulitzer was a youth of twenty years of age at this time, soon to start on his famous career with the *New York World.*

"That's a great place — a plate of cakes, a cup of coffee, and a Russian bath, for ten cents!" exclaimed Borst as they reached the sidewalk on this intensely hot night. Edison said that this was "fifty per cent of his entire conversation for two days."

Whether he was to spend the nights in the telegraph offices, or to find a place where he could sleep so that he could make his "invasions of the city" during the daytime, was his first problem. This was solved by securing permission to pass the nights in the battery room of the Gold Indicator Company, a concern that supplied a newly invented electrical indicator to record the quotations on the floor of the Gold Exchange in Wall Street. Three days he lived on the borrowed dollar, until, at the most unexpected moment, he walked directly into his first opportunity.

First Job in New York — Meets an Emergency

This first opportunity lay at his very feet — right where he was sleeping, in the battery room. On the third day after his arrival, there was a sudden commotion in the offices of the Gold Indicator Company — the transmitter which was sending quotations to the floor of the Gold Exchange suddenly stopped during an exciting moment in the market. Pandemonium broke loose — not only in the Indicator office but in the three hundred brokerage offices which were depending upon these quotations. The financial district was thrown into panic.

"Within three minutes," explained Edison "three hundred boys — a boy from every broker in the Street — were rushing up the stairs shouting the information at once that the quotations had stopped in their offices."

The inventor of the instrument — Dr. S. S. Laws, who had been Vice President of the Gold Exchange — rushed into the room in tense excitement. He demanded to know what had happened. The superintendent stood speechless. Young Edison, at this moment, volunteered the statement that he thought he could fix it.

"Fix it! Fix it! Be quick!" burst out Laws.

The young inventor from Boston stepped up to the instrument and found that a contact spring had been broken and dropped between the two gear wheels. He removed the broken spring and set the contact wheels at zero. Orders were issued for the entire force of men to rush to the three hundred offices of the financial district to set the instruments. Two hours later the system was again in perfect operation and peace was restored in the brokers' offices. The importance of this can be realized when it is considered that this was before the invention of the telephone and speculators were dependent on the new telegraph system or messenger boys.

"What's that boy's name?" demanded Dr. Laws, pointing at Edison.

Gets $300 a Month and Is Made Manager

On the following day when the inventor, Laws, entered his office, he sent for Edison. Sitting in the midst of stacks of books on science and physics, he attacked him with a barrage of questions: "What are you doing? Where did you come from? What do you know about telegraphy? What do you know about my indicator? How does it work?"

Edison answered promptly the severest examination he had ever been up against (it was a questionnaire that equaled his own famous tests for boys which he was to inaugurate some fifty years later). It ended with orders to Edison to "come in early in the morning" — he did not have far to go, for he was sleeping in the battery room.

"I have decided to put you in charge of my whole plant," announced Inventor Laws. "Your salary will be $300 a month!"

Loaned by Edison Family from Private Collection

A PAGE FROM EDISON'S RAILROAD NEWSPAPER

Edison, while a newsboy on the train, printed and published the *Weekly Herald*, "the first traveling newspaper."

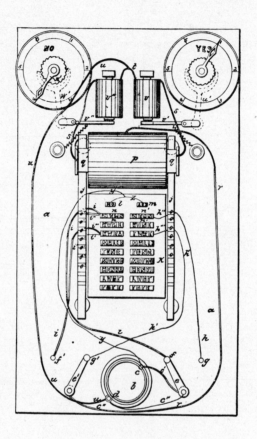

Inventor.
Thomas A. Edison.

EDISON'S FIRST PATENT

The intricate workings of the ingenious device which was made for Congress, but which Congress didn't want. Thereupon Edison vowed that he would never make anything people did not want.

Edison admitted that this violent jump from anything he had ever received before almost paralyzed him. He thought it was too good to last, but started to live up to his reputation and give full service for the money. He accepted the position with "becoming gravity." This opened for him the opportunity to utilize his inventive ingenuity and he worked day and night on improvements and developments for the indicator, until he was becoming an important figure along the Street.

"Black Friday" — Edison in Midst of the Panic

Then came the sensational day — "Black Friday," September 24, 1869. Speculators were thrown into panic. Jay Gould and Jim Fiske had cornered the gold market. Frenzied throngs stood on the sidewalks along Wall Street; the crowds reached through Broad Street and New Street and the entire financial district. It was a surging, crazy crowd — Speyer, the banker, became so excited that it took five men to hold him down. Fortunes were made and lost in a minute. Gould and Fiske manipulated the market with great profits to themselves and fearful consequences to the rest of the world. Quotations went up and down faster than the indicator could follow, and Edison's men were forced to meet the emergency. It was a severe test for the Gold Indicator, but by one o'clock Edison had managed to get the machines up to the correct figures. Then, with his crew sending the right quotations to the boards, he sat down calmly and watched the frenzied crowds.

One of the operators walked over to Edison and, extending his hand, exclaimed: "Shake, Edison — we're O. K. — we haven't a cent to lose!"

It is interesting to note here that, while right in the midst of these enormous transactions, with fortunes being

9

made and lost, Edison never speculated. He had invented a stock ticker and was general manager of an indicator company, with closest inside information concerning pools and the manipulations on the market, but never was drawn into the whirlpool. His invention were to build industries which were to be the center of tremendous activities on the market, and twelve years later, after the installation of the first central station of his incandescent light system, he was to watch the shares of the first Edison Electric Light Company advance in price from $100 to $3,500 and stand calmly by as his new invention forced gas stocks to drop with amazing results.

STARTS FIRST FIRM OF "ELECTRICAL ENGINEERS" IN AMERICA

Six days after "Black Friday," there appeared in the columns of the *Telegrapher* of October 1, 1869, the first professional card ever issued in America by a firm of electrical engineers: "Pope, Edison & Co.— Electrical Engineers and General Telegraph Agency — Office, Exchange Buildings, Nos. 78 and 80 Broadway, Room 48." A young telegraph engineer, Franklin L. Pope, who had been a fellow worker with him in the Gold Indicator Company, was the partner, while J. N. Ashley, publisher of the *Telegrapher*, was the "Co." The Gold Indicator Company had been consolidated with the Gold and Stock Telegraph Company, which was now absorbed by the Western Union.

The new concern started out energetically, with visions of great prosperity. Edison, in order to be in constant touch with his partner, Pope, boarded with him at his home at Elizabeth, New Jersey. They began their experiments in the small shop of Doctor Bradley, in Jersey City

— because it was located near the station of the Pennsylvania Railroad and they could "jump off the train and go to work" on their way to and from New York.

These were the hours of the daily schedule: leaving New York about 6.00 P.M. — arriving in Jersey City and working until about 1.00 A.M. — going to Elizabeth and then walking to the Pope house to sleep — getting up at 6.00 A.M. for breakfast — and catching the 7.00 A.M. train for return to New York. This continued throughout the winter of 1869, and frequently, as Edison said, "I was nearly frozen on the walk in Elizabeth."

This progressive young firm of electrical engineers was watched very closely by General Marshall Lefferts, President of the Western Union. Its first invention was an improved "Gold Printer," along with the installation of private telegraph lines, with the result that the concern was soon taken over by the Western Union, and the partnership dissolved with "some profit."

OPPORTUNITY KNOCKS AT DOOR — AND HE OPENS IT

Marshall Lefferts now engaged Edison to concentrate his time on the improvement of the stock ticker. This ticker was then a very crude instrument, and Edison immediately developed a number of important improvements on which he secured patents. Among other devices, he succeeded in developing a unison stop. We find, in the Patent Office at Washington, these records: "Printing Telegraph (Boston), January 25, 1869 — Apparatus for Printing Telegraph (New York), August 17, 1869 — Electrical Switch for Telegraph Apparatus, August 27, 1869 — Printing Telegraph (Pope and Edison), September 16, 1869 . . ." And so the record continues until we find, "Edison's Universal Printer."

Fortune stood knocking at young Edison's door, but he himself admitted that he did not realize it at the time and it came most unexpectedly. The first "break" of good fortune in his life had come — the result of all the industry and energy and determination from the days of the first laboratory back in the cellar of the home in Port Huron. Fortunate it was in many ways, for the big house had burned down in Port Huron and the family had removed to a modest little home not far away, where his mother, Nancy Edison, now in her sixtieth year, was lying, a confirmed invalid, waiting eagerly for the weekly letters that told her of the progress of her beloved son in New York.

On one eventful day, Edison was summoned to General Lefferts' office. As he entered, he noted from the expression of the general's face, that something of consequence was on his mind. He had faced his "superiors" so many times with dire results, that he was prepared for better or worse.

"Edison," exclaimed General Lefferts, "how much do you want for your 'Universal Printer?'"

This was a vital moment — Edison had figured that $5,000 would be about right, but when faced by the bargaining general he was about to drop his figure to $3,000, or even less, when he blurted out: '

"Well, General, suppose you make an offer."

"How Would $40,000 Strike You?" Asked Lefferts

Edison was so startled that he could almost feel his heart stop beating, and came as near fainting as he ever did in his life. Finally he managed to collect himself and reflectively answered:

"I think that is fair."

"All right," exclaimed General Lefferts, "I will have a contract drawn; come around in three days and sign it and I will give you the money."

When Edison went out of that office, he admitted he had to "pinch himself to see if he was alive." That night he began to reflect on the matter and could not believe that his work was worth such a huge sum; he sat down and estimated the value of his time and trouble, without apparently any realization of what the invention was worth to the Western Union. He even consulted his conscience as to whether or not he should talk it over again with the general and tell him that possibly the price was too high.

"Three days later, however," said Edison, "I walked into General Lefferts' office. He handed me the contract and I signed it without reading it."

First Check Edison Ever Received Stuns Him

General Lefferts handed him the check for $40,000 — the first check he had ever received. He walked out of the office and down the street with the "piece of paper" in his hand and entered the bank. Stepping up to the paying teller's window, he handed him the check like a business man. The paying teller looked at it — then looked at him — and handed it back. Edison believed for a moment that he had been cheated and hurried out of the bank "to let the cold sweat evaporate."

Hurrying back to General Lefferts' office, he walked in and told him what had happened. The general sat back in his chair and laughed uproariously.

"All that's the matter is this — the check must be indorsed!" explained General Lefferts. "That is probably what the bank teller told you and you did not hear

him because of your deafness. I will send my secretary
over to identify you."

When the paying teller saw Edison return with the
secretary of General Lefferts, he was quite surprised.
While his keen knowledge of signatures had told him that
the signature was genuine, he had been somewhat perplexed by this strange young man, rather poorly dressed,
entering the bank with a check for so large an amount;
moreover, he was more amazed when he had asked the
youth to indorse it and had seen him shoot out of the
door.

The secretary explained the situation and introduced Edison as one of the "coming inventors." The
paying teller, however, evidently had a sense of humor,
for he decided to give the youth another jolt. He
counted out the amount in small bills — a bundle which
made a cubic foot, or which in a pile would have stood
six feet high.

Pockets Bulging with Bills — First Bank Account

Edison stood there, gazing at this "mountain of
money" — and then gravely proceeded to stow it away in
his pockets. He had difficulty in finding pocket room —
every pocket was bulging with bills. He said he felt as
if he himself was a "walking bank," and as he hurried
down the street, he imagined that everybody was looking
at him and feared that the policemen would take him up
for robbing a bank. He hurried to his room which was
then in Newark, rushed into it and locked the door. There
he sat up all night to guard his fortune.

Again, General Lefferts' office was in an uproar in the
morning, when Edison appeared with his pockets bulging
and asked him what to do with the money. The general

then gave him his first practical advice in financial matters
and issued orders for the deposit of the money to Edison's
account — *his first bank account.*

The young electrical engineer interviews the president of the Western Union.

CHAPTER XIII

THE YOUNG INVENTOR ON THRESHOLD OF GREAT DISCOVERIES

One of the early forms which Edison's stock ticker took. He called it grandly, " Edison's Universal Printer."

FORTY THOUSAND DOLLARS! "Black Friday" had been "Good Friday" to young Edison. He had seized the opportunity to turn adversity into prosperity in the worst panic Wall Street had ever known.

From a cup of tea to financial independence in a few weeks (not through speculation but by hard work), by a young man of twenty-two years, is a notable achievement. Coming as it did out of a long period of poverty and struggle, it was sufficient to turn his head.

"Money means nothing," said Edison, "but a means to an end." Without taking an hour's vacation, he went to work harder than ever. He plunged into his day-and-night habit — with half an hour to sleep on a workbench three or four times out of the twenty-four hours — and entered upon the work schedule which he was to follow for the next sixty years, a record of unparalleled endurance and industry.

The forty thousand dollars was invested in machinery; he started a small shop and was soon lost in experiments. Securing large orders to build stock tickers for General Lefferts, he was compelled to move to larger quarters and set up his plant in Newark, New Jersey. Business increased; he put on a night force — fifty men were employed — then two hundred fifty. He acted as his own foreman on both shifts.

The prodigious labors of this young inventor can be comprehended only by the fact that in this period, from 1870 to 1876, beginning when he was twenty-three years of age, he created 122 patented inventions, keeping up an average of an invention every month for six years. The patent office referred to him as "That young man in New Jersey who has made the path to the Patent Office hot with his footsteps." This was the beginning of the more than 1,000 patents which were to create industries valued at $25,000,000,000 by the time of his death.

Scenes at Edison's First Shop in Newark

There probably was not a busier hive of industry in the world than this shop of Edison's in Newark as far as activity and hours of labor were concerned. Edison never asked his men to do anything that he would not do himself; his one order was "follow me" — and that meant through endless hours. It is said that on one occasion he even locked himself and his men in until the job had been finished and "all the bugs taken out" — sixty straight hours. The men worked largely on piecework and this allowed them to make high wages.

A true inventor, he kept no books, but jabbed all his records on two hooks — the bills that he owed on one hook, and the accounts that were owed him on the other hook. When bills fell due, he paid them — if he had the money; otherwise, he gave them a note. These notes, he admitted, generally went to protest and there was "a regular path trod by bank messengers with protested notes demanding a fee of one dollar twenty-five cents. The result was frequent visits to the bank with Edison persuading the money powers to take small payment and renew his notes until he was able to meet them.

This "Siege of the Protested Notes" continued for two years, and during the entire time his credit was good — a man of integrity who will meet his obligations. To avoid the pressure, however, and the time consumed, Edison finally hired a bookkeeper. It took him three months to go over the books or hooks — and ascertain how much Edison had made or lost. His report was three thousand dollars profit — and Edison gave a supper to some of his men to celebrate. Two days later the bookkeeper informed him that he had made a mistake — he had lost five hundred dollars. Within a week the bookkeeper, finding new records tucked away in all sorts of places, finally announced that "the profits are over seven thousand dollars."

"That taught me another lesson," declared Edison. "I learned never to count anything real profit until I had paid all my bills and the money was in the bank."

At one time in the Newark shop he was working on forty-five inventions at once. Most of them were connected with the development and expansion of the science of telegraphy; he took the telegraph up where Morse left off. Its tremendous period of expansion came largely out of Edison's "invention shop," the automatic telegraph — duplex — quadruplex — sextuplex, and multiplex telegraph systems, all of which greatly increased speed and distance until they saved the telegraph companies some twenty million dollars in cost of line construction in

America. Through his efforts it became possible to send and record three thousand five hundred words a minute between New York and Philadelphia — and one thousand words a minute between New York and Washington. Automatic messenger boxes and automatic printers that recorded the messages in roman letters for immediate delivery saved both time and expense.

EDISON DEVELOPS TYPEWRITER WITH SHOLES

This was not all — other inventors were coming to him for coöperation in working out their problems. Sholes came from Milwaukee with the first crude model of a machine which he called "the typewriter." It was placed in Edison's hands to perfect. He immediately saw its tremendous possibilities as a revolutionary force in the world's business. The first model was full of "bugs"; there was no alignment of the letters as they wandered across the page; the ribbons failed properly to distribute the ink, and it took much longer to write a letter on this new device than it did by hand. Finally, Edison delivered the machine in "fair working order." The first regular typewriters were made and installed in the office of the Automatic Telegraph Company.

"I predict that some day all business letters will be written on the typewriter," declared Craig, one of the company's officials. His farsightedness proved accurate, but he did not live to see it take place. The typewriter made its way gradually against many difficulties; it required the creation of a new profession called *stenography*. Moreover, there was a general feeling that it was not exactly courteous to send typewritten letters. But when the new process finally got under way, it changed the whole system of the business world. The typewriter that

Edison put into commercial shape is now known as the Remington.

DEATH OF EDISON'S MOTHER IN MICHIGAN — AGE SIXTY-ONE YEARS

It was at this time, while Edison was at work on the typewriter, that the first real tragedy in his life occurred. His mother died in 1871, back in the little village of Gratiot, near Port Huron. After years of patient invalidism, she passed away at sixty-one years of age, at the moment that her son stood on the very threshold of world fame, which she never lived to witness. The loss was so keenly felt by the young inventor, now twenty-four years old, that for years he could seldom speak of her; only to those nearest to him could he even mention her goodness. Then it was that he said: "The memory of her will always be a blessing to me."

The following year was one of loneliness and mourning; the words of Shelley came to his mind: "If winter comes can spring be far behind?" And toward the summer of 1873, Edison, now twenty-five years of age, married. There are many stories regarding this romance. The version that is most generally accredited is typical of the genus known as the inventor, for it came as a natural sequence to the developments in the shop where his life was being spent. He was engaged in inventing the apparatus which would transmit 3,000 words a minute over a single wire. This was accomplished by the use of paraffin paper (which he also invented). With him in his experiments on this paper was an assistant, Miss Mary G. Stillwell, an able and brilliant young girl who was daily amazed at the industry and genius of her employer. Suddenly, she turned, while at work, and found Edison at the back of her chair.

"I always know, Mr. Edison, when you are near me"; she is reported to have said.

Edison stood regarding her for a moment, and then, with the timidity of an adolescent, stammered:

"Miss Stillwell . . . I have been thinking about you a great deal lately . . . I should like you to marry me . . . if you will have me."

Young Inventor Marries Mary Stillwell in 1873

There is another version which states that the courtship progressed in the parlor of a mid-Victorian boarding house. The inventor was constantly dismayed by the continued occupation of the parlor by the other boarders. There seemed to be no place where he and Miss Stillwell could be alone. Finally he drew a quarter from his pocket and started to tap out the words that discretion would not allow him to give voice. Miss Stillwell reached across the table and took the quarter from his hand, and started to tap the desired answer on the marble top.

It is further said that shortly after, a friend on entering Edison's attic room one morning, found him painfully well groomed, shined, and brushed, but pacing the floor in a quandary. Inquiring into the cause for this deep perplexity of mind, Edison told him that he was trying to remember something that had to do with his unusually good appearance. The floor pacing went on for some minutes — when finally Edison, in a shout of triumph, declared:

"Oh, yes, now I know what it was . . . this is the day I am going to be married."

Edison and his bride laughed at these stories goodnaturedly, but refused to commit themselves. When he saw that the tales were becoming established as folklore he declared that they were only figuratively true, and that he did not forget his wife. He did admit, however, that as he seldom carried a watch and did not then use a clock in his workshop, he might have been somewhat delayed in the matter of time, but he thought it was after the marriage and not before.

"It must be understood," explained Mr. Edison, "that I never watched the clock."

EDISON MAKES TESTS IN ENGLAND IN 1873

Events were following in rapid succession. With Edison's automatic telegraph system meeting with great success in America, it was agreed, in 1873, that he would make a trial of the system in England. We find Edison aboard the famous *Jumping Java* of the Cunard line — with "one small satchel of clothes, three large boxes of instruments, and his bright fellow telegrapher, Jack Wright." It was a rough voyage; one of the passengers was thrown violently against the iron wall of the smoking room and received a bad scalp wound. Edison stated that he was able to get on deck but two days.

"I was not familiar with the sea," said Edison in describing this voyage, "as my longest voyage before had been on the night boat from Boston to New York. Occasionally, I had taken short sails on the Great Lakes and along the Mississippi River in the 'show boat' days. The operation of this ocean liner interested me, and I spent much of my time in the engine room and with the captain. I wondered how an ocean steamer could be made to pay with so few passengers, as there were only ten or twelve people at the table in the dining room, but I was informed that there were nearly three hundred in their staterooms, for reasons quite obvious during the stormy voyage."

Upon his arrival in London, the American inventor reported to Colonel George E. Gouraud and set up his American apparatus at the Telegraph Street headquarters, while his fellow worker was sent on with the instruments to the other end of the wire in Liverpool. Severe conditions were imposed upon him; he must record one thousand words a minute and tests must be made every half hour for six hours. He soon found that the wire and batteries placed at his disposal were not in the best condition.

ENGLISH SCIENTISTS CHALLENGE AMERICAN SYSTEM

"You are not going to have much show," hinted one of the men assigned to watch the test for the officials. "They are going to give you an old Bridgewater Canal wire that is so poor we don't work it, and a lot of 'sand batteries' at Liverpool."

"I thanked my English friend for the information," said Edison later. "Then I decided to find some way to try to get out of the hole. I was living at a little hotel in Covent Garden, where they were feeding me on roast beef and flounders. This was not what I needed for my imagination — I could think better on pastry. My search led me to a little French pastry shop in High Holborn Street, where I loaded up with proper inspiration. That night I laid out my plan of action."

When he met Colonel Gouraud the next morning, he told him that it would be necessary to buy a powerful battery for the Liverpool end. He agreed and telegraphed to Jack Wright in Liverpool to come down to get it. It was finally installed, just two hours before the test began according to the conditions. Much to the amazement of many of the officials, the test was a complete success.

The officials then requested that he attempt to secure speed through submarine cables with his new system. Twenty-two hundred miles of cable, under water in tanks, was placed before him, with the testing hours between eight at night and six in the morning. He worked for more than two weeks on this cable, but was unable to get more than two words per minute. He afterward discovered that the coiled cable, owing to induction, was no test whatever as to what it would do when laid out straight. His speed, under the conditions, was equal to, if not better than, the British system then in use.

He Returns to America and Plunges into Work

"I returned to America in apparent defeat," explained Edison, "only to find, later, that they had adapted my principle to their system — the automatic was finally adopted in England and I never got a cent for it."

Upon his return to America, Edison plunged into the development of multiple transmission, which he carried to successful achievement until messages could be sent in opposite directions over one wire at the same time. So engrossed did he become that, when he was notified that if his taxes were not paid immediately, in Newark, he would be fined $12\frac{1}{2}$ per cent extra, he admitted: "When I was suddenly asked at City Hall for my name, I actually forgot it and lost my place in the line."

"I reached a place where I needed money much more than the glory," explained Edison. "I was trying to sell my quadruplex system to the Western Union. The chief electrician of the company told me he thought he could put the deal through if he could claim to be joint inventor and also have a percentage of the money. They gave me a room with a marble tile floor in which to work

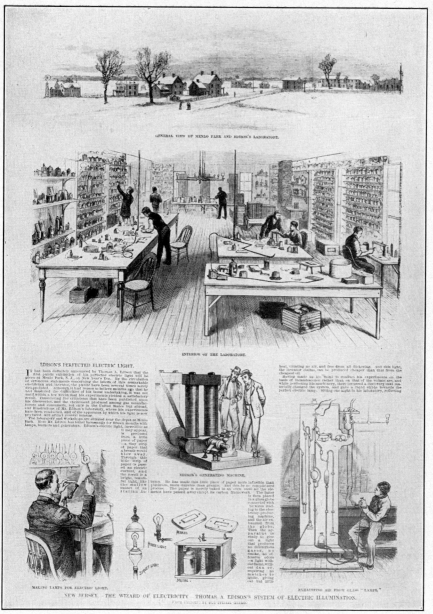

GENERAL VIEW OF MENLO PARK AND EDISON'S LABORATORY.

INTERIOR OF THE LABORATORY.

EDISON'S PERFECTED ELECTRIC LIGHT.

EDISON'S GENERATING MACHINE.

MAKING LAMPS FOR ELECTRIC LIGHT.

EXHAUSTING AIR FROM GLASS "LAMPS."

NEW JERSEY.—THE WIZARD OF ELECTRICITY—THOMAS A. EDISON'S SYSTEM OF ELECTRIC ILLUMINATION.

MENLO PARK AND THE LABORATORY THAT BECAME FAMOUS

A page from *Leslie's Weekly* of the year 1880, giving a graphic idea of the epoch-making experiments that were conducted by Edison and his associates in the Menlo Park days.

FIRST CARBONIZED PAPER EXPERIMENT

A reproduction from *Frank Leslie's Illustrated Newspaper*, 1879.

EDISON'S ORIGINAL GLASSBLOWING SHOP

A vital part of the equipment at Menlo Park. In later years it was transported, with the soil, and re-erected at Henry Ford's Edisonia Museum at Dearborn, Michigan.

out my apparatus, and while it was all right to stand on, I found it very hard to sleep on. With a detail of eight operators, it required two months of hard work before we got it to working, over a wire to Albany and back."

MEETS VANDERBILT — GETS $5,000 AT CRUCIAL TIME

The day came for the test. The directors flocked in — such men as William H. Vanderbilt and the leading financiers of the time, with President Orton. A terrific storm broke over the line and the chances of success became less and less. Moreover, Edison was then paying five dollars a day to the sheriff to withhold execution of judgment and was in danger of foreclosure on his machinery. However, the fates were with the inventor for the moment.

"We will give you $5,000 as part payment on your invention," decided the board of directors. Edison took the money and paid his debts, without leaving a dollar for himself. Then another of those unexpected situations developed; he had done his part and successfully installed the apparatus on the lines of the company, but no more funds were forthcoming.

"You will never get another cent," General Eckert informed him. "I know that they do not intend to go through with it, but I will introduce you to a man who has large capital and I think I can interest him."

MEETS JAY GOULD — GETS CHECK FOR $30,000

On the very next day, General Eckert appeared at the Edison shop in Newark with Jay Gould. It was the first time that Edison had met the famous financier. Gould watched the apparatus in operation and then left without committing himself. The general appeared on the following day, however, and stated that Gould would like to see

Edison that evening at his house on Fifth Avenue. Eckert, fearing that they might be watched, took Edison into the Gould mansion through the servants' entrance in the basement, where he found Gould installed in a secret office.

"How much do you want?" asked Jay Gould, the master manipulator of finance.

"Make me an offer," answered the young inventor.

"I will give you $30,000," replied Gould sharply.

"I have a partner," explained Edison, "but I will sell my interest for that amount of money if you will take care of him to his satisfaction."

Again good fortune seemed to be turning toward Edison. He met Gould in the offices of his lawyers, Sherman & Sterling, the next morning, and the check for $30,000 was waiting for him.

"You have got the steamboat *Plymouth Rock*," remarked Gould, as he handed him the check. "I just sold her for $30,000 and am turning over the money to you."

The celebrated fight between Gould and the Western Union was now on. Gould controlled the Atlantic & Pacific Telegraph Company and had purchased Edison's quadruplex system as a wedge with which to get control of the Western Union. To get further control of Edison's automatic system, which was owned by the inventor and his associates in the Automatic Telegraph Company, the daring financier made a staggering offer.

EDISON PATENTS IN $4,000,000 DEAL — AND THE RESULTS

"I will pay $4,000,000 in stock," offered Gould, "for the Automatic Telegraph Company." The deal was made and Edison was engaged in establishing his automatic system, which was to revolutionize telegraphy. Gould believed there was a great future in the young inventor and called him frequently to his office. He would sit for four hours at a time with maps and explain to Edison the great future of the Union Pacific Railroad.

The "money king" seemed to be "money mad." He worked until one o'clock in the morning to devise new schemes for securing control of valuable properties. He hammered the Western Union with his opposition company and the Edison inventions until he tired William H. Vanderbilt out, and Gould took control through consolidation. It was at this point that Gould repudiated his contract with the Automatic Telegraph Company.

"We never got a cent for our patents or wires," said Edison. "I lost three years of hard labor."

Then began one of the most famous lawsuits in the history of American jurisprudence, which arose out of the Edison patents and the Gould transactions. The action was brought by Edison and his associates to recover the contract price of $4,000,000 for his invention and the wires of the company; it remained in the courts for thirty-five years and not one dollar was ever recovered.

EDISON EXPERIMENTAL SHOP FIRST IN THE WORLD

This ended Edison's interest in the telegraph — it had practically ruined him financially, but the value of his services to the world at large were beyond calculation. We find him now inventing "everything and anything that came into his mind as possible for general utility": the Mimeograph, which is universally used to multiply letters; the "Edison Electric Pen," which, attached to an electric motor traveling at high speed, could produce three thousand copies from a stencil; paraffin paper, which is in general use in covering confectionery and food products; district messenger call boxes, which he improved from other inventions as used today for police calls, fire alarms, and many other services — his inventive genius seemed to know no bounds.

At one time — before he was thirty-nine years old — he was conducting experiments in five workshops. His "invention shops" were the first of the kind in the world — the beginning of the modern laboratories which are operated by all great industries today, with large staffs of the ablest scientists, in continuous research and experiment. Edison was the first of the "masters" who took young men of ability under his direction and trained them for future service to science.

At one bench in Newark were three young men who became famous in later years: Sigmund Bergmann, who became head and principal owner of the great electrical works in Berlin, employing ten thousand men; Schuckert, who founded the electrical factories which became the third largest in Germany; John Kruesi, later engineer of the great General Electric Works in Schenectady, New York, and whom we shall meet in these pages when we observe Edison giving the "talking machine" to the world. Hundreds more of men who accomplished big things started with Edison as we shall find them as this story of achievement develops.

It is now — in 1876 — that we move to Menlo Park where the development of Bell's telephone through the Edison transmitter — the phonograph — and the incandescent electric light are literally to "startle the world."

CHAPTER XIV

CREATING A NEW ERA IN HUMAN LIFE — THE TELEPHONE

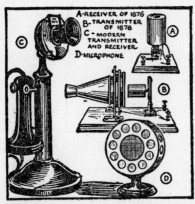

A-RECEIVER OF 1876
B-TRANSMITTER OF 1876
C-MODERN TRANSMITTER AND RECEIVER
D-MICROPHONE

Edison's carbon transmitter made the modern telephone and the radio microphone possible.

TREMENDOUS financial problems besieged Edison from the age of twenty-three to thirty years. His enormous capacity for hard work and the rapidity of his inventions (all requiring large capital), crowding upon him, were enough to floor the most sagacious financier.

So great were the demands upon his energy that, in 1876, he sought seclusion by setting up his laboratory at Menlo Park to concentrate on his many projects — only soon to find the throngs beating a track to the laboratory of the "wizard." Little did he realize that in his amazing improvements on other inventions he was at the door of original discoveries that were to startle the world.

Menlo Park — on the arrival of Edison — was to become more famous as the scene of epoch-making inventions during the next ten years. It was a little railway station twenty-five miles from New York, in Middlesex County, New Jersey, on the line of the Pennsylvania Railroad between Elizabeth and Metuchen. There was nothing to distinguish it, excepting its seclusion, an ideal place in which the young inventor could concentrate on the problems before him.   Here, Edison set up his *first real laboratory* for inventive and scientific experiment.   He had found, according to one of his associates, that "the combined work of manufacturing and inventing taxed even his superhuman strength; in fact, the two occupations proved irreconcilable.   If a new idea struck him, it had at once to be tested in a thousand different ways, with the help of every man within call; but this would hardly do in a factory run on a regular time schedule and expected to yield an immediate return for every dollar."

When Edison Was at His Laboratory in Menlo Park

We find Edison at his laboratory in Menlo Park in the year of the great Centennial Exposition at Philadelphia (1876), in celebration of the hundredth anniversary of the signing of the Declaration of Independence, which his great-grandfather had given his most loyal support.   This was a time of unusual excitement.   The famous Tilden-Hayes presidential campaign was arousing the country, with James G. Blaine as one of the leading figures of the day.   The "Boss Tweed scandals" were creating a sensation in New York.   The massacre of General Custer, out in Little Big Horn in Montana, by the Sioux Indians under Sitting Bull, furnished additional news of the moment. Nothing had happened since the "Great Fire " in Chicago and the "Big Fire" in Boston that so excited the people. In the field of sport, this same year saw two great American sports coming into the life of the nation — the organization of the National Baseball League and the beginning of college football.   P. T. Barnum's "greatest show on earth" was also establishing itself as an institution.

But events of far greater consequence than all these were in the making.   Three great American inventors were working independently, to give the world a new system of communication in which the human voice would speak over wires stretching across continents — the telephone. This race is one of the most interesting in the history of invention. We find Edison filing a caveat for the "first telephone" in the United States Patent Office on January 14, 1876. Exactly a month later, on February 14, 1876, Alexander Graham Bell, of Salem, Massachusetts, filed his application for a patent for his first telephone; and two hours later, on the same day, Elisha Gray, of Chicago, Illinois, filed his application for an invention "transmitting vocal sounds through electrical propulsion." Gray had been beaten by two hours — Edison had beat them both by thirty days with a caveat proving that he was working on such an invention, while Bell was ready for a patent on his completed model.

AMERICANS AND EUROPEANS WHO CLAIM TELEPHONE

The "GREAT TELEPHONE WAR," resulted — a situation unparalleled in the annals of invention. It involved as it progressed many noted inventors, such as Berliner, Blake, Hughes, and Dolbear — all of whom were working on the same principle at the same time. It was found that as far back as 1837 an American named Page had made elementary discoveries along the same line; Charles Bourseul, a young French soldier in Algeria, had given a lucid description of what he called "electrical telepathy," in a newspaper in Paris, in 1854. Philipp Reis, a professor in Germany, had built an electrical telephonic apparatus imitating the human ear, in 1860, and this instrument was brought to America for exhibition in Cooper Union, New York, in 1868, by Dr. Van der Weyde. There were claimants in England, where inventors were working during this same period, on the new science of communication.

The war was bitterly waged — great corporations were drawn into it, with a terrific financial battle between the old telegraph systems and the new telephone company for control of the great invention. The decision gave the patent rights on the telephone to Alexander Graham Bell, whose place thereby is secure as *the* inventor. The Edison caveat was insufficient to hold his claims, and the hand of Fate had worked against Gray. The decision of the Supreme Court of the United States, eleven years later, gave due credit to Reis for his discoveries and for the first use of the word *telephone,* but held that as his apparatus "could not be made under any circumstances to reproduce the delicate forms of the air vibrations caused by the human voice in articulate speech . . . Reis failed to transmit speech telegraphically. Bell did and he succeeded. Under such circumstances, it is impossible to hold that what Reis did was an anticipation of the discovery of Bell. To follow Reis is to fail, but to follow Bell is to succeed. The difference between the two is just the difference between failure and success." A little oversight of failing to "turn a screw a fractional rotation on its axis, and not connecting two particular binding posts by a wire" proved the defeat of Reis — "no man ever escaped fame by so narrow a margin."

Fate, too, had worked against Bourseul: he had been in reach of the epoch-making discovery but had failed to put it into operation. He had originated the idea without giving it either a name or an apparatus. Here are his words: "I have asked myself if what is spoken in Vienna may not be heard in Paris. This thing is practicable in this way: suppose that a man speaks near a movable disc sufficiently flexible to lose none of the vibrations of the voice; that this disc alternately *makes and breaks* the connection from a battery; you may have at another distance another disc, which will simultaneously execute the same vibrations." His prophecy was sound, but his principle, in which he speaks of "makes and breaks," was proved erroneous by Reis. He neglected to develop his idea into practical form. Later he became superintendent of telegraph lines at Auch, France; and the French Government later created him Chevalier of the Legion of Honor as a reward for his treatise on telephony.

Edison's attitude during this entire conflict was typical of the man: he gave full credit to Bell for being "the first to transmit articulate speech over an electric current." The first words to pass over a telephone wire, a message from Bell to his assistant, Thos. A. Watson, merely passed from one room to another; Bell had no transmitter, and the instrument was capable of sending the voice but a very short distance — it required propulsion to make the new invention of any value whatsoever.

Undismayed by his apparent defeat as the original inventor, when the patent was granted to Bell, Edison went into the laboratory at Menlo Park and continued his work as if nothing had happened. He saw tremendous possibilities in the new invention — an opportunity to develop it into practical use for the people of the world.

Edison Invents Transmitter Making Telephone Practical

Secretly "locked up" for several months, working day and night, Edison finally appeared with the invention that was to bring the telephone into practical utility — *the carbon transmitter*, which was to solve the problem and, with his electromotograph, create amplification, which was to carry the vibrations of the human voice to the ends of the earth, for it is this transmitter which, as we shall see, made possible the succeeding era of the wonders of radio, the instrument known as the *microphone*. The millions of telephones used all over the world were thus to bear the genius of Edison, as his transmitter took the "feeble voice left by Bell's original telephone" and gave it almost unlimited power. The name of "Edison" was stamped on the instruments in nearly every home and office for a generation to come until the telephone represented the combined geniuses of Bell and Edison.

"HELLO!" — STORY OF HOW IT ORIGINATED WITH EDISON

It was Edison who originated the salutation "HELLO!" over the telephone. This historic fact was verified by Frederick P. Fish, late President of what is now the American Telephone and Telegraph Company: "Years ago," said Mr. Fish, "when the first telephones came into use, people were accustomed to ring a bell on the box and then say, ponderously: 'Are you there?' 'Are you ready to talk?' . . . Mr. Edison did away with that awkward, un-American way of doing things. He caught up the receiver one day and yelled into the transmitter one word — a most satisfactory, capable, soul-satisfying word — 'HELLO!' It has gone around the world. The Japs use it; it is heard in Turkey; Russia could not do without it, and neither could Patagonia."

Edison frequently told the story of these days: "Bell invented the first telephone, which consisted of the present receiver, used both as a transmitter and a receiver (the magneto type). It was attempted to use it commercially, but it failed on account of its faintness and the extraneous sounds which came in on its wires from different sources. Orton, of the Western Union, with whom I had developed the telegraph, asked me to take hold of it and make it commercial. As I had also been working on it simultaneously with both Bell and Gray, I was pretty familiar with the subject. I started in, and soon produced the carbon transmitter, which is now universally used."

"When we made our first tests with the original Bell telephone between New York and Newark, a short distance, hardly a word could be heard," explained Edison. "We made our tests between New York and Philadelphia, and also between New York and Washington, using regular Western Union wires. We succeeded in getting remarkable results as soon as I developed the transmitter."

FIRST PUBLIC EXHIBITION AT PHILADELPHIA IN 1876

The first public use of the telephone was in Philadelphia, during the Centennial Exposition, when the first recorded telephone message was sent over the wire. Alexander Graham Bell, the inventor, was on one end of the wire and a distinguished guest, Dom Pedro, Emperor of Brazil, was on the other end. The voice of Bell came, indistinctly. He spoke the lines from "Hamlet":

> "To be, or not to be: that is the question:
> Whether 'tis nobler in the mind to suffer
> The slings and arrows of outrageous fortune,
> Or to take arms against a sea of troubles,
> And by opposing end them? To die: to sleep;
> No more; and by a sleep to say we end
> The heart-ache and the thousand natural shocks
> That flesh is heir to, 'tis a consummation
> Devoutly to be wish'd. To die, to sleep;
> To sleep: perchance to dream: ay, there's the rub . . ."

The successful transmission of this famous soliloquy created quite a sensation at the Centennial Exposition.

The war between the two inventors now waged furiously. Bell organized his Bell Telephone Company, in Massachusetts; the Western Union took over the Edison patents and used these as a weapon against the Bell interests. Gould and Vanderbilt appear again in this "fight to a finish." The new "Telephone Department" of the Western Union was placed in charge of W. K. Vanderbilt's able son-in-law, Hamilton McK. Twombly, and progressed rapidly. Theodore Pukas, of Budapest, Hungary, was the first to suggest a telephone exchange and it was immediately put into operation. The Bell Company started an exchange.

"The Bell Company pirated the Edison transmitter," explained Edison later, "and the Western Union pirated the Bell receiver — it was 'fifty-fifty.'" In the midst of this fight the Western Union sent for Edison.

Edison Gets $100,000 for His Telephone Invention

"Edison," exclaimed Mr. Ort, "what do you want for your transmitter?"

The young inventor felt that the work he had done on the telephone was worth $25,000 — and he intended obstinately to stick to that figure.

"What offer will you make?" asked Edison.

"We will give $100,000," replied Ort.

"All right," answered Edison. "It is yours on one condition — and that is that you do not pay it all at once, but pay me at the rate of $6,000 a year for seventeen years, the life of the patent."

Edison in explaining this strange request said: "I knew what I was doing. I always had an ambition about four times too large for my business capacity. If I got all that money at once I would spend it on experiments. I deliberately fixed it so that this could not happen. By this stroke I saved seventeen years of financial worry."

It was about this time that an inventor named Page had secured a patent on the principle of the electromotograph, which Edison had utilized in telegraphy. Jay Gould was hammering the Western Union down on the Stock Exchange and raising havoc with railroad contracts. He bought the Page patent believing that it would strengthen his strategical position and prove the final blow to Western Union.

$12,000 A YEAR FOR SEVENTEEN YEARS

Edison again was called in to save the day. Ort beseeched the young inventor to create "something that will make Gould's patents worthless." Again he sought refuge in Menlo Park that very night. Some weeks later he appeared with his motograph — a device which made the instrument and the combination claim of the Page patent valueless.

"What do you want for it?" asked Ort.

"Make me an offer," replied Edison in his usual manner.

"I'll give you another $100,000," exclaimed Ort.

The terms again were fixed at $6,000 a year for seventeen years. He was secure at last in his own livelihood, at least, with a total of $12,000 a year for the next seventeen years.

FIRST TELEPHONE EXHIBITED IN ENGLAND CREATES AMAZEMENT

The first telephone shown in Europe was at the meeting of the British Association in Glasgow, 1876. Sir William

Thompson, the scientist, after hearing the first message exclaimed, "It is the greatest of all marvels!" There are many interesting anecdotes regarding it; one scientist declared: "For men's low, deep voices the plate of a telephone should be larger than for the shriller voices of women and children."

A scientific jury investigated the telephone in England to ascertain whether or not it was practical. Eminent foreign electricians were members of this jury. As they tested a telephonic apparatus before Dr. Werner Siemens they had difficulty in making it answer to their voices. Various names of foreign savants were shouted into the mouthpiece of the telephone, but it would not respond. Professor Hughes, who was an accomplished musician, stepped forward, and secretly ascertained the fundamental note of the telephone by tapping its plate. Turning to his fellow jurors with a smile, he remarked:

"There is a peculiarity about this telephone; it is an anglophile and will only respond to the honored name of Faraday (the famous British scientist whose works Edison had read as a boy). We will test this strange phenomenon and I will prove it to you."

The jurors laughed in amiable derision — but this was soon changed to wonder. They spoke into the telephone the names of the famous pioneers in electricity — "Benjamin Franklin — Ohm — Volta — Ampère." The telephone remained obstinately silent until at last Professor Hughes approached, and pronounced the magic syllables, *Far-a-day!* The mysterious instrument delivered the words distinctly. There was no mystery to it; the word Faraday had simply been spoken by him in the same tone of voice as the fundamental note of the telephone plate.

Exhibition of Telephone in America a "Sensation"

The first exhibition of Edison's "marvelous electrochemical telephone" at Saratoga, on the evening of August 30, 1879, created quite a furore. The news even was carried prominently on the front pages of the newspapers of the country. This record from the columns of the *New York Tribune* indicates the sensation that Edison was creating:

"The town hall was crowded with people, who were all interested and amused by the exhibition and description of the new chemical telephone, Mr. Edison's latest invention. On the platform were Professor Barker, Professor A. Graham Bell, Professor Borton, and Mr. Edison. Professor Barker, in a clear, simple, and popular way, gave a history of the telephone.

"Then the comparative powers and qualities of the various forms of transmitters were tested for the enlightenment of the audience. Mr. Batchelor, Mr. Edison's assistant, who is blessed with a most powerful and resonant voice, but was afflicted last night with a cold in the head, was in a distant room in the building, to which the telephone wires were conducted. In the first place, experiments were tried with the magneto transmitter and magneto receiver, and it was shown that only one person, and he only when holding the receiver to his ear, could hear Mr. Batchelor's vociferous remarks and thunderous songs, even though that worthy gentleman strained his lungs to the utmost.

"Then the carbon transmitter and the magneto receiver were used, and a few persons close to the instrument could hear faintly Mr. Batchelor's shouts into the transmitter. The sounds were much louder than when the magneto transmitter was used, but could not be heard at all a little distance from the receiver.

"Finally the electrochemical telephone was used with brilliant results. Mr. Batchelor's talk, recitations, and singing could be heard all over the hall, and the audience was delighted with such enchanting novelties as 'Mary Had a Little Lamb,' and 'Jack and Jill Went Up the Hill,' 'John Brown's Body,' 'There Was a Little Girl' and the like. However, the assembly was spared one infliction — no selections from 'Pinafore' were given. The telephone gave distinctly the singing of two and three persons at once, the talk of one person and the singing of another at the same time, whistling, airs on the cornet, laughter loud and long, repetition of the alphabet, and many other sounds. Mr. Edison described the machine which worked these wonders and drew a plan of it on the blackboard.

"Mr. Edison's explanation of it pleased the people greatly. His quaint and homely manner, his unpolished but clear language, his odd but pithy expressions, charmed and attracted them. Mr. Edison is certainly not graceful nor eloquent. He shuffled about the platform in an ungainly way, and his stooping, swinging figure was lacking in dignity. But his eyes were wonderfully expressive, his face frank and cordial, and his frequent smile hearty and irresistible. If his sentences were not rounded they went to the point, and the assembly dispersed with great satisfaction at having seen and heard the renowned inventor, and having seen and heard his most recent invention. It is certainly a remarkable instrument."

Edison Sends His Men to "Invade England"

The inventions that were coming out of Menlo Park were putting tremendous impetus behind the development of telephony — the electromotograph — the microphone — and a long flow of patents which were to expand its usefulness. England had taken up the telephone with its own scientists, and Professor Hughes was working on the microphone. A controversy arose concerning which Edison made the following statement: "I sent one of my men over to London especially to show Preece (the English scientist who later invented low-frequency wireless telegraphy) my carbon transmitter. Hughes first saw it and heard it—then, within a month, he came out with a microphone, without any acknowledgment whatever. Published dates will show that Hughes came long after me." Edison's patent was sustained in the British courts, also in the contest with Bell.

Edison's "invasion of England" is an interesting experience in this telephone fight. He sent representatives abroad to establish exchanges in Great Britain and on the Continent. This was at the time when Gladstone and Disraeli were the great British figures; the Suez Canal deal had been put through. It was in the aftermath of the Franco-Prussian war, with the fall of Napoleon III and the establishment of the Republic of France. William I had been proclaimed Emperor of Germany and Bismarck was in his power.

The Edison "Loud Speaker" created quite a sensation in London. The Edison Telephone Company crowded into the basement of offices in Queen Victoria Street. Edison had placed Col. Gouraud, his old English manager in the automatic telegraph, in charge of his forces in England. Threats of litigation met the arrival of the first American instruments, both by the English and the Bell interests. Gouraud called for help. Edison cabled him to hold the fort. A crew of twenty men was sent on early steamers, and the war in England was on. The "Loud Speakers" won the day. A cable came to Edison from Gouraud stating:

"Will you take 30,000 for your interests?"

Edison cabled back that he would accept, and, when the draft came, he was astonished to find that it was 30,000 pounds not dollars — $150,000 in American money. Many of the men sent over from Menlo Park stayed in England and established telephone exchanges all over the Continent, some of them making large fortunes.

George Bernard Shaw Gets Job with Edison

G. Bernard Shaw now appears in the Edison forces. The inimitable Irishman, who has since become a famous littérateur and the "playboy of the world," secured one of his first jobs as lecturer or demonstrator of the "Edison Loud-speaking Telephone" at wages amounting to about $10 a week. Shaw claims, however, that he "never got a cent" (evidently he never made a sale or performed services worth such high wages). This is the famous Shaw's story of his experiences as he recorded them in one of his admirable books, *The Irrational Knot:*

"The American invention was much too ingenious . . . a telephone of such stentorian efficiency that it bellowed your most private communications all over the house, instead of whispering them with some sort of discretion, was not what the British stockbroker wanted; so the company was soon merged in the National Telephone Company, after making a place for itself in the history of literature, quite unintentionally, by providing me with a job. These deluded and romantic men gave me a glimpse of the skilled proletariat of the United States; and their language was frightful even to an Irishman. They worked with a ferocious energy which was out of all proportion to the result achieved. Indomitably resolved to assert their republican manhood by taking no orders from a tall-hatted

Englishman whose stiff politeness covered his conviction that they were, relatively to himself, inferior and common persons, they insisted on being slave-driven with genuine American oaths, by a free and equal American foreman. They utterly despised the artfully slow British workman, who did as little for his wages as he possibly could; never hurried himself, and had a deep reverence for anyone whose pocket could be tapped by respectful behavior. Need I add that they were contemptuously wondered at by this same British workman, as a parcel of outlandish adult boys, who sweated themselves for their employer's benefit instead of looking after their own interests?"

"They adored Mr. Edison as the greatest man of all time in every possible department of science, art, and philosophy," explains Shaw, "and execrated Mr. Graham Bell, the inventor of the rival telephone, as his satanic adversary; but each of them had (or pretended to have), on the brink of completion, an improvement on the telephone, usually a new transmitter. They were free-souled creatures, excellent company; sensitive, cheerful, and profane; liars, braggarts, and hustlers; with an air of making slow old England hum, which never left them even when, as often happened, they were wrestling with difficulties of their own making, or struggling in no-thoroughfares from which they had to be retrieved by Englishmen without imagination enough to go wrong."

"In this environment I remained for some months," records the Irish iconoclast, "as I was interested in physics and had read Tyndall and Helmholtz, besides having learned something in Ireland through a fortunate friendship with a cousin of Mr. Graham Bell, who was also a chemist and physicist, I was, I believe, the only person in the establishment who knew the current scientific explanation of telephony; and as soon as I struck up a friendship with our official lecturer, a Colchester man whose strong point was prescientific agriculture, I often discharged his duties for him in a manner which, I am persuaded, laid the foundation of Mr. Edison's London reputation: my sole reward being my boyish delight in the half-concealed incredulity of our visitors (who were convinced by the hoarsely startling utterances of the telephone, that the speaker, alleged by me to be twenty miles away, was really using a speaking trumpet in the next room), and their obvious uncertainty, when the demonstration was over, as to whether they ought to tip me or not: a question they either decided in the negative, or never decided at all; for I never got anything."

The first manager of a telephone exchange on the European continent was Samuel Insull, an enterprising young Englishman, who later came to America and joined the Edison forces at Menlo Park where he remained until he became the greatest force behind the development of the power industry in America, and probably in all the world. He will appear in our records of the "Edison Pioneers."

GREAT TELEPHONE WAR ENDS — TERMS OF COMPROMISE

After a long and costly fight, the war between the Bell interests and the Western Union forces (with the Edison patents) was ended. Under the terms of peace, a compromise was reached whereby the Western Union agreed to keep out of the telephone field and the Bell company withdrew from the telegraphic field. Profitable concessions were exacted by the Western Union because of the value of the Edison improvements, including "twenty-per-cent royalty on the earnings of the Bell system until the Bell patents expired." The yearly revenues for the following years amounted to several hundred thousand dollars from these royalties alone — and into millions of dollars in their total sum.

Bell made a fortune with his telephone, largely through his stock holdings rather than on the patent rights. He had a difficult time at the beginning in securing money with which to finance it. Going to a friend, he offered "a half interest in my invention for $2,500"; the friend declined. Bell offered a tenth interest for $100 to an official in the Patent Office; this was refused. That tenth interest in fifteen years was worth $1,500,000.

Edison had done for Bell's telephone what he had done for the Morse telegraph — he had expanded them into enormously profitable properties. When Alexander Graham Bell died — forty-six years after his invention of the telephone — at his country house in Nova Scotia, the old controversies had passed away, all bitterness was forgotten, and Bell and Edison were firm friends. Edison spoke of him with affection and highest esteem as "a great man who had done a great work."

Bell and Edison became firm friends.

How "Hello!" became the telephone call.

CHAPTER XV

A MODERN MIRACLE AMAZES THE WORLD—
THE "TALKING MACHINE"

With the original Edison cylinder phonograph, home-recording was a popular pastime.

"THOMAS EDISON has invented *a machine that talks!*" The news flashed through the country in 1877. It taxed the credulity of the people. "There must be some trick about it," they said. "It is absurd . . . impossible!" It came upon the scientists without warning and they, too, were skeptical.

The public press made it the sensation of the day: "Here is a machine that is almost human — speaks like a human being. You can speak into it, or sing into it, and it will repeat your own words so clearly that you can recognize your own voice. It is even said that records can be preserved so that your voice can be heard a hundred years after you are dead!"

Thousands of people, curious to see and hear for themselves, flocked to Menlo Park. So great was the interest in this uncanny device that the Pennsylvania Railroad ran special trains to accommodate the crowds.

How this miracle was performed is a wonder story in itself. Edison, with the men who were present when the experiments were being made, has given this historic account:

Edison Tells How He Came to Invent Phonograph

"It was the result of discoveries I made while working out the principles behind the telegraph and the telephone," explained the inventor. "I was singing to the mouthpiece of a telephone when the vibrations of the voice sent the fine steel point into my finger. That set me thinking. If I could record the actions of the point and send the point over the same surface afterwards, I saw no reason why the thing would not talk. I tried the experiment first on a strip of telegraph paper. I shouted the words 'Hello! Hello!' into the mouthpiece, ran the paper back over the steel point, and heard a faint 'Hello! Hello!' in return. I determined to make a machine that would work accurately, and gave my assistants instructions, telling them what I had discovered. They laughed at me. That's the whole story. The phonograph is the result of the pricking of a finger."

But it was the result of much more than this — it was the cumulative knowledge and genius of Thomas Edison which discovered a new principle and gave to the world one of its most startling and original inventions, out of which we shall see the talking picture develop and the radio age come into existence. For it was at this same time that Edison was making his first discoveries in sound waves, to which he gave the name "Etheric Force."

It was on a day in the autumn of 1877 that Edison called John Kruesi, one of his most skilful coworkers, into a private room at the laboratories in Menlo Park. He handed him a sketch which he had completed during the night. It was one of the typical Edison drawings, with definite directions and all details worked out. There was a memorandum on the margin stating that he thought the job was worth about $18. Kruesi was a model maker, with piecework wages. He studied the drawing and tried to figure out what the queer contrivance was intended to do. Finally, he went to Edison and told him that his curiosity was aroused.

"I am going to make a machine that talks," stated Edison, decisively. "You complete that model and I will show you what it will do." Kruesi, who had seen Edison perform what was considered the impossible, admitted that for the first time he was skeptical of the inventor's claims. The idea looked preposterous. He knew that it had been prophesied in Europe, but that scientists in general considered it a wild concoction of the imagination.

His job, however, was to follow the directions and produce the model. He worked thirty hours without sleep (with only a bite to eat), and then called Edison to look upon the strange but simple mechanism. It was nothing more than a wooden base with a metal shaft — a thread cut in it like a horizontal screw, and a handle at one end. The shaft ran through the metal drum with a spiral groove cut on its surface. There was a little tube on the sides of the drum; a parchment diaphragm was stretched over the inside end of each little tube; a steel needle was placed in the center of the diaphragm.

Edison stood looking at the crude instrument with a smile on his face. His men gathered about him with good-natured jibes of incredulity.

"I'll bet a box of cigars that that thing won't work," declared Carman, foreman of the machine shop.

"MEIN GOTT IM HIMMEL!" — THE MACHINE TALKS

Edison laughed, and then placed a thin sheet of tin foil around the drum. Looking up at his men to observe the expressions on their faces, he started to turn the crude handle of the shaft, and at the same time he leaned over one of the little tubes and in stentorian tones began to recite:

> "Mary had a little lamb,
> It's fleece was white as snow —
> And everywhere that Mary went
> The lamb was sure to go . . ."

The absurdity of the situation aroused loud laughter from the men around him. The inventor looked up and smiled as he turned the shaft backward to the starting point. Drawing the first tube away, he adjusted the other tube, and then again began to turn the shaft forward.

"*Mein Gott im Himmel!*" shouted John Kruesi. The machine talked! Faintly, but unmistakably, out of the crude mechanism, came the voice of Edison — "His Master's Voice."

The workers in the Menlo Park laboratory were actually astounded for the first time in their lives. They gathered about Edison and his talking machine with awe and admiration.

"I was never so taken aback in my life," admitted Edison finally. "I was always afraid of things that worked the first time."

"Well," exclaimed Carman, the foreman of the machine shop, "I guess I've lost my bet again!" He pulled out a cigar and handed it to the "Master," who put it in his mouth, lighted it, and walked away.

Throughout that night Edison and Kruesi were locked up in the laboratory; all night long the inventor talked into little pieces of tin foil on the cylinder — reciting over and over again the words of the classic adventure of Mary and the lamb. Edison sang into it — whistled into it — and shouted at it. Kruesi took his turn in talking his

Swiss-German dialect at the "foolish tin foil." Each time the little talking machine spat back their words at them. They both admitted, at daybreak, that they were astonished at the results of the experiment.

About nine o'clock in the morning, Edison wrapped up the "queer instrument" in a package and, taking it under his arm, started for New York — he had had no sleep. When he walked into the offices of the *Scientific American*, the leading scientific journal in the world, he looked like "a tramp who was carrying a bundle of clothes under his arm." The story of this strange intrusion has been told by F. C. Beach, the editor of the publication which every inventor approached with fear and trembling, as it was a violent exposer of hoaxes and fakes.

OFFICIAL STORY OF FIRST DEMONSTRATION IN NEW YORK

"I had not been at my desk very long that morning," said Mr. Beach, "when Mr. Edison was announced. He came in, and set his parcel, which he appeared to handle somewhat carefully, on my desk. As he was removing the cover, I asked him what it was.

" 'Just a minute!' replied young Edison.

"Presently with a 'here you are,' he pushed the quaint-looking little instrument toward me. As there was a long shaft having a heavy wheel at one end and a small handle at the other, naturally I gave the handle a twist, and, to my astonishment, the unmistakable words, emitted from a kind of telephone mouthpiece, broke out, 'Good morning! What do you think of the phonograph?'

"To say that I was astonished is a poor way of expressing my first impressions, and Edison appeared to enjoy his little joke on me immensely. Like a flash the news went among the staff that Edison had brought in a machine which could talk, and soon there was an excited crowd around my desk.

"We watched the inventor wrap his little sheet of tin foil (this was the medium used for recording the sound waves in the first machine) around the cylinder and adjust the stylus. Intently we followed the operation as he shouted the lines of the nursery rhyme, 'Mary had a little lamb,' into the mouthpiece. We listened just as surprisedly when, instantly this was completed, the machine was started again and the well-known words were repeated. Time after time the machine was handled first by myself and then by my colleagues, one and all testing the instrument both in recording and reproducing.

"Information respecting this remarkable demonstration leaked out, and in a short time the office was inundated with excited reporters despatched in hot haste from the various newspapers to examine the machine and witness the tests. Edison was kept going for two or three hours, but at last the crowd attained such proportions that I feared the floor would give way under the abnormal weight, and I requested the inventor to stop."

News Flashed Around World Creates
Skepticism

The newspapers on the following day hailed "the greatest invention of the age — a machine that talks." The amazing news soon traveled around the world and the inventor was flooded with letters from all parts of the globe. Managing editors of the leading journals believed their reporters were being "hoaxed," and ordered investigations. Edison was besieged in his laboratory at Menlo Park, by doubters who came as heretics and went away converts — and the headlines of the press proclaimed him "the wizard of Menlo Park." No other invention had aroused such a furore.

"Edison's latest invention, which he calls the 'phonograph,' is destined to turn the old groove of everyday routine topsy-turvy!" declared *Leslie's Weekly*. It captured the world like a *tour de force* and its tremendous possibilities were prophesied in glowing terms. Jules Verne had just created a sensation with his *Twenty Thousand Leagues under the Sea* and his imaginative "projectile train," shooting through the ether with its human freight, "From the Earth to the Moon." But Edison had surpassed even this in the popular imagination — he had made a machine that talked! Special trains, as we have stated, were run to Menlo Park, to see both the invention and the genius who had created it.

Edison started to work day and night improving the ability of the machine to speak. Tens of thousands of records were made. The machine, it is said, had a tendency to lisp and Edison would shout into it, "Mary had a little lamb — *lamb* — LAMB — *LAMB* — !"

And it is further said that when the instrument answered, it frequently added such sentences as, "You gol-swingled beast, can't you say LAMB!" More than fifty new machines were built, and destroyed in subsequent experiments. He finally succeeded in making several larger instruments which he considered safe for exhibition.

Inventor Proves His Machine Talks at Nation's Capital

A telegram from Washington reached Menlo Park, urging Edison to come to the National capital and exhibit his phonograph to members of Congress and also at the White House, as President Hayes was deeply interested. There are many interesting stories relating to this adventure. The young inventor, now thirty-one years old, was quite a curiosity as he arrived at the home of a member of the family of James G. Blaine, the leading statesman of the time. His hostess was Mary Abigail Dodge, a famous author who was writing under the pseudonym, "Gail Hamilton."

It was a brilliant assemblage of Senators and celebrities who came all day long and late into the evening to see this inventor and his invention. Senator Roscoe Conkling, of New York, arrived and was introduced to Edison, who, however, did not catch his name owing to his deafness. Conkling was the subject of caricaturists because of his eccentric manner of wearing a curl of hair on his forehead. Edison, perhaps subconsciously, noting this curl, began to recite into the phonograph as the distinguished guests listened in wonderment:

> "There was a little girl, who had a little curl
> Right in the middle of her forehead;
> And when she was good she was very, very good,
> But when she was bad she was horrid."

The listeners caught the significance as the phonograph shouted back the words, and broke into laughter. But the august Senator, who was a man of exceedingly great self-esteem, considered it an insult. It is said that he thought Blaine, who was his bitter political enemy, had deliberately placed him in this embarrassing situation.

About eleven o'clock that night, a messenger came from the White House and said: "President Hayes would consider it an honor if Mr. Edison could come to the Executive Mansion immediately."

The young inventor, with his invention under his arm, hurried down Pennsylvania Avenue to the White House. When he entered, he found the President waiting with several guests. Carl Schurz, the exiled patriot, soldier, and philosopher, was sitting at the piano in the library, playing from Beethoven, when Edison entered the room. He greeted the young man cordially and with expressions of admiration for the great achievements of so young a man.

President Hayes became so enthusiastic when he heard the machine talk that, at about 12.30 A.M., he hurried to the chamber of Mrs. Hayes and urged her to get up and dress and come down and see this marvel. Mrs. Hayes aroused the other ladies who were guests at the White House and they, too, came down. It was 3.30 A.M. when the party broke up and young Edison left the White House.

It was still difficult to convince the skeptical world that there was no trickery about this new invention. The insinuations of fraud became so current that the leading bishop of the Methodist Episcopal Church decided to investigate.

BISHOP VINCENT, OF CHAUTAUQUA, MAKES RIGID TEST

The arrival of the Reverend John H. Vincent at Menlo Park was an important event. With Lewis Miller, one of the most farsighted men in the country, and an educational philanthropist of note, Bishop Vincent had founded the Chautauqua Movement, which became one of the greatest educational forces in the country. This meeting of Miller and Edison is also historic because it cemented a friendship which resulted, in later years, in the marriage of Edison to a daughter of the Miller family, after the death of his first wife.

"I think it would be more satisfactory if you talked to the machine yourself," remarked Edison to Bishop Vincent.

The Bishop stepped up to the tube and, without hesitation, began to shout at top speed the longest proper names from the Bible that he could command — "Mahalaleel — Methuselah — Arphaxad — Hazarmaveth — Chedorlaomer," and a list of names that Edison said would "stop a clock." The little machine did not even shiver or stutter — it shot back the Biblical "begats" at the good Bishop with such rapidity that it astonished him.

"*I am satisfied!*" exclaimed Bishop Vincent. "There isn't a man in the United States who could recite those names with the same rapidity." It is said that he had been warned to search for "a ventriloquist concealed somewhere about the premises," but he defied any ventriloquist to keep pace with him when it came to his Biblical lore.

Edison Gets Patent for Original, Startling Invention

The first patent on the phonograph was filed in the United States, December 24, 1877, and was granted February 19, 1878, No. 200521. The examiners in the Patent Office stated that the invention was so absolutely new that no attempt ever before in the United States had been made to record and produce speech or other sound, and the patent was immediately granted. An application had been filed in Great Britain on July 30, 1877, even prior to that in the United States, and it is because of this that Edison's model of "the world's first phonograph" was treasured for years in the British Museum, until returned to the valuable Edison Collection at Orange.

Many claimants began to contest the honors, but there was no basis for their claims. An unidentified author, believed to have been the poet, Hood, had made this imaginative statement in 1839: "In this country of inventions, when a self-acting drawing paper has been discovered for copying invisible objects, who knows but that a future Niepce, or Daguerre, or Herschel, or Fox Talbot might find out some sort of Boswellish writing paper to repeat whatever it hears?" The other writer to predict the phonograph was Jean Ingelow, who, in 1872, while forecasting events a hundred years hence, describes a "great invention in acoustics which you are going to find out very shortly."

Two Frenchmen also entered claims: Edouard-Leon Scott de Martinville, who had invented a "phonautograph" in 1857; and Charles Cros, who invented an instrument in 1877 which his friend, the Abbe Leblanc, called the "phonograph," thus creating the word. These crude devices failed to produce results, and Edison had never heard of them.

The first manufacture of phonographs for sale to the public was done in the little shop of Sigmund Bergmann on Wooster Street, in New York. He had worked at the same bench with Kruesi in the old Edison shop in Newark, and, saving money on his "piecework," had started a shop for himself. The first exhibition manager was Dr. John Redpath, the famous Lyceum lecturer, who laid out the country in territories which were leased on a percentage basis. Rights to Great Britain and the European continent were assigned to Professor Fleeming Jenkin, about whom Stevenson wrote his "Memoir." He created wide attention when he exhibited the first Edison phonographs before the Royal Society of Edinburgh and the scientists in London, Paris, Berlin, and the continental capitals.

The first exhibition headquarters for the phonograph in America were opened at 203 Broadway, New York, and

Photo by Underwood

EDISON AT THE AGE OF THIRTY-TWO

This photograph was made during a demonstration of his speaking
phonograph before the National Academy of Science in April, 1878.

Photo by Underwood

EDISON LISTENING TO HIS "EDIPHONE"

The little wax cylinder of the early days which recorded speech was regarded as "almost
supernatural." The phonograph knows no other parent than Edison, and he brought
it to its present condition by devotion and tireless skill.

EDISON AND HIS "INSOMNIA SQUAD"

A picture taken in 1912. These men labored for several months averaging only three and a half consecutive hours' sleep a day. Left to right are: (seated) John Lamont, Wm. Fulton, S. Moore, and Mr. Edison; (standing) Edward McGlynn, Robert Spahle, and Al Hoffman.

demonstrators were sent out to all parts of the country. Interesting stories are told in Philadelphia and in Chicago and New Orleans, in fact in nearly every large city at the time, of the crowds that thronged these exhibitions. Famous prima donnas sang into it, and Edison once stated: "People may think some of these folks are great singers. Lots of little defects don't sound in the concert hall, but when they come out of that hole they do! They can't fool my phonograph! I've got them!"

INVENTOR EXPERIMENTS AT HOME ON HIS FIRST BABY BOY

It was about this time that the first baby was born in the Edison home, and the proud father determined to make a record of his firstborn's lusty crying — the first record ever made by a baby. The story is recorded in the *New York Herald* in 1877:

"The phonograph came to the Edison laboratory and the first baby to the Edison home about the same time, and when the baby was old enough to say 'Goo-goo' and pull the great inventor's hair in a most disrespectful manner, the phonograph was near enough perfection to capture the baby talk for preservation among the family archives. So Mr. Edison filled up several rolls with these pretty articulations and laid them carefully away.

"But this was not sufficient. The most picturesque thing about the baby's utterances was its crying, and the record of this its fond father determined to secure. How it would entertain him in his old age, he thought, to start the phonograph a-going and hear again the baby wails of his firstborn! So one afternoon Mr. Edison tore himself away from his work and climbed the big hill leading to his house. He went in a great hurry, for he is a man who grudges every working moment from his labors. A workman followed at his heels, carrying the only phonograph that at that time had been sufficiently completed to accomplish really good results.

12

"Reaching home and the nursery, Mr. Edison started the phonograph and brought the baby in front of it. But the baby didn't cry. Mr. Edison tumbled the youngster about, and rumpled its hair and did all sorts of things, but still the baby didn't cry. Then the inventor made dreadful faces, but the baby thought they were very funny, and crowed lustily. So back to the laboratory went Mr. Edison in a very unpleasant frame of mind, for the baby's untimely good humor had cost him an hour of work. The phonograph was also taken back.

"But he didn't give it up. The next afternoon he went home again, and the phonograph with him. But if the baby was good-natured the day before, this time it was absolutely cherubic. There was nothing at all that its father could do that didn't make the baby laugh. Even the phonograph with its tiny whirring wheels the baby thought was meant for its special entertainment, and gurgled joyously. So back to work the inventor went again with a temper positively ruffled. The next day and the next he tried it, but all to no purpose. The baby would not cry even when waked suddenly from sleep.

"But to baffle Edison is only to inflame his determination, which, as has been remarked before, is one of the secrets of his success. So at length, after much thought, he made a mighty resolve. It took a vast amount of determination on his part to screw his courage to the point of committing the awful deed, but he succeeded at last, and one morning, when he knew his wife was down town, he went quietly home with the phonograph and stole into the nursery, where the baby greeted him with its customary glee.

"Starting the machine, Mr. Edison ordered the nurse to leave the room. Then he took the baby on his knee and bared its chubby little leg. He took the tender flesh between his thumb and finger, clenched his teeth, shut his eyes tight, and made ready to — yes, actually to pinch the baby's leg. But just at the fateful moment the nurse peeped through the door, and, perceiving the horrid plot, flounced in and rescued the baby in the nick of time. Mr. Edison breathed a mighty sigh of relief as he gathered up the phonograph and went back to the laboratory. He then gave up the project of phonographing the baby's crying.

"But not long afterwards he accomplished his purpose in spite of everything, and quite unexpectedly, too. As soon as the baby was old enough to take notice, its mother took it down to the laboratory one sunny day, and when the big machinery was started a-roaring, the baby screwed up its face, opened its mouth, and emitted a series of woeful screams that made Mr. Edison leap to his feet. 'Stop the machinery and start the phonograph,' he shouted, and the record of his baby's crying was there and then accomplished."

EDISON MAKES OFFICIAL STATEMENT ON WHAT PHONOGRAPH WILL DO

Edison recorded his opinions regarding the future of his invention in the *North American Review* in 1878:

"Among the many uses to which the phonograph will be applied are the following: (1) Letter-writing and all kinds of dictation without the aid of a stenographer — (2) Phonographic books which will speak to blind people without effort on their part — (3) The teaching of elocution — (4) The reproduction of music — (5) The Family Record (a registry of sayings, reminiscences, etc., by members of a family in their own voices), and of the last words of dying persons — (6) Music boxes and toys — (7) Clocks that should announce in articulate speech the time for going home, time for meals, etc. — (8) The preservation of languages by exact reproduction of the manner of pronouncing — (9) Educational purposes, such as preserving the explanations made by a teacher so that the pupil can refer to them at any moment; and spelling or other lessons placed upon the phonograph for convenience in committing to memory — (10) Connection with the telephone so as to make that instrument an auxiliary in the transmission of permanent and invaluable records, instead of being the recipient of momentary and fleeting communication."

His farsightedness is shown by his further prophecies: "The phonograph will undoubtedly be largely devoted to music — either vocal or instrumental — and may possibly take the place of the teacher. It will sing the child to sleep, tell us what o'clock it is, summon us to dinner, and warn the lover when it is time to vacate the front porch. As a family record it will be precious, for it will preserve the sayings of those dear to us, and even receive the last messages of the dying. It will enable the children to have dolls that really speak, laugh, cry, and sing, and imitation dogs that bark, cats that meow, lions that roar, and roosters that crow. It will preserve the voices of our great men, and enable future generations to listen to speeches by a Lincoln or a Gladstone. Lastly, the phonograph will perfect the telephone and revolutionize present systems of telegraphy."

Spends $2,000,000 to Perfect the Talking Machine

About this time — in 1878 — Edison was suddenly seized with a new idea. He set the phonograph aside, went out to the ranches of Wyoming, returned and again locked himself up in his laboratory at Menlo Park until he appeared with his next new world wonder — the incandescent electric light. This story will be told in the next chapter, but to sustain the narrative of the phonograph we take up its story in 1888, when Edison appeared — after working five days and nights without sleeping — with his second or "improved" phonograph with the voice preserved first on wax and then composition cylinder and disk; and with continuous improvements which required sixty-five new patents. The perfection of the talking machine finally cost more than $2,000,000.

This new Edison phonograph swept the country and

revived the interest of a decade before. The chords of "Sweet Adeline," and "Home, Sweet Home," rang through nearly every home. It became the craze to sing or talk into the wax record and then hear one's own voice. There is the story of a quartet in Philadelphia that sang all the popular songs and then exhausted the religious hymns. Charles F. Kint, President of The John C. Winston Company, was a member of one of these first quartets to sing into the phonograph. Edison's name was on everybody's lips and became a household word; he had brought entertainment and delight to the whole world.

The inventor, himself, took great pleasure in "playing with his own phonograph"; such as reproducing songs backwards and mixing up serious speeches with hilarious jokes. The story is told how he once hid a phonograph in a guest's room at his own home. At eleven o'clock at night the guest was suddenly awakened by a voice calling: *"One hour more!"* The clock ticked through the hour, and then the sleeper was awakened at the stroke of midnight by a voice which groaned: *"Prepare to die!"* It is said that the guest fled from the room in terror, while Edison stood near by shaking with laughter.

FIRST PUBLIC EXHIBITION IN ENGLAND CAUSES EXCITEMENT

The first public exhibition of the "New Edison Phonograph" in England drew great crowds to Crystal Palace in 1888. This was opened with a private exhibition at Norwood, with such distinguished guests as William E. Gladstone, the Earl of Aberdeen, Sir Morell Mackenzie, Sir William Hunter, Sir John Fowler, Lord Rowton, and a brilliant gathering of notables. The guests were amazed as Edison's voice came from the phonograph in a message to the British people. Here is the exact transcript, as the phonograph delivered it:

> "Gentlemen — In the name of Edison, to whose rare genius, incomparable patience, and indefatigable industry I owe my being, I greet you. I thank you for the honor you do me by your presence here today. My only regret is that my master is not here to meet you in the flesh as he is in the voice. But in his absence I should be failing in my duty, as well as in my pleasure, did I not take this, my first opportunity, to thank you and all the press of the great city of London, both present and absent, for the generous and flattering reception with which my coming to the Mother Country has been heralded by you to the world."

At the London exhibition at Crystal Palace, the first phonographic letter was delivered — a talking letter. Edison had dictated it in America to Colonel Gouraud, his European manager. The record spoke these words:

> "June 16, 1888, 3 o'clock A.M.
>
> "Friend Gouraud — Ahem! This is my first mailing phonogram. It will go to you in the regular United States mail from New York via Southampton, North German Lloyd Steamer *Eider*. I send you by Mr. Hamilton a new phonograph, the first one of the new model, which has just left my hands.
>
> "It has been put together very hurriedly, and is not finished, as you will see. I have sent you a quantity of experimental phonogram blanks, so that you can talk back to me. I will send you phonograms of talk and music by every mail leaving here until we get the best thing for the purpose of mailing.
>
> "Mrs. Edison and the baby are doing well. The baby's articulation is quite loud enough, but a trifle indistinct; it can be improved, but is not bad for a first experiment.
>
> "With kind regards,
>
> "Yours,
>
> "Edison."

The stirring event which had thrilled the hearts of the distinguished guests and the British people, was when the phonograph spoke its "salutation" — the words which had been composed and spoken into the machine three thousand miles away by Horatius Nelson Powers, an eminent doctor of divinity, at Piermont-on-the-Hudson. Gladstone was said to have been deeply affected as the clear tones came from the record:

THE PHONOGRAPH'S SALUTATION

I seize the palpitating air, I hoard
　　Music and speech.　All lips that breathe are mine;
I speak, the inviolable word
　　Authenticates its origin and sign.

I am a tomb, a Paradise, a shrine,
　　An angel, prophet, slave, immortal friend;
My living records, in their native tone,
　　Convict the knave, and disputations end.

In me are souls embalmed.　I am an ear,
　　· Flawless as truth, and truth's own tongue am I.
I am a resurrection; men may hear
　　The quick and dead converse, as I reply.

Hail! English shores, and homes, and marts of peace,
　　New trophies, Gouraud, yet are to be won.
May sweetness, light, and brotherhood increase;
　　I am the latest born of Edison.

GLADSTONE, BRITISH PREMIER, MAKES FIRST ENGLISH RECORD

The great Gladstone was deeply admired by Edison, and the latter had given orders that every effort should be expended to persuade Gladstone to make a record for posterity.　The British statesman felt honored by the request, and, standing impressively before the marvelous invention of this American genius, he spoke these words fervidly, addressing them direct to Edison far across the sea:

> "I am profoundly indebted to you for, not the entertainment only, but the instruction and the marvels of one of the most remarkable evenings which it has been my privilege to enjoy. Your great country is leading the way in the important work of invention. Heartily do we wish it well; and to you, as one of its greatest celebrities, allow me to offer my hearty good wishes and earnest prayers that you may long live to witness its triumphs in all that appertains to the well-being of mankind. — Gladstone."

This is the first phonogram made for posterity, by one of the world's great statesmen. It remains among the priceless treasures in the collection of "Voices of the Great," now preserved at the Edison home at Llewellyn Park. Here, today, the members of the Edison family may place the records on the machine and hear the voices of Bismarck — Tennyson — Browning — Henry Ward Beecher — and the famous men of two continents who were living at the time that Edison was perfecting his phonograph. The famous explorer, Stanley, who found Livingstone when he was lost in Africa, and his wife, were guests at the Edison home; and while listening to these records, Mrs. Stanley turned to Edison and asked:

"Whose voice of all the great men of the past would you like best to recall and register?"

Edison sat thoughtfully for a moment, his mind running up and down the centuries of human history. Should it be King Solomon — or Cæsar — or William the Conqueror?

"Napoleon," Replied Edison, Decisively

The argument that ensued lasted through the evening and the Stanleys were amazed at the wide fund of knowledge which Edison possessed; history seemed to be a living thing to him, as if he were intimately acquainted with all the great characters who have lived through the centuries. Edison stood his ground: Napoleon was his choice, and for a record of his voice he was willing to barter "the entire collection of records in my possession." And the record which Edison treasured most affectionately was that of the voice of John Kruesi, the model maker who had made his first phonograph, "the cleverest mechanic I ever knew." After Kruesi died — twenty-two years after the invention of the phonograph — it is said by Edison's intimates that, when alone, he would take down records of his coworker's voice and listen intently as it "spoke from the grave."

All Europe was enthralled by the new American invention. Queen Victoria spent many evenings with it at Buckingham Palace; William II, the young emperor (Kaiser Wilhelm), had just taken the throne of the German Empire and admitted that he was "astonished by the invention." Franz Josef, Emperor of Austria, commanded that he be given an audition. Czar Alexander III, of Russia, ordered it installed in his private room. King Leopold II, of Belgium, considered it "the wonder of the age." King Humbert I, of Italy, had many official records taken. Royalty, and populace alike, were thrilled by the discovery of Edison. His triumph reached its zenith at the great Paris exposition in 1889, when forty thousand people a day flocked to hear the phonograph — even Eiffel Tower did not so completely astound them.

First Exhibition in Germany Before Emperor William II

The first exhibition ever given of the phonograph in Europe was before Emperor Wilhelm at his palace in Berlin in 1888. The young Emperor greeted Edison's emissary and coworker, A. T. Wangemann, a German who worked with Edison in America, in his private apartments. After listening to it speak, he asked that it be taken apart and then put together again, and listened intently to an explanation of the scientific principles which gave it voice. Wilhelm was not satisfied until he had examined every detail and had made many records himself. He then requested that the Edison phonograph be exhibited before his court at the palace that evening. A brilliant assembly gathered and to their amazement the young emperor himself appeared as lecturer and explained its mechanism as skilfully as though he had been "educated in the Edison laboratory." For two hours, Wilhelm discoursed on acoustics before some of the ablest scientists in Germany, including his army staff and statesmen. He later had records taken of the Royal Court Orchestra as they rendered the symphonies of the great German masters.

When, some years later, Kaiser Wilhelm was requested to make a record for posterity, to be deposited in the archives of Harvard University, he expressed his delight and extended his highest admiration for Thomas Edison. The request was made through the American ambassador in Berlin by Dr. Edward Scripture, an eminent American psychologist of Yale University. The official memorandum sent to the Emperor read:

"The Phonographic Archives are to include records from such persons as will presumably have permanent historical interest in America. The importance of the undertaking can be estimated by considering what would have been the present value of voice records by Demosthenes, Shakespeare, or Frederick the Great. I wish to record his Majesty's voice as the first European record deposited in the Archives."

It was on Sunday morning following religious services at the palace, that Kaiser Wilhelm received the American scholar. He recalled to Dr. Scripture the delightful occasion on which the Edison phonograph was first shown him by Dr. Wangemann. The Emperor ordered all persons from the room and stood alone as he spoke into the phonograph. His first record was on the career of Frederick the Great (made for the Archives at Harvard University), and the second record was an essay on "Fortitude in Pain" (for the National Museum at Washington). The Imperial family was then called into the room and gathered devoutly around the American invention as they listened to it repeat the Emperor's orations.

First Demonstrator Sentenced to Prison in Russia

There are stories told in Russia of when the Edison phonograph was exhibited in the pavilion of the public gardens; the crowds gathered about it as it sang and talked and laughed undisturbed, until it began to recite one of Kirloff's famous fables. A police officer suddenly became suspicious and ran and got Kirloff's book to "check it up." Horror of horrors! The "speaking mechanical beast" was reciting the fable that had been prohibited by the censor more than half a century ago, and was telling "the peaceful inhabitants many undesirable things." The guilty demonstrator was placed immediately under arrest, put to trial, and sentenced to three months' imprisonment with a heavy fine. And the innocent little "talking machine" was smashed to pieces at the feet of the Czar's august officials.

BUDDHISTS IN SACRED TIBET SAY PRAYERS TO PHONOGRAPH

This "Eighth Wonder of the World" found its way into the farthest corners of the earth. A traveler returning from Tibet was amazed to find Edison's phonograph in far-off Lassa, the religious capital of the Buddhist faith. This is the experience he relates: "Travelers of the Buddhist faith may visit Lassa if they are under no suspicion of being emissaries of the Christians. Among such travelers was a certain Burmese merchant, who, familiar with the resources of civilization, took with him to show the Grand Lama or sacred and miraculously appointed head of the Buddhist Church, an Edison phonograph. This was a good idea on the part of the Burmese trader, for in the Buddhist cult great account is made of mechanically repeated prayers. Praying wheels to reel off printed or written prayers are employed, and it struck the merchant that if he could introduce a machine which would actually repeat the prayers aloud he might make a fortune in supplying the apparatus.

"He succeeded in getting the Grand or Dalai Lama and the dignitaries that surround him to inspect the phonograph, and, as he had read into it a chapter of the sacred writings of the Buddhists, he was able to make it repeat this chapter aloud to the great astonishment of the Grand Lama, who thought he was witnessing a miracle. The merchant asked the Dalai Lama to speak into the machine, and he did so proclaiming the beautiful prayer called 'Om mani padme cum,' or 'Jewel in the Lotus.' Then the cylinder being put in place, the phonograph repeated the prayer in the Dalai

Lama's voice, to the great amazement and edification of all the auditors. For many days thereafter the phonograph was kept busy with this and other utterances holy to the Buddhists, and now the phonograph has taken its place as the favorite 'praying machine' of Lassa."

A visit to the "Voices of the Dead" in the Edison laboratories — or to vaults of the National Museum at Washington and at Harvard University — would be like visiting the tombs of kings or going to Westminster Abbey. Here, great statesmen, soldiers, scientists, educators, artists, famous opera singers and violinists and pianists — long since gone — still raise their voices and speak from the dead in these treasure houses of preserved records.

"I have set my heart on reproducing perfectly Beethoven's Ninth Symphony," declared Edison on the twenty-fifth anniversary of the phonograph, "with seventy-five people in the orchestra. When I have done that I'll quit."

So these "wonder stories" might be told endlessly — Edison's private scrapbooks and records contain thousands of them — but the wizard of Menlo Park was performing new miracles, and we must return to the laboratories.

Familiar trade-marks of other days, one showing the famous Edison signature, the other a child determined to find out where the band came from.

CHAPTER XVI

THE "WIZARD OF MENLO PARK" LIGHTS THE WORLD

All the world came to Menlo Park to see the "Wizard" at work.

MENLO PARK was becoming a place of mystery. It was a modern Pandora's box. What would come out of it next?

The "Wizard" was working on his usual schedule of eighteen to twenty hours a day and something must result. Invention, heretofore, had been a matter for mechanics, but now it was beginning to appeal to the popular imagination as it entered into fields which belonged for centuries only to the realms of magic.

Edison, in the meantime, went West in July, 1878, for a much needed rest, out to the ranches in Wyoming — his first vacation, at thirty-one years of age. Two months later he came back "reborn," as he said, with many tales of his adventures. The cowboys had ridden a hundred miles over the plains to meet him. "Texas Jack," the two-gun man, inebriated, had come to demonstrate his marksmanship by firing through an open window at a distant sign, and only after much persuasion could he be induced to leave. Broncho-busters displayed their skill. On a hunting trip into the Ute country, Edison, the tenderfoot from the East,

was permitted to ride on a cowcatcher.   The locomotive
hit an animal about the size of a bear.   Hurled upward,
it struck just under the headlight.   Edison admitted,
"I ducked and probably saved my life."

Edison Tests His Tasimeter on Plains of Wyoming

This vacation, however, proved to be but another
scientific investigation, for Edison's real purpose was to
test a delicate instrument which he had just invented —
the tasimeter.   The chief purpose of his trip was to accompany an expedition of scientists who had gone to Wyoming
to observe an eclipse of the sun.   Astronomers from nearly
every nation were present on July 29, 1878, when this
event took place.   The new tasimeter measured down to
the millionth part of a degree Fahrenheit.   Its sensitive-
ness amazed the scientists.   Experiments proved that the
heat from the corona of the sun was ten times the index
capacity of the instrument.   The *Scientific American*
reported:

"Seeing that the tasimeter is affected by a wider
range of etheric undulations than the eye can take cogni-
zance of, and is withal far more acutely sensitive, the prob-
abilities are that it will open up hitherto inaccessible regions
of space, and possibly extend the range of aërial knowledge
as far beyond the limit obtained by the telescope as that
is beyond the narrow reach of unaided vision."

The young inventor had joined the expedition at the
urgent request of Professor George F. Barker, Professor of
Chemistry and Physics in the University of Pennsylvania,
who was convinced that in Edison the world had one of
its great future scientists.

"I watched the scientists as they started to take their
calculations," said Edison.   "They first set up their

instruments to determine their exact position upon the earth and its relation to the sun. I was amazed at the immense amount of mathematics, and preserved one of their sheets — it looked like the time-table of a Chinese railroad. They found they were not in error more than 100 feet. It was a revelation to me on the precision of the astronomers and the physicists, as I had always been fascinated when I read about the exact distances between the planets and the vastness of the solar system."

With the completion of the records on the eclipse of the sun, Edison and Professor Barker, with some of the army officers from the near-by military post, went on a hunting expedition into northwestern Colorado. The inventor's intimate relations with Jay Gould, who then controlled the Union Pacific, gave him "right of way" through the country — even to the extent of riding on the cowcatchers of the locomotives. Like a sentry on duty, he took this position of vantage and scouted the Great West — from Omaha to the Sacramento Valley.

"I deserted my post on the cowcatcher but once," explained Edison. "I was driven into the cab of the engine when we passed through the snowshed on the summit of the Sierras in the Rocky Mountains."

BACK AT MENLO PARK WITH GIANT TASK BEFORE HIM

Two months passed and, in the last of August, Edison was back at Menlo Park, plunging more deeply than ever before into scientific problems; his tasimeter and his "voice-engine," or "phonomotor," which could "actually talk a hole through a board," were temporarily set aside. He was engaged upon new and vital discoveries — the problem of subdividing the electric current for illuminating purposes. If this could be accomplished, the system of

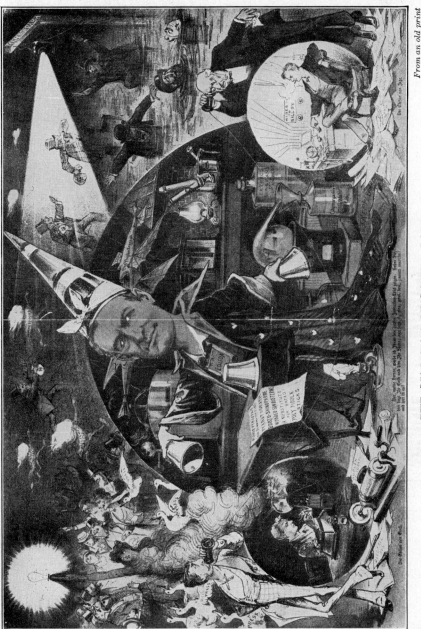

From an old print

THE MAGICIAN OF MENLO PARK

The phonograph and the electric light instantly brought world fame to Edison. This is a German artist's dream of the wonder-
worker saying "One, two, three," and presto! here it is.

Photo by *Wide World*

A CORNER OF THE OLD CARBON HOUSE AT MENLO PARK

From the smoking chimneys of the kerosene lamps, Edison derived his carbon, to be compressed into buttons on the hand press, and weighed on the scales seen in the background.

lighting the world could be revolutionized. It is said that Professor Barker urged him to concentrate his genius on this problem which had challenged the scientists of Europe and America since the discovery of electrical forces.

"Let there be light," is one of the first recorded commands in Scriptural history. Edison, as a boy, had read and reread the first words in Genesis, following the creation of the earth: "Let there be light: and there was light. And God saw the light, that it was good: and God divided the light from the darkness. And God called the light Day, and the darkness he called Night. And the evening and the morning were the first day."

It seemed like a superhuman task, even supernatural, for man now to attempt to turn the darkness of night into the light of day. The world had groped along through the centuries in the darkness. Primitive man, when he first discovered fire, used torches; then he held burning pine chips between his teeth to guide him; finally he had burned the fats of animals in utensils called lamps. Ancient Egypt, Greece, and Rome, long before Christ, had molded clay and then hammered metal into shallow urns in which they burned oils. Through the Medieval Ages the progress was slow until the invention of tallow candles, the discovery of petroleum, and the wonders of gas.

Great Discoveries of Men Who Had Blazed the Trail

The slow march of civilization made its way through the diffusion of light — and then more light. We find Otto von Guericke, in 1650, building the first machine for generating electricity, a crude sulphur ball rotated at high speed on a shaft. Francis Hawksbee, in 1700, produced light with a similar machine; Von Kliest invented the

Leyden jar, about 1745, when he first "stored" electricity
in a bottle of water and was knocked off his feet.   Benjamin Franklin made tests with this Leyden jar and finally
drew sparks from a key attached to a kite during a thunder-
storm, in 1752.

The search for "electric light" now began.   Sir Hum-
phry Davy, at the Royal Institute, in London, was the
first to produce it when he discovered the principle of
the arc light, in 1809–10.   Michael Faraday discovered the
principle of the magneto machine, in 1831.   Frederick de
Molyns, an Englishman, made the first decisive step toward
the development of the incandescent light, in 1841.   J. W.
Starr, an American, with E. A. King, an English associate,
made the next forward step when he substituted carbon
filaments for platinum, in 1845.   Then, in rapid succession,
came W. E. Staite, in 1848, and J. J. W. Watson, in 1853,
and Moses G. Farmer, in 1859, until we reach Joseph W.
(later Sir Joseph) Swan, in England, who made an important discovery by devising a lamp with a conductor formed
by a strip of carbonized paper, in 1860.

Edison Starts Where the Pioneers Left Off

These are the conditions with which Edison was confronted when he entered his laboratory at Menlo Park in
1878, to find the solution which would give the incandescent electric light to the world for practical utility.   Ingenious schemes had been proposed by many inventors —
Roberts, Lodyguine, Konn, Kosloff, Khotinsky, Bouliguine,
in Europe, and Wallace, Sawyer, and Mann, in America.

The glaring arc light was the furthest that inventive
genius had been able to develop, with such skilled scientists as Elihu Thomson, Edward Weston, and Charles F.
Brush.   At the Centennial Exposition at Philadelphia, in

1876, these brilliant arc lights created quite a sensation. The old kerosene and gas street lights were doomed as Brush placed his new arc lights in the public squares of his home town of Cleveland, Ohio, and in Madison Square and Union Square, New York. These lights burned with a hissing sound, almost blinding the eyes, and rapidly burned themselves out.

Grounded in knowledge of what had been done before him, and with full realization of the almost insurmountable problems, Edison made a trip to Ansonia, Connecticut, in September, 1878, to witness experiments in arc lighting by William Wallace and Moses G. Farmer, two of the greatest pioneers in the electrical age. He was greeted as a fellow scientist by these great characters who were giving their lives to human progress. Present on this historic occasion was Edison's friend, Professor Barker, who was also an intimate friend of Wallace, also Charles Batchelor, one of Edison's assistants in his laboratory, Professor Charles F. Chandler, then a famous Professor of Chemistry in Columbia University, and Doctor Henry Draper, the scientist who gained world renown in the field of celestial photography.

This was a distinguished gathering of geniuses, all working in harmony to find the secrets that could be utilized for the benefit of mankind. Wallace turned over to Edison one of his Wallace-Farmer dynamos and a set of Wallace arc lamps to light his laboratory at Menlo Park. To commemorate the memorable gathering, each member of the party inscribed his name with a diamond point on goblets used at that time in toasts to success. The Edison goblet is still treasured by his family and bears the inscription: "Thomas A. Edison, Sept. 8, 1878, made under the electric light."

"Wallace," exclaimed Edison, as they shook hands when parting, "I believe I can beat you making electric light. I do not think you are working in the right direction."

"I believe in the arc light," replied Wallace. "I do not believe that the electric current can be subdivided, but I wish you all the good fortune in the world."

Edison returned to Menlo Park with renewed confidence that he was working on the right lines. He entered into a thorough investigation of the subject of gas lighting, analyzing the "transactions" of the associations of gas engineers. The data he gathered at this time was in itself astounding. Among the treasures in the possession of his family are two hundred notebooks, containing over 40,000 pages, filled with his handwriting during these electric-lighting researches. There are such entries as these, which show his keen observation:

"So unpleasant is the effect of the products of gas that in the new Madison Square Theatre every gas jet is ventilated by special tubes to carry away the products of combustion . . ." — "Object: Edison to effect exact imitation of all done by gas so as to replace lighting by gas by lighting by electricity . . ." — "Edison's great effort — not to make a large light, or a blinding light, but a small light having the mildness of gas."

GETS FINANCIERS TO BACK HIM FOR $40,000

Activities in the Edison laboratories were speeded up to the limit of human endurance. He called several noted financiers around him and told them what he intended to do. Among the men were J. P. Morgan, Henry Villard, and Grosvenor P. Lowry, legal adviser for the inventor.

"We will give you a certain sum of money each week," they decided. "It will be enough to keep you going and employ your men. Go ahead and see what you can do."

As the months went on, the financiers became more cautious with their funds. When $40,000 was expended, they met and seriously considered whether to continue or not. Edison was forced to "resell" them — there was nothing left for them to do but to put up more money or to take their loss and they generally left enthusiastic, but always with a warning:

"I'm afraid this is the last money I can get for you," Lowry, the legal adviser, would state. "If I have to go back to them again, I will probably have to guarantee them with my own signature. But — go ahead. I believe in you and feel confident that you will win out." To protect the inventors, a syndicate was formed under the name, "The Edison Light Company," capitalized at $3,000. A flood of patents began to appear at Washington and the curiosity of the scientific world, which was now watching every move made by Edison, was aroused.

Scientists Challenge Edison to "Subdivide Electric Current"

All sorts of rumors became current throughout America and Europe. London newspapers obtained copies of every patent specification and commented incredulously, as their sympathies were with their own inventor, Swan.

"This document," reports one British journal, "reveals for the first time authoritatively the line on which Edison is experimenting. It reveals nothing new, however, for in one manner and another the substantial facts in regard to Edison's experiments had all been obtained previously . . . Scientific men may judge for themselves as to the probable success of the Edison light. The weak point of the lamp is this, that in order to be luminous, platinum must be heated almost to the point of melting. With a slight increase in the current, the lamp melts in the twinkling of an eye, and in practice the regulator is found to short-circuit the current too late to prevent the damage. It is this difficulty which must be overcome. Can it be done?"

Scientific men in America and Europe positively declared it to be impossible. The British Parliament appointed a committee to investigate and called before them nearly all the prominent scientists as witnesses. "The subdivision of the electric light is a problem beyond the power of man to solve," was their decision.

"The subdivision of the light is an absolute *ignis fatuus*," asserted the great Sir William Preece, eminent English electrician.

"I am sorry that I cannot agree with you," retorted Dr. John Tyndall, the distinguished scientist. "Edison has the penetration to seize the relationship of facts and principles and the art to reduce them to novel and concrete combinations. Hence, though he has thus far accomplished nothing new in relation to the electric light, an adverse opinion as to his ability to solve the complicated problem on which he is engaged would be unwarranted . . . Knowing something of the intricacy of the practical problem, I should certainly prefer seeing it in Mr. Edison's hands to having it in mine."

AMERICAN INVENTOR IGNORES CHARGES — AND GOES AHEAD

Edison, however, made no reply to these charges, but merely put more days and nights into his experiments at Menlo Park. The European press called him "fool" — "visionary" — "ignorant" — "dreamer" — and even "boaster." Mathematicians pointed out that he was attempting the utterly impossible. Even the American scientists sidestepped the controversy and refused to commit themselves, except those who were his personal friends and declared their faith in him.   The patent claims in which he recorded that he had succeeded in solving the problem, caused much editorial comment in the American newspapers.   We find this warning in the *Scientific American*, February 15, 1879:

"The Philadelphia *Bulletin* suggests that if Mr. Edison wishes public faith in that electric light of his to remain steadfast, he will have to give an early demonstration of the truth of his claim that it is a practical success.   When he first announced that he had solved the problem of dividing the light and of adapting it to domestic uses, there was a very general inclination to accept the story with absolute confidence because Mr. Edison had proved by his previous inventions that he could achieve some things which had been regarded by other men as impossible.   But, after all, the proof of the pudding is in the eating, and the world, after waiting patiently for the public display of an invention which sent gas stocks down as soon as it was heralded, will be disposed, unless Mr. Edison shows his hand, to suspect that the Edison Electric Light and the Keely Motor will have to be ranked together as enterprises which contained more of promise than of performance."

EDISON'S BACKERS STOP FALSE AND MALICIOUS RUMORS

Aroused by these slurs, Lowry, who, with his friends, was backing Edison, showed his fighting spirit.   Spending much of his time at the laboratories, his enthusiasm daily increased.   He kept in touch with the newspapers and warned them against misstatements.   Here is one of the historic documents issued to the press:

"Dear Sir,—Your columns this morning contain the following, which you will undoubtedly be glad to correct:

"'It is understood that Mr. Edison is suffering from ill health, and has given up his experiments with the electric light.'

"My relation to Mr. Edison in respect to his inventions and discoveries in electric lighting gives me opportunity to know the truth about these matters, and the public interest concerning them makes it seem a duty to correct statements which I know to be erroneous. *Mr. Edison has been daily and nightly, as usual, at work in his laboratory upon the electric light. I spent several hours with him a few days since.* He seemed in the highest spirits and in excellent health, and very enthusiastic over the results of his work in electric lighting. Since the state of progress in this work is of interest to the public, I may avail myself of this occasion to state my view of the matter as it now stands, promising that I am not an expert . . .

"His first invention, as it will appear in the first patents to be issued, will but inadequately show the novel discoveries and devices which he has made even to this time, when, according to his own views, he is comparatively only upon the threshold of a new and wonderful development of electrical science . . .

"In the meantime there is an interest somewhere to set on foot false reports affecting Mr. Edison's light, one of which, recently circulated in an up-town club, I beg space to correct. It was stated that an official paper emanating from the British Patent Office had been seen which denied a patent to Mr. Edison. The author of the report would, perhaps, have been more careful had he known that the legal period fixed for the issue or denial of such a patent has not yet been reached, and that the existence of such a paper at this time is, therefore, impossible."

With the "Valiant Little Army" at Menlo Park

Stirring scenes were being enacted at the Edison laboratory in Menlo Park during these tense days. From floor to ceiling it was piled high with batteries of cells, chemicals, instruments, and apparatus — every conceivable substance that he could use in his experiments. Some fifty men were at work at the benches through long stretches, without sleeping, and food was brought in to them. Edison stood in the midst of his "loyal army" and directed operations while he made every original experiment himself. Thousands of tests resulted only in failure. He would throw himself down on a hard bench to catch a few minutes sleep and then arise to go to work with renewed energy; his labors were ceaseless and tireless.

A great general, directing his troops, never showed a more unconquerable spirit. We shall meet some of these men in the following chapter on "Days and Nights with Edison in his Laboratory," and these old "Edison Pioneers" will tell their personal stories; it is in itself an epic in the faithfulness and fidelity of men to their leader, his ideals and principles. Their stories of Edison, suddenly stopping to "play tunes" on an old organ in the laboratory, how they sang at their midnight meal, how "everyone was keyed up to concert pitch," and their relaxation from the "great intensity," are classics in themselves.

First Attacks on Impregnable Forces of Nature

The almost "unscalable mountain" that challenged the progress of Edison was the problem of finding the right filaments for the glass bulbs. Every substance seemed to be too delicate and broke at the point where success seemed near. The glass blower had done his work and the bulb idea had been proved practical. The experiments with filaments, however, seemed endless; he tried everything that gave any indication of proving workable. The early experiments with carbon were set aside, although he never lost faith in it.

When he tried platinum, he was sufficiently encouraged to complete his model and take out a patent, in April, 1879 — the *first incandescent-lamp patent obtained by Edison*. As one of his workers has said: "Time after time we broke our filaments when the glass blower tried to fit them into

the lamp; time after time the delicate loop would break
when taken out of the mold. Batchelor, with Edison
following, finally reached the glass-blower's bench with
one carbon still intact. At the moment he handed it to
the glass blower it broke. Again and again they tried,
and finally succeeded — but it would hiss, sputter, and
burn itself out and dissolve into ashes."

It was in April, 1879, that the first barrier was overcome — the first step that led to the modern incandescent
light. This was when Edison conceived the idea of the
all-glass globe, or bulb, hermetically sealed, with all air
exhausted. He found that by inserting a piece of platinum
wire into this bulb, he could pass the electric current through
and secure a light equal to "25 candle-power without
melting." All other experiments had resulted in the wire
melting in the open air when the light reached 4 candle-
power. This required continuous experiment in passing
the current through the platinum while the vacuum was
being obtained; finally, he succeeded in improving his
pumps to the point where he could produce a vacuum up
to the one-millionth of an atmosphere. At this point he
retreated, setting aside the platinum filaments, and went
back to experiments with carbon. This proved the strategical move that won the victory.

Thirteen months had passed and their funds were nearly
exhausted — the financiers demanding results. Edison
sat in his laboratory alone, in deep thought. Thousands
of times he had tried and failed, and now he had reached
the moment of decision. With one hand running nervously
through his hair as was his custom, he was tapping the
fingers of his right hand on the table when they touched a
little pile of lampblack mixed with tar, which was used in
his experiments with the telephone transmitter. He gazed

at this substance and began rolling it between his finger and thumb. This continued for nearly half an hour, when he suddenly arose and quickly called a boy.

The Great Idea — Solution at Ends of His Fingers

"Go out and get me some spools of cotton thread," he exclaimed, and it is said that he added, "Be quick about it!" He had a habit of getting what he wanted immediately — and the spool of thread was soon in his hands.

"Batchelor," he said to his untiring assistant, "I am going to see if this will do it — we have tried everything else."

As they proceeded to carbonize the thread, it seemed impossible that it could withstand an electric current that melted the hardest of metals. The task was one that required unlimited patience; a short piece of thread was bent into the shape of a hairpin and placed in a nickel mold — the mold was placed for five hours in a muffle furnace. Removing the mold from this furnace, they stood by it until it cooled, and then opened it. They must now withdraw this delicate carbonized thread and seal it into a bulb. Throughout the night, during the entire day and the next night, Edison and Batchelor kept at the critical task. Time and time again the thread broke, until at last, on the third day, one short piece from the whole spool was saved that "did not break while being taken from the mold."

Let Edison relate the story of this crucial moment: "We had to take this piece of carbonized thread to the glass-blower's house," he said. "With the utmost precaution Batchelor took up the precious carbon, and I marched after him, as if guarding a mighty treasure.

To our consternation, just as we reached the glass-blower's bench the wretched carbon broke. We turned back to the main laboratory and set to work again. It was late in the afternoon before we had produced another carbon, which was again broken by a jeweler's screw driver falling against it. But we turned back again, and before night the carbon was completed and inserted in the lamp. The bulb was exhausted of air and sealed, the current turned on, and the sight we had so long desired to see met our eyes."

The first successful incandescent electric light in the world was invented — Historic date: October 21, 1879. What the scientists declared to be "impossible" was a reality! Edison had successfully subdivided the electric current for illuminating purposes. A new light had come into the world — a new power that was to start a new era in human progress.

Three Days Without Sleep or Rest — to Triumph

Again let us listen to the simple words of Thomas Edison: "The day was — let me see — October 21, 1879. We sat and looked, and the lamp continued to burn, and the longer it burned, the more fascinated we were. None of us could go to bed — there was no sleep for any of us for forty hours. We sat and just watched it with anxiety growing into elation. It lasted about forty-five hours."

"If it will burn that number of hours now, I know I can make it burn a hundred hours," exclaimed Edison. Bets were laid as to how long it would burn. The frail thread filament stood through the hours like a soldier, bearing heat under which platinum would have instantly melted. Through the forty-five hours it gleamed "like an evening star" — then, "with a suddenness that was startling, the light vanished!"

The three days without sleep or rest were ended. Edison stood looking at Batchelor a moment, put his hand on his shoulder, and then turned and walked out of the laboratory door. It was nearly twenty-four hours before he came back — he had been sleeping and thinking. He had established a new principle and he intended to pursue it to the ends of the earth, in search of the right substance for the filament that would light the world. He knew that the fragile little thread could not undertake this gigantic task, but it had served its purpose nobly in proving a scientific fact.

The newspapers again began to proclaim the story of the "Wizard": "Edison has invented a light that will burn night and day for more than a week," announced the press, and thousands again took up the journey to Menlo Park to see the light that outrivaled Aladdin's lamp. So large were the throngs that it was necessary to close the gates at Menlo Park and put watchmen on guard.

Conflicting stories appeared throughout Europe and America: "Edison's new invention is a brilliant success" — "A dead failure" — "An infringement on Swan's patents" — and even that the inventor had "broken down under the strain and was in a dangerous condition." A letter was addressed to the press for the purpose of showing that the incandescent light was used way back in the thirteenth century, by quoting from an old book on Sorcery and Magic:

"During the thirteenth century, for profit of the common people, Virgilius, on a great mighty marble pillar, did make a bridge that came to the palace. The palace and bridge stood in the middle of Rome, and upon this pillar made he a lamp of glass that always burned without going out, and nobody might put it out; and this lamp lightened over all the city of Rome from the one corner to the other; and there was not so little a street but it gave such a light that it seemed two torches there did stand; and upon the walls of the palace made he a metal man that held in his hand a metal bow that pointed over and upon the lamp to shoot it out; but always burned the lamp and gave light over all Rome . . . And this forsaid lamp was abyding after the death of Virgilius by the space of three hundred years or more."

Myths, Legends, and Rumors Begin to Surround Edison

These stories created hearty laughter at the Menlo Park laboratories, where they had seen the "Wizard" create one of the most revolutionary inventions in the world's history. For experimental purposes, lights were strung on wires around Menlo Park where they burned brightly. A newspaper despatch written by a man with a sense of humor, stated that "What everyone thinks is the evening star is really an electric lamp which Edison sends up attached to a balloon every night."

Thousands of people gazed into the night skies to see this mysterious light. People from other states began to declare that they could see the wonderful sight. Letters were received from all over the country asking for further information. It became necessary, finally, for the press of the country to assure the people that "the evening star is not Edison's," but the myth became so firmly established that it persisted for years and is still told to children. Hundreds of letters are filed among Edison's private papers asking him whether or not the story of the "Edison star" is true. The absurdity of the legend was such that he never answered the letters.

Stories of the "lights strung on wires in Menlo Park" jolted the temper as well as the credulity of some newspaper editors. The *New York Herald* published a statement about these lights on the morning of December 21, 1879, and it created an uproar even in the James Gordon Bennett offices. An old journalist of the time, F. M. White, has told the story in his inimitable way and it also has been recorded by George S. Bryan in his excellent work on Edison.

Edison's personal friend, Albert E. Orr, was city editor of the *Herald*. He was at his desk on the eventful morning of this story of the electric light when Thomas D. Connery, the managing editor, rushed in and demanded excitedly:

"How did that stuff get into the paper? Lights strung on wires! You've made a laughingstock of the *Herald!* What will Bennett say?"

"He'll probably say that it is the biggest newspaper beat of the times," replied Orr.

"But don't you know that it has been absolutely demonstrated that that kind of light is against the laws of nature? Who wrote the article?"

"Marshall Fox," replied Orr, "our star reporter who went with Edison on the eclipse expedition to Wyoming last year."

"How could he allow himself and the paper to be so imposed upon?" demanded the managing editor. "Where is he? Send for him. We must do something to save ourselves from ridicule. No — don't try to explain — just find Fox and send him to me."

This actual episode tremendously interested Edison and he frequently related it. He decided, immediately upon hearing it, to give a public exhibition and settle all doubts for all time.

Throngs at Menlo Park to See First "Great White Way"

The great event occurred on New Year's Eve, 1879-80, and lasted through midnight to welcome the New Year. More than three thousand visitors arrived on special trains to participate in the celebration. Arriving at Menlo Park after dark, their vision was greeted by a brilliant spectacle — hundreds of glowing incandescent lights stretched on wires among the leafless trees — the first "Great White Way." Distinguished guests marveled at the "Celestial vision." The New York Board of Aldermen went to Menlo Park on a special train at Edison's invitation.

The patents on the incandescent lamp were granted to Thomas Edison on January 28, 1880. These were but the beginning of one hundred sixty-nine patents on electric lights which he finally was to take out. The specifications are written clearly in Edison's own handwriting, and begin as follows:

"Be it known that I, Thomas Alva Edison, of Menlo Park, New Jersey, United States of America, have invented an improvement in electric lamps and in the method of manufacturing the same . . ."

"This was the beginning of litigation," stated Edison in later years, "which lasted almost through the life of the patents, but I finally won a complete victory . . . I speak without exaggeration when I say that I constructed three thousand different theories in the development of the electric light, each one of them reasonable and apparently likely to be true. Yet in two cases only did my experiments prove the truth of my theory. My chief difficulty was in constructing the carbon filament, the incandescence of which is the source of the light."

THE BIRTH OF THE INCANDESCENT LIGHT

Preparing the first successful incandescent lamp for its life test at the Menlo Park Laboratory. This lamp was lighted in the evening of October 19, 1879, and burned continuously for over forty hours. Young Edison is seen driving the last of the gases from the filament with current from a battery.

THE GREAT WHITE WAY

Made possible by the development of Edison's original invention of the incandescent lamp. This is a night view of Times Square, at the intersection of Seventh Avenue and Broadway, New York.

The sensation in the newspapers began to die down, except among the adherents of Swan, in England, who continued to charge Edison "with characteristic effrontery in claiming the invention." These charges, however, were grossly unjust when it is understood that Swan had never produced a practical light on which the great industry was built. The American press became enthusiastic, and we find in *Leslie's Weekly*, January 10, 1880, this comment:

> "Edison's electric light, incredible as it may appear, is produced from a little piece of paper — a tiny strip of paper that a breath would blow away. Through this little strip of paper is passed an electric current, and the result is a bright, beautiful light, like the mellow sunset of an Italian autumn. He has made this little piece of paper more infusible than platinum, more durable than granite (!). And this by no complicated process. The paper is merely baked in an oven until all the elements have passed away except its carbon framework. The latter is then placed in a glass globe connected with the wires leading to the electricity-producing machine, and the air exhausted from the globe. Then the apparatus is ready to give out a light that produces no deleterious gases, no smoke, no offensive odor — a light without flame, without danger, requiring no matches to ignite, giving out but little heat, vitiating no air, and free from all flickering. And this light, the inventor claims, can be produced cheaper than that from the cheapest oil."

The world search for a filament now began. Expeditions of more than twenty men were sent out from Menlo Park to search all parts of the earth, under orders from Edison to "find a substance that will make a practical filament, so that the electric light may be developed to its fullest powers."

These explorations cost Edison more than $100,000. William H. Moore started out for the Orient in the summer of 1880, and made his way into the interiors of Japan and

14

China to test bamboo.   John C. Brauner sailed for Para, Brazil, and traveled 2,000 miles through the swamps and forests on foot and by canoe to collect grasses and palms. C. F. Hanington traveled through Argentina, Paraguay, Uruguay, and other South American countries, in search of fibrous plants.   Segredor went to Cuba, and died of yellow fever.   James Ricalton went to England and through the Suez Canal to Ceylon and India, Burma, the Malay Peninsula, and on through China and Japan, around the world, covering 30,000 miles and fighting for his life against wild beasts in the jungles.   Frank McGowan went into the wilds of Colombia, Ecuador, Peru, lived without removing his clothes for ninety-eight days, fighting venomous reptiles, wild beasts, and hostile tribes.   Stricken with fever, deserted by his guides, he returned to Menlo Park after fifteen months, where he greeted his friends, related thrilling incidents of his wanderings, bade them all good night at the door of a restaurant, in New York — and from that moment never was seen or heard from again.   Just before his strange disappearance, the *New York Evening Sun* gave a page to his thrilling adventures and commented editorially upon them:

"The narrative given elsewhere in the *Evening Sun* of the wanderings of Edison's missionary of science, Mr. Frank McGowan, furnishes a new proof that the romances of real life surpass any that the imagination can frame.

"In pursuit of a substance that should meet the requirements of the Edison incandescent lamp, Mr. McGowan penetrated the wilderness of the Amazon, and for a year defied its fevers, beasts, reptiles, and deadly insects in his quest of a material so precious that jealous Nature has hidden it in her most secret fastnesses.

"No hero of mythology or fable ever dared such dragons to rescue some captive goddess as did this dauntless champion of civilization.   Theseus, or Siegfried, or any knight of the fairy books might envy the victories of Edison's irresistible lieutenant.

"As a sample story of adventure, Mr. McGowan's narrative is a marvel fit to be classed with the historic journeyings of the greatest travelers. But it gains immensely in interest when we consider that it succeeded in its scientific purpose. The mysterious bamboo was discovered, and large quantities of it were procured and brought to the Wizard's laboratory, there to suffer another wondrous change and then to light up our pleasure haunts and our homes with a gentle radiance."

Throughout this world search Edison remained in his laboratory, testing everything that came to him on ships from the Seven Seas. He estimated that "practically everything on earth was tried" and he finally utilized the bamboo from Japan, which furnished the filaments for millions of Edison lamps. He believed, however, that the final solution was in the chemical laboratory, and, after years of continuous tests, he developed an artificial filament better than bamboo — a "squirted" filament made of a cellulose mixture. The search was ended. And the electric light began to reach out into all corners of the globe, until it was "lighting the world."

Turning from the phonograph to the electric light.

The First Dynamo

A forerunner of the Edison bipolar dynamo.

CHAPTER XVII

THE NEW POWER BEHIND HUMAN PROGRESS—
THE ELECTRICAL AGE

Long days of experiment ended happily when Edison and his associate saw the glow of the first incandescent light.

THE eighteenth and early nineteenth centuries saw the work of the world revolutionized by the steam engine, the spinning jenny, and other inventions. In the last half of the nineteenth century the world entered a second New Era—the Electrical Age, in which Edison was one of the foremost figures, while scientists in all parts of the world were building the new civilization. Another industrial revolution was about to reconstruct human life and change the mode of living, opening up new systems of communication and transportation, and developing the whole economic and social organization of the nations.

The power of invention is greater than that of wars or statesmanship; invention creates new political systems; even changes the forms of governments. The Machine Age today, where one machine is doing the work of hundreds of men, is causing readjustments in every country.

Here, in the United States, we are working out the problems of the Electrical and Machine Age with intelligence and wisdom, building the future on the solid foundations of our Constitution, a practical, coöperative working plan which gives every individual the opportunity to work out his own future and secure his just rewards for the services rendered to the benefit of the whole community.

Great Pioneers Behind the Electrical Age

Let us see how this Electrical Age began: Foundations are laid deep — nothing merely happens. Every forward step in human progress is the result of the cumulative knowledge behind it. There is no record of the discoverer of electricity, but its existence was known far back in the ancient civilizations of India and China, 4,000 years before Christ. Two thousand years ago it was not known that lightning was an electrical force; it was considered a flash of anger from the gods. During the reign of Queen Elizabeth, while Shakespeare was writing his plays, one of the court physicians, Dr. William Gilbert, christened this mysterious phenomenon "*electricity.*" He was the first to give it a name. The first recognized form of electricity came from amber under friction; and the Greek word for *amber* is *elektron.* It was from this that Dr. Gilbert, three hundred years ago, coined the word *electricity.*

This started the era of electrical research, and in the centuries to follow many great names appear who live today in the terminology of the science — Galvani, of Italy (1737–98), Volta, of Italy (1745–1827), Ampère, of France (1775–1836), Ohm, of Germany (1787–1854). The inventors whom we have mentioned came down through the years: Franklin with the lightning rod (1752), Henry with the electromagnet (1828), Morse with the electric telegraph (1835), Wheatstone with the electromagnetic telegraph (1836), Vail with the electric locomotive (1851), Gintl with duplex telegraphy (1853), Edison with quadruplex telegraphy (1874), Bell and Edison with the telephone (1876), Brush with the arc light (1879), Edison with the first successful incandescent lamp (1879). These names stand out foremost, with a legion of other inventors in the ranks.

EDISON TAKES UP WORK WHERE FARADAY LEFT OFF AND STARTS GREAT INDUSTRY

The birth of the electrical industry, which was to revolutionize human life, got its first momentum from Menlo Park. The struggling, infant industry, in units hardly larger than blacksmiths' shops in various parts of the country, was to set its pace from Edison. He was besieged from all parts of the world to "light our cities." Surrounded by more than a hundred coworkers, the young inventor, now but 32 years old, began to create a beehive industry. More than three hundred patents came out of the Edison laboratories on this early development of the electrical age. He became known as the "Twelve Million Dollar Brain." His energies were now directed toward electrical technology rather than new public sensations.

"There were no high-speed engines in these days," stated Edison. "I decided that the magneto should be taken up where Faraday had started it. There was no way to build a great electrical industry until the machinery was developed. I conceived the idea of a direct-coupled machine, and wanted to hitch the dynamo direct to the engine without belting. The engine builders held up their hands and said, 'Impossible!' I called C. H. Porter and said to him:

" 'Mr. Porter, I want a 150-horse-power engine to run 700 revolutions a minute.'

"He hummed and hawed a bit and then agreed to

build it. We set the machine up in the old shop, and I had some idea of what might happen. So we tied a chain round the throttle and ran it out through a window into the woodshed, where we stood to work it. The shop stood on one of those New Jersey shale hills, and every time we opened up the engine and she got to about 300 revolutions, the whole hill shook under her. We shut her off and re-balanced, and tried again, and, after a good deal of trouble, we finally did run up to 700, but you should have seen her run! Why, every time the connecting rod went up, she tried to lift that whole hill with her! After we got through with this business we tamed her down to 350 revolutions (which was all I wanted) . . . We closed a bill with Porter for six engines.

"While all this was going on in the shop, we had dug ditches and laid mains all around the district (through which to supply power). I used to sleep nights on piles of pipes in the station, and I saw every box poured and every connection made on the whole job. I had to! There was nobody else who could superintend it. Finally we got our feeders all down and started to put on an engine and turn one of the machines to see how things were. My heart was in my mouth at first, but everything worked all right and we had more than 500 ohms insulation resist-ance. Then we started another engine and threw them in parallel.

"Of all the circuses since Adam was born, we had the worst then. One engine would stop, and the other would run up to about a thousand revolutions and then they would seesaw.

"What was the matter? Why, it was these Porter governors! When the circus commenced, the men who were standing round ran out precipitately, and some of them kept running for a block or two. I grabbed the throttle of one engine, and E. H. Johnson, who was the only one present who kept his wits, caught hold of the other and we shut them off. Of course I discovered then that what had happened was that one set was running the other one as a motor.

"I then put up a long shaft connecting all the governors together, and thought this would certainly cure the trouble, but it didn't. The torsion of the shaft was so great that one governor managed still to get ahead of the others. Then I got a piece of shafting and a tube in which it fitted. I twisted the shaft one way and the tube the other, as far as I could, and pinned them together. In this way, by straining the whole outfit up to its elastic limit in opposite directions, the torsion was practically eliminated, and after that the governors ran together all right.

"Somewhere about that time I got hold of Gardiner C. Sims, and he undertook to build an engine to run at 350 revolutions and give 175 horse power. He went back to Providence and set to work and brought the engine back with him. It worked, but only for a few minutes, when it busted. That man sat around that shop and slept in it for three weeks until he got his engine right and made it work the way he wanted it to.

"When he reached this period, I gave orders for the works to run night and day until we got enough engines, and when all was ready, we started the main engine. The date was September 4, 1882, a Saturday night. That was when we first turned the current on to the mains for regular light distribution, and it stayed on for eight years with only one insignificant stoppage. One of these engines that Sims built ran twenty-four hours a day for 365 days before it was stopped to give it a rest."

This was the beginning of the first electric motor ever made for commercial circuits of 110 to 120 volts, which was constructed by Edison in 1879. It is still in existence in the Edison laboratories and capable of operation. Out of this workshop also came immediately the first practical generator for distribution of current for light, heat, and power, which is the foundation of the great power systems today. Mechanical devices came out of the brain of Edison with startling rapidity: sockets — switches — insulators — devices for the generation, regulation and measurement of electric current — all new and revolutionary.

His Brain Begins to Think of Gigantic Power Houses

The idea of "central stations or power houses" now entered Edison's mind. He was thinking in terms of hundreds of millions of dollars — even billions. Great financiers again were called in and warned the young inventor about going "too fast." The investors who had supplied the original money for the development of the inventions, refused to take the risk of manufacture, but demanded to be allowed to remain as the original syndicate, to issue "licenses and rights" to new corporations. The brain of J. P. Morgan can be seen in these operations, for he was one of the original Edison backers. A corporation was finally formed with a capitalization at $1,000,000, under the name of "The Edison Electric Illuminating Company of New York." This corporation proposed to enter into the "distribution of light, heat and power" (and later became the present New York Edison Company).

Getting the First Political Franchise in New York

A vigorous character, Norvin Green, of the Western Union forces, was the first president of the new Edison holding corporation. Political influence was required to secure a franchise from the New York Board of Aldermen, which would allow the laying of main wires through the streets. This idea of "underground" was another of Edison's new methods, and it was even feared that it might "blow up the city." The inventor, to gain the goodwill of these jovial but practical politicians, invited them out to Menlo Park as his guests and gave them a royal feast. He even made a speech — one of the few in his life — and regaled them with stories. The franchise was granted. Under this charter none of the million dollars could be used by Edison for manufacturing. A vigorous discussion followed in which Edison arose and declared:

"If there are no factories to make my inventions, I will build the factories myself. Since capital is timid, I will raise and supply it."

HE RAISES HIS OWN MONEY TO PRODUCE HIS INVENTIONS

The young inventor then plunged into financing, putting in his own resources to the limit and securing money from friends. He became so hard pressed that he was forced to sell his holdings in the original syndicate, known as "The Edison Electric Light Company," and here, again, is the amazing story of a lost fortune. The business began to boom, and the Edison patents rose in value to where financiers were no longer timid, but were maneuvering to get control. The day came, in less than nine years, when the Edison companies were merged into the General Electric Company, with a capital of $12,000,000 on an 8 per cent dividend basis. If Edison had retained his holdings, they would have created almost immediately an immense fortune, for the General Electric has become one of the greatest industrial organizations in the world.

The first Edison offices in New York were opened at No. 65 Fifth Avenue, in 1881, and Edison began to establish his workshops wherever he could find a plant, with Menlo Park running full blast as the laboratory for new inventions.

"I took over the old Etna Iron Works on Goerck Street, surrounded by tumbled-down old tenement houses, on the East Side of New York," he said. "We ran this as the Edison Machine Works, my first factory for dynamos, but the business grew so fast that we finally removed to Schenectady. We began to manufacture our meters, chandeliers, sockets, and switches in the little shop of Sigmund Bergmann, in Wooster Street. Bergmann had worked at the bench for me in Newark and then started the Wooster Street shop, where he built some of my phonographs. This is the Bergmann who finally became owner of the great electrical industries in Berlin."

"Our shops were all so busy," explained Edison, "that John Kruesi was brought over from Menlo Park and put in charge of a factory at 65 Washington Street, known as the Electric Tube Company; here we manufactured our underground tube conductors and junction boxes. The lamp factory was removed from Menlo Park to Harrison, New Jersey, and we had our hands full."

Turning Great Losses into Huge Profits

Edison had agreed to make lamps for the syndicate and deliver them at 40 cents, on a contract for the life of the patents. The first year the lamps cost him, to manufacture, $1.10 — the second year they cost him 70 cents — the third year he got the price down to 50 cents — and the losses on these contracts were piling up disastrously. Again he concentrated his energies on improved machinery and production, and in the fourth year got the cost down to 37 cents — and then 22 cents — and in one year made all the money he had lost in the preceding years.

"Whereupon," said Edison, "the Wall Street people thought they would like to own this profitable business and bought us out."

The Harrison works were on a profit-sharing basis, but produced nothing but losses for the first four years. When the profits did begin, they flowed in like a river. Edison had divided the stock into 100 shares at a par value of $100 a share, and most of the "boys" had become partners. During the period of the losses, some of them sold out for anything they could get. One of the workmen sold two shares to Robert Cutting, who took the certificates and proceeded to forget them. Finally, when the profits began to roll in, Edison declared a "dividend every Saturday night." Cutting received checks by mail for three weeks in succession and then called up on the phone:

"I want to know what kind of concern it is that pays a weekly dividend!"

The Harrison works were sold out to the Wall Street group for $1,085,000. The "boys" felt as if they had all become suddenly rich. Edison, in his characteristic manner, began to pay off all his accumulated debts and mortgages. Another period of financial stress was over and he had met it with the same integrity and industry that marked his entire career.

Historical record should be made here of the "firsts" in the beginning of this new electrical age: (1881) First business house to be lighted by Edison, in New York — First mill, at Newburgh, New York — First newspaper

plant, *New York Herald* — First electrical exposition in
the world, at Paris — First central power station, at London;
(1882) First incandescent electric light central station, at
Appleton, Wisconsin — First Edison central station, in
New York — First Edison lighting corporation, in France
— First church lighted by Edison, in London — First
theater lighted, in Boston — First electric sign, in London
— First steam yacht to be equipped with electric light was
James Gordon Bennett's; (1883) First permanent station
in Europe, at Milan, Italy — First central Edison station
in South America, at Santiago, Chile — First Edison
central station, at Berlin.

Story of First Large Power House in America

The first time that any city in the world was lighted
by the Edison incandescent system was on September 4,
1882, when the current was turned on from the first central station of the Edison Electric Illuminating Company
and flashed through "four hundred lamps." This event
created tremendous interest and crowds came to witness it.
It is said that Edison was garbed for the occasion in a
"Prince Albert" for the first time in his life, with collar
and cravat; but he was later found by one of the newspaper reporters with his white, high-crowned derby and
collarless shirt.

"My heart was in my mouth at first," said Edison,
"but everything worked all right. For a time it was a
terrifying experience as I wasn't sure what was going to
happen. The engines and dynamos made a horrible
racket, from loud and deep groans to a hideous shriek, and
the place seemed to be filled with sparks and flames of all
colors. It was as if the gates of the infernal regions had
been suddenly opened."

The great electric light, heat, and power industry was started in America, and was soon to reach around the world. Great industries were to rise, with geniuses of organization behind them, and create properties valued at many billions of dollars. Edison began to experiment with the electric railway, which was soon to take the place of the horse car. Experiments had been made by Vail in 1851, and an exhibition line had been built in Berlin, which convinced Edison that it had tremendous possibilities.

THE BEGINNING OF ELECTRIC RAILWAYS IN AMERICA

During what he called "lulls" in his work with electric lighting, Edison built an electric railway on the grounds of Menlo Park. The little locomotive, powered by one of his dynamos, chugged along with twelve horse power and pulled three cars: a flat freight car in front, an open awning car, and a box car called the "Pullman." This electric railway was equipped with all sorts of devices invented by Edison. There was a holiday when it made its first trips along its third-of-a-mile route on May 13, 1880. A letter in existence, written by Grosvenor P. Lowry, the inventor's legal adviser, is an interesting exhibit:

"Goddard and I have spent a part of the day at Menlo, and all is glorious. I have ridden at forty miles an hour on Mr. Edison's electric railway — and we ran off the track. I protested at the rate of speed over the sharp curves, designed to show the power of the engine, but Edison said they had done it often. Finally, when the last trip was to be taken, I said I did not like it, but would go along. The train jumped the track on a short curve, throwing Kruesi, who was driving the engine, with his face down in the dirt, and another man in a comical somersault through some underbrush. Edison was off in a minute, jumping and laughing, and declaring it a most beautiful accident. Kruesi got up, his face bleeding, and a good deal shaken; and I shall never forget the expression of voice and face in which he said, with some foreign accent: 'Oh, yes! pairfeckly safe.' Fortunately no other hurts were suffered, and in a few minutes we had the train on the track and running again."

The success of these first tests in electric railroads resulted in building a line three miles long, with sidings, turntables, freight house, car house, like a miniature steam railroad line. Two locomotives were used, one for passenger service and the other for freight. This was opened in 1882, and again drew crowds to Menlo Park. The locomotive was speedy and hauled ninety passengers at a time. Thousands of people rode over the line. It had been built at the request of Henry Villard, who was considering adopting it for the Northern Pacific Railroad. It was declared by engineers as "absolutely and utterly impracticable." This is the system that is now used on the New York Central and the New Haven roads.

The first American electric locomotive had made its trial trip on April 29, 1857, with the inventor, Prof. C. C. Page, of the Smithsonian Institution. At a speed of nineteen miles an hour, it ran over the tracks of the Washington and Baltimore Railroad. But the first electric railroad in America, built for that purpose, and carrying passengers and freight, was the Edison road at Menlo Park. The Villard agreement with Edison was that he should develop a passenger locomotive that could travel at the rate of sixty miles an hour; Villard entered into a contract to reimburse Edison for the cost of the experiments when he succeeded in obtaining this rate of speed. During these experiments, Villard's fortune was swept away by the crash in the Northern Pacific Railway, and he was forced to begin the rehabilitation of his large estate as one of the first American millionaires.

Electric railways began to appear in Germany, constructed by Siemens and Halske; while Stephen D. Field, in America, was working on his idea of the third rail. Litigation again developed: Siemens and Field both attacked Edison's position and claimed infringements on their patents; Siemens was beaten in the courts, while Edison and Field came together and put into operation an electric railway for the Chicago Railway Exposition. Van de Poele, of Belgium, came to the front, while Sprague, an ex-lieutenant in the United States army, appeared with his electric trolley — and Edison, with his "thousand and one" ideas demanding his attention, began to lay plans for the creation of his storage battery.

Capitalists came from South America to negotiate with Edison for electric engines to climb the steep grades of the mountain ranges and replace the mules that were then being used. Tests were made that solved all the problems. The promoters then disappeared, stating that they would raise the funds in South America and return.

"I have never seen them since," declared Edison in later years. "As usual, I paid for the experiment."

From Franklin with his kite —   — to the giant generator.

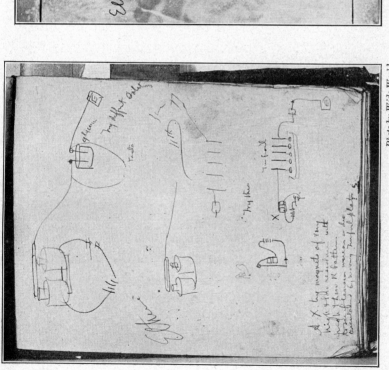

Photo by Wide World

Loaned by Edison Family from Private Collection

NOTES AND DRAWINGS FROM EDISON'S NOTEBOOK

As far back as 1877, when these diagrams were made, Edison was working on "etheric force," the basis of long-distance telegraphy and the radio.

FIRST EDISON ELECTRIC LIGHTING STATION IN NEW YORK
A reproduction of an old drawing, showing the dynamo room.

THE MODERN GENERATOR
This huge turbine generator is at the East River Station (New York) of the General Electric Company. The two pictures indicate what marvelous advances have taken place since Edison started the great electric power-development industry.

CHAPTER XVIII

THE WHOLE WORLD PASSES BEFORE YOUR EYES—THE MOTION PICTURE

An early type of Edison Projecting Kinetoscope for motion pictures.

WHAT Edison did for the world in the span of one lifetime seems almost inconceivable. He seemed to be a hundred men in one — each with a different idea on which he was working. We find him moving so fast from thirty to forty years of age that it is impossible to follow him chronologically, so many are the directions in which he was reaching out, so versatile his interests.

He was working on the discovery of a new phenomenon which he called the "Edison Effect," the principle behind wireless and radio, as we shall see in a later chapter. He was the first of the great American inventors to apply his genius to the problem of aërial navigation, while at the same time conceiving ideas for gigantic machinery in the electrical industry. He actually "stormed" the Patent Office at Washington with more than three hundred patents in a period of four years, covering so many phases of human life that it bewildered the Government officials. And now we shall see him give that universal entertainment, the motion pictures, to the world, with their development into talking pictures.

It was during this amazing period of activity that his wife, Mary Stillwell Edison, died, in 1884, leaving three children. The story of this bereavement and of his marriage to the brilliant Mina Miller, in 1886, is told in the chapter on "The Home Life of Edison with His Family." At this time, too, he found that his future plans would require a larger arena for his activities and so he bade "good-by" to historic little Menlo Park and in 1887 moved on to new laboratories in West Orange, which were the scenes of his future life achievements.

Edisons on Tour of Triumph in Europe

In the midst of these events, we find him in Europe with his wife and Marion Edison, the inventor's oldest daughter, being hailed as "The Genius of the Age." He was acclaimed at the great Paris Centennial Exposition, in 1889, as the man who had "Organized the Echoes" and "Tamed the Lightning." The Edison exhibit covered about an acre — one-third of the space allotted to the United States — and was the sensation of the exposition. There was a monster incandescent lamp — forty feet high and mounted on a pedestal twenty feet square — with the American flag in red, white, and blue lamps on one side and the French flag on the other, and the name "Edison" shining brilliantly above. The "Phonographic Temple" drew throngs where Edison's talking machines were speaking every European language — a linguistic event that rivaled the Tower of Babel. The crowds broke into cheering when he appeared and he was greeted with greater enthusiasm than any member of the royalty of Europe.

President Carnot conferred on him the Order of the Legion of Honor. The Edisons occupied the President's private box at the opera, which was brilliantly illuminated with Edison's lights, and the distinguished French audience rose in tribute as the orchestra played the "Star-Spangled Banner." Throughout the capitals of Europe the Edisons were greeted with demonstrations: Berlin, Rome, London —all paid him the highest tributes.

Upon his return to America, Edison was greeted with an enthusiasm that rivaled that of Europe. In making his statement, he said:

"It was a magnificent experience and I feel that the honor belonged to America, not merely to me. And I escaped without even making a speech. Once I got Chauncey Depew to make a speech for me, and I got Whitelaw Reid to make three or four. Dinners, dinners, dinners — I looked down from the Eiffel Tower on the biggest dinner I ever saw, given to the mayors of France by the Municipality of Paris — 8,900 people dining at one time. I ate but one American dinner while abroad — it was given by Buffalo Bill . . . Now I feel I must starve for a few months in order to get straight again, after all those dinners. I wonder they didn't kill me."

Inventor Plunges into New Fields of Conquest

When Thomas Edison arrived back home, he plunged immediately into his experiments in his new laboratories at West Orange. His mind was set upon a new and great achievement; he had made a machine that talked, and now he would make pictures that move — motion pictures. His first tests of the new principle which had been made in 1887, had led him in the right direction. He calculated that if a number of photographs could be taken of a moving object at the rate of fifteen per second, these same photographs, under mechanical motion, would reproduce exactly the movements of the original object. It was a simple calculation in mechanical motion — a scheme to beat the eye by moving so fast that it could not see the fractional movements in each of the photographs. He proposed to "do for the eye what the phonograph does for the ear — and by a combination of the two produce sound and motion simultaneously." This had been attempted by many ingenious schemes during the years, but had failed to produce practical results.

Daguerre and Niepce, of France, invented photography, in 1839. Dr. William Horner, of Bristol, England, worked on "dancing images," in 1858. Desvignes, a Frenchman, patented a device called the "Zoetrope," or Wheel of Life, with drawings of a galloping horse, in 1860. Coleman Sellers, of Philadelphia, made a device which showed stereoscopic pictures and called it the "Kinematoscope," in 1861, utilizing the word "Kinema," which spread through the world until in every language it means motion picture. M. Ducos, of France, obtained a patent for motion pictures, in 1864, but never got further than paper.

Two inventions appeared that seemed to be almost on the threshold of "motion pictures," but just failed to produce practical results. In France, a device known as the "photochronograph," was produced by E. J. Marey, in 1877, in which he showed a cat falling and landing on its feet, and objects swimming and walking, but it was a toy device. In America, Eadweard Muybridge, of California, with the coöperation of John D. Isaacs, actually developed animal motion in photography, such as a horse trotting, birds in flight, and performances of athletics, in 1878. These were all spectacular stunts almost in the nature of magic, without any definite goal toward bringing them within reach of the people.

EDISON WITH EASTMAN — AT THE DOOR OF AN AGE-LONG SOLUTION

It was at this time that Edison went into conference with George Eastman, of Rochester, New York, to discuss the new transparent celluloid roll film, which Eastman had placed on the market in 1889. He believed this was the solution — the film in motion in a camera. With this solved, the matter of a projector, with the film passing with the same rapidity past a powerful magnifying lens, would be comparatively simple. Eastman agreed with him that this seemed to be the solution of the long quest.

EDISON GIVES MOTION PICTURES TO THE WORLD

Edison was at the moment of another great victory, and in the summer of 1889 the first practical motion-picture camera in the world was invented. Since that day, the principle of the Edison camera has been the established method for securing pictures in motion — and at that moment began another gigantic industry that has reached to the ends of the earth. It is thus that historians record:

"Thomas A. Edison, inventor of the motion-picture camera and the kinetoscope, with the practical adaptation of the motion-picture film — the technological foundation of all motion pictures." The application for United States patent was filed on August 24, 1891, and granted after a contest with the Muybridge claims, on August 31, 1897.

The story of what followed, with its litigation and counterclaims as a giant young industry sprang into existence, is told by William K. L. Dickson, who was an associate with Edison at this time, and Terry Ramsaye, the historian of motion pictures. Here, we can but establish the fact that Thomas Edison was the father of the motion-picture industry. He claimed only the technological credit and left the production as it is known today to the newcomers in the field — the showmen. Edison could have easily controlled the entire industry if he had desired to follow it through.

Hundreds of fascinating stories might be told of his early experiences in setting up the greatest system of popular entertainment that the world has ever known. He produced the first projecting kinetoscope to throw pictures on the screen. He built the first motion-picture studio, in the yard of his laboratory at West Orange — a wooden, barnlike structure with a roof that could be raised and lowered. It was called the "Black Maria," and revolved on a circular track so that it could be swung with the sun.

The first pictures ever filmed were those of Fred Ott sneezing, of the famous Carmencita dancing, and of bears performing. Acrobats were brought to the studio to do their trapeze stunts; fencers entered into combat before the lens; blacksmiths hammered on their forges; and, finally, horsemanship was successfully reproduced. The public marveled at these amazing scenes.

Then came the day when James J. Corbett, who had become the world's champion when he defeated the great John L. Sullivan, appeared at the "Black Maria," to make the first sensational action picture ever known. A Negro fighter had been employed for the event, but when he recognized his famous opponent, he was paralyzed with terror and began to tremble. Finally recovering the use of his legs, instead of entering the ring in the studio, he shot out of the door and did a Marathon back to Newark. The old-timers are laughing at it yet. The Corbett picture was finally made, however, with another opponent, and "Jim" holds the honor as well as the title of being the world's first motion-picture actor.

CHAPTER XIX

FLASHING THE HUMAN VOICE AROUND THE WORLD — THE RADIO

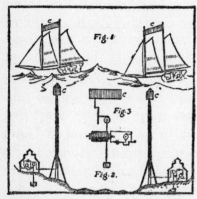

Radio owes much to the inventive genius of Edison. This is reproduced from an Edison patent in the early days of wireless.

THREE epoch-making scientific discoveries came with the dawn of the twentieth century: aërial navigation, after five thousand years of man's struggles to conquer the air; the Motor Age, with its "horseless carriage," which was to begin a new era in transportation; and then what was to furnish the untold resources of music and education to all the world and to bring all mankind within the sound of a single voice — the radio. Even Shakespeare himself could hardly have dreamed how the Prospero of Science would fulfil his delightful fantasy in "The Tempest":

"Be not afeard; the isle is full of noises,
  Sounds and sweet airs, that give delight and hurt not.
  Sometimes a thousand twangling instruments
  Will hum about mine ears; and sometime voices
  That, if I then had wak'd after long sleep,
  Will make me sleep again: and then, in dreaming,
  The clouds methought would open and show riches
  Ready to drop upon me, that when I wak'd
  I cried to dream again."

We find Thomas Edison in his laboratories working out scientific principles which were to aid their inventors in the practical development of these new and powerful factors in human progress. He was working on what he called the "Edison Effect" and "etheric forces" in 1875, years before Preece, Marconi, De Forest, and the inventors who followed. He was engaged on the helicopter as a flying machine in 1880, long before the historic day when the Wright brothers made the first successful flight of an airplane in the world's history, on December 17, 1903. He was patenting galvanic batteries in 1872, and later developing storage batteries for auto transportation many years before the first automobile appeared on the streets of our cities.

Edison's famous notebooks, preserved in his laboratory, show many interesting entries in his handwriting, which record his discovery of what he called "etheric force"; the entries are dated 1875. Here he observed the phenomena of sound waves. He believed that he was on the trail of important revelations and developed a "dark box," which was exhibited at the Paris Exposition in 1881. It was a few years later that Heinrich Hertz, the famous physicist, identified these phenomena as "electromagnetic waves" and developed the science which resulted in the modern Radio Age.

"ETHERIC FORCE" DISCOVERED BY EDISON LONG BEFORE RADIO

Edison was given credit for his pioneer observations by Sir Oliver Lodge, who, when describing the "Hertzian waves" to a group of British scientists, declared: "Many of the effects I have shown — sparks in unsuspected places and other things — have been observed before. Henry observed things of the kind, and Edison noticed some curious phenomena, and said it was not electricity but 'etheric force' that caused these sparks; and the matter was rather pooh-poohed. It was a small part of *this very thing;* only the time was not ripe; theoretical knowledge was not ready for it."

Lord Kelvin, one of the greatest of the British scientists, while discussing the experiments by Faraday with his "insulated cage," said: "His [Faraday's] attention was not directed to look for Hertz sparks, or probably he might have found them in the interior. Edison seems to have noticed something of the kind in what he called 'etheric force.' His name, 'etheric,' . . . seemed to many people absurd."

THE ALL-IMPORTANT "MICROPHONE"

Two fundamental principles in the modern radio belong to Edison: The microphone, which he patented in 1877, and the "Edison Effect," on which every radio "tube" is based, in 1883. The microphone again appealed to popular imagination when it became known that it could magnify sound so that "one could hear a fly walk many miles away." It was reported that "a pin dropped in front of the microphone can be made to sound like a bomb exploding," and that "the human voice can be made to roar like thunder." Controversy waged over this invention, with Hughes, in England, claiming that he had invented it, but investigations proved that Edison was working on it in America and had exhibited it in London a month before Hughes appeared with his microphone. It was about this time, too, while Edison was working on "voice engines," that he invented the modern megaphone, which is now universally used in speaking to large audiences at sporting events and in acoustic devices for magnifying the voice in great auditoriums and stadiums.

EDISON GETS FIRST PATENT ON WIRELESS LONG BEFORE MARCONI

The first patents on "wireless telegraphy" were filed by Thomas Edison, on May 23, 1885. He perfected a wireless system which he used on trains in motion, or moving trains between railway stations, and invented a wireless system of communication between ships at sea that allowed them to communicate with the land. This was the forerunner of all wireless telegraphy.

"We made our first experiments on wireless telegraphy at Menlo Park during the first days of the electric light (1879–83)," recorded Edison. "We succeeded in transmitting messages through the air for a distance of about two and one-half miles. We then tried it out on a thirteen-mile stretch of the Staten Island Railroad. I placed an operator named King on the train, and he found he could send messages when the train went in one direction, but could not make them go in the opposite direction. There were many attempts to work out this strange phenomenon. We decided to put it up to King, and telegraphed him asking what suggestions he had to offer. We got back this reply:

"'The only thing I can suggest is to put the island on a pivot so it can be turned around!'"

Edison succeeded in solving his own problem, and wireless telegraphy was installed in 1886 on the construction trains of the Lehigh Valley Railroad. From the top of the car, the electric wave passed from a piece of metal into the air and was taken up from the telegraph wires and went on its way to the despatcher's office. It was known as the "grasshopper" telegraph. He joined forces with Ezra T. Gilliland and Lucius J. Phelps, and several joint patents were taken out. The system was finally sold to a wealthy

leader in the scientific world. His system became rapidly established, and civilization owes a great debt to him. Attempts were made to obtain the Edison patents by rival groups, and Edison thoroughly investigated the critical situation. Strong influence was brought to bear upon him and his associates to dispose of their rights as a basis for setting up a competitive war against the Marconi company. Edison stepped into the fight, blocked the deal, and forced the sale of his patents to Marconi, in 1903.

Beginning of the Motor Age — Its Early Pioneers

The Motor Age was developing at this time, with the new invention of the "horseless carriage," which was to revolutionize transportation, bringing towns and people together out of their isolation, and setting up new modes and standards of living which were to affect the whole social and economic structure of civilization. The fight was between three powers; steam — gas — electricity. Otto, in Germany, had invented his gas engine in 1877; Selden, in America, patented his gasoline motor (auto) in 1879; Carl Benz invented his two-stroke motor in 1879, and drove the world's first motor car through the streets of Munich in 1886. This three-wheeled vehicle is now in the Munich Museum.

The first gasoline automobile in the United States was operated by its inventor, C. A. Duryea, in 1892; while Ellwood Haynes drove a gasoline automobile of his own invention at Kokomo, Indiana, in 1894. Both machines are on exhibition in the Smithsonian Institution at Washington; Winton came along with his "steam carriage" in Cleveland, Ohio, in 1894; Stanley, with his "steamer," in Massachusetts, in 1897.

Edison watched these developments with the keenest interest. It was at this time that he met a young inventor who was to become the greatest power in the automobile world — Henry Ford. This was August 11, 1896. Ford was then Chief Engineer of the Detroit Edison Company. An Edison convention was being held at Manhattan Beach, near New York, and Ford had come on from Detroit to attend it. Edison sat at the guest table, and the discussion was largely on the matter of turning the rapidly developing "horseless carriage" into the new field of electricity, by the charging of storage batteries for these vehicles. Ford had just built his first car, and it created wide interest. He was introduced to Edison, who attacked him with his usual barrage of questions: "Do you explode the gas in the cylinder by electricity? Do you do it by contact or by spark?"

Ford answered every question with directness and a keen mastery of the new science of automotive engineering. He relates the historic meeting in his book, *Edison as I Know Him*, which he wrote in collaboration with Samuel Crowther, telling how, when he had finished, Edison brought his fist down on the table with a bang and said:

"Young man, that's the thing — you have it. Keep at it. Electric cars must keep near to power stations. The storage battery is too heavy. Steam cars won't do either, for they have to have a boiler and fire. Your car is self-contained — carries its own power plant — no fire, no boiler, no smoke, and no steam. Gasoline! You have the thing. Keep at it!"

START OF LONG SEARCH FOR THE GREAT STORAGE BATTERY

This was the beginning of a friendship as epic as that of Damon and Pythias. From that moment Edison took Ford into his friendship — a comradeship that lasted until his last day, when Ford, who had become one of the greatest industrial geniuses in the world, stood at his bier at the

funeral services at historic "Glenmont" after the great
Edison passed away at 84 years of age.

After this first meeting with Ford — following the
death in 1896, of Edison's father at the age of 92 years —
Edison started his long searches for the storage battery
which was to come into this new age of transportation.

The search started and lasted through the years. The
"insomnia squad" got to work and after long hours without
sleeping, Edison would crawl into a roll-top desk and take
a nap with Watt's *Dictionary of Chemistry* as his pillow.
His "boys" said that he "absorbed the contents during his
sleep, judging from the flow of ideas afterwards."

Then came the big day — the Edison storage battery
was perfected — the best storage battery that had ever been
made. It took its place immediately in general use on the
huge motor trucks used by the American Express and the
large trucking companies; on short-line street cars where
there was no trolley or power line; to operate the flashing
lights of buoys and marine signals, and for lighting service
on yachts. It became established on the signal systems for
railways and subways — all signals on the New York subways are operated by Edison storage batteries. It was
welcomed by homes in rural districts, where there were no
power stations, and farms were finally able to be lighted by
electricity from the Edison batteries. Its most important
use is in the submarines of the world, which are brilliantly
lighted by Edison batteries as they dive down under the
seas.

Edison was once asked how many laboratory experiments it was necessary for him to make to perfect the storage
battery. "Goodness only knows!" he replied. "We used
to number our experiments consecutively from 1 to 10,000.
When we got up to 10,000, we turned back to 1 and ran up

to 10,000 again — and so on. I don't know how many
experiments we made. I lost track of them — but it was
not far from 50,000. It took ten years and cost $3,000,000."

BEGINNING OF AËRIAL AGE — EDISON'S "FLYING MACHINE"

The Aërial Age, which was now developing, also was to
embody the genius of Edison. The great dirigibles, which
had been invented by Zeppelin in 1900, were to carry dynamos and to be lighted with his electric lights, and to send
their wireless messages, as they made their journeys around
the world. The large fleets of airplanes, with their batteries
worked from the ignition boards, were to come out of these
electrical discoveries; while the huge "flying ships," with
their cargoes and passengers, with aërial drawing-rooms and
sleeping compartments, were to be lighted by electricity and
keep in touch with the earth through radio.

Years before, the newspapers had heralded "Edison's
flying ship to tour the world," but this was a phantasy,
inasmuch as while Edison did design a flying machine
somewhat along the lines of the "rocket ship," the construction was never completed. While the writer of this biography was working on a history of aëronautics, for which
Edison wrote the "Preface" as the last service of the kind
he ever rendered, shortly before his death, he made this
statement:

"I conducted researches sometime before the Wrights
on certain aëronautic principles. James Gordon Bennett
requested me to make designs and paid me $1,000. I laid
out roughly a general plan for a flying ship. I did construct
a helicopter, in which I used guncotton, made from stock-
ticker paper, which was fed into the cylinder of the engine
and exploded with a spark.

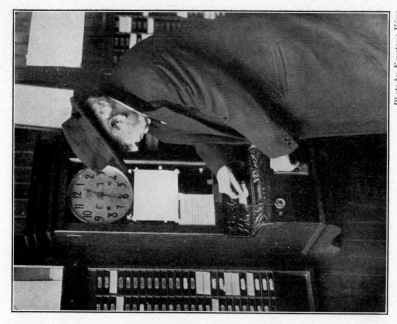

Photo by Keystone View

A CONSCIENTIOUS WORKMAN — ON TIME

A snapshot of Edison, at seventy-four, grimly doing what he had done for many years—punching the time clock.

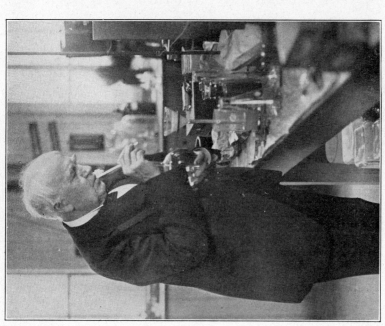

Photo by Underwood

A CORNER OF THE EDISON LABORATORY

Edison once declared "My greatest luxury would be a laboratory more perfect than any we have in this country."

THE DISCOVERER OF THE "EDISON EFFECT"

In 1883 Thomas Edison patented what became known as the "Edison effect," the passage of electricity from a filament to a plate of metal inside a glass tube. He is shown here with the first "Edison effect" lamp with second element (plate).

"I got good results," stated Edison, "but burned one of my men pretty badly, and burned off some of my own hair, and decided that the experiments were too dangerous at the time. It was like playing with dynamite. I became assured, however, that the solution to aërial navigation was only a matter of experiment. I reported to Mr. Bennett that when an engine could be made that would weigh only three or four pounds to the horse power, the problems of the air would be solved. I have not changed my mind — but I have had to wait a long time."

AMAZING SCIENTIFIC INSTRUMENTS INVENTED BY EDISON

During these years also, we find Edison, as usual, engaged in many scientific explorations. He developed his microtasimeter, which he had invented for the purpose of measuring temperatures down to the millionth of a degree Fahrenheit. This instrument would register the heat from a human hand thirty feet away. This led to his invention of the odorscope, for testing gases. It was so sensitive to moisture that it would detect odors so faint that no human being could smell them.

His enthusiasm for the new Electrical Age was increased as he saw the great power stations rise all over the world, and cities and homes being brilliantly lighted. When he first viewed the Statue of Liberty, unveiled on October 28, 1886, standing in the harbor of New York with a torch raised high as a greeting to ships from the sea, he felt that this truly symbolized the new age. He believed, too, that the brilliantly lighted Grand Court at the World's Columbian Exposition, in Chicago, in 1893, celebrating the four hundredth anniversary of the discovery of America, was a fitting tribute to human progress. These were monuments worthy of the genius of man.

16

CHAPTER XX

GREAT INVENTOR RISING TO THE HEIGHT OF HIS POWER

THESE years from the beginning of the twentieth century — up to the outbreak of the World War — set a pace that is almost incomprehensible in the extent of their activities (1900–1914).

From the Edison kilns came the cement that built the Yankee Stadium.

Edison, an intensely practical man, who had dedicated his life to creating only that which was a "necessity to the people," started on new and daring enterprises. He struck out into new fields—far removed from the mediums of transportation, communication, entertainment, and education — and concentrated his energies on the solution of two tremendous national problems: The increase of the nation's wealth through its natural resources, and the building of homes that would be within reach of the

(242)

people at a cost which would allow every family to own its own home.

No greater achievement was ever conceived by an inventor, and this alone demonstrates the spirit which finally earned him the title: "Benefactor of Mankind."

Starts Gigantic Enterprise in Magnetic Mining

Edison realized that the production of iron ore was one of the greatest needs in American industry. He believed that magnetic separators could be developed which would allow him to extract low-grade ores by grinding mountains to dust without the necessity of going far out to the mines in the West, which were being taxed to their fullest capacity. This idea had first come to him when he was devising the machinery for distribution of electric light, heat, and power with the establishment of the central-station system, which is considered one of his greatest achievements.

"Greater even than the invention of the electric light," says one authority, "is the system of distribution which carries it under our cities to our factories, our business establishments, and the homes of the people. If Edison had done nothing but this, his name would stand as a great industrialist."

How the inventor came to extend his field of operations into mining is told in his own words: "I had been down to Quogue, Long Island, to get away from the laboratory 'and think.' When pressure became too great at Menlo Park, we used to go down and hire a sloop and go fishing off Sandy Hook. [It is said that on one of these trips Edison fished two days and nights without a bite and the "boys" had to hoist the anchor to make him quit.] I noticed the immense deposits of black magnetic sand along the shore. It lay along the beach for miles, in layers as deep as six inches. There were hundreds of thousands of tons going to waste. I decided to see what could be done with it and put up a little magnetic separating plant, when a tremendous storm came up and swept the black sand out to sea."

CRUSHING MOUNTAINS IN GIANT ROLLS TO OBTAIN IRON

But this was the beginning of another great idea. Later, he sent William H. Meadowcroft, one of his able and valued associates (who is mentioned in the story of the Pioneers and in the preface of this book), to Rhode Island, where the first "magnetic separating mine" was put into operation. The results proved the theory, and the sands of the Rhode Island shores produced more than a thousand tons of concentrated iron ore of excellent quality. This test was recorded in the Edison laboratory records, where it remained for many years while he was engaged in other enterprises.

Economic conditions in the United States, about the time of the Spanish-American War, created a condition where the iron mills of the East were suffering from the need of ores at a reasonable price. Edison decided that this was the time to meet an emergency and also show that it could be done on a colossal scale. He ordered a great magnetic survey throughout the East for the purpose of locating large bodies of rock that contained magnetic iron ore. It was the most comprehensive survey of the kind ever made and covered territory from North Carolina to lower Canada.

"The results even amazed me," said Edison. "They were simply fabulous. There was untold wealth lying all

around us. In three thousand acres immediately surrounding us, in New Jersey, there were over 200,000,000
tons of low-grade ore. I leased 16,000 acres near by, which
contained sufficient ore to supply the whole United States,
and leave a surplus for export, for more than seventy
years."

New Mining Town Named "Edison" Rises
in the East

A mining town now arose in the hills of New Jersey,
and the railroad station was named "Edison." Machinery
was set up. Magnetic ore separators with giant rolls
weighing seventy tons, with a thunderous noise began to
grind to pieces eight tons of rock in a minute. New
machinery was constantly required — none was in existence — and Edison was forced to invent it as his iron
mills were grinding. The story is told by one of his most
intimate associates, Arthur J. Palmer:

"Everything was done on a gigantic scale. Three-
inch holes twenty feet deep in the mountain side were
filled with dynamite. A single blast would dislodge thirty-
five thousand tons of rock. Steam shovels scooped this up
and loaded it on cars, which carried it to the giant crushing
rolls. The giant rolls were made of solid cast iron, six feet
in diameter and five feet long, and fitted with chilled-iron
knobs. They traveled at terrific speed and crushed boul-
ders weighing six tons. Their power is illustrated by the
fact that pieces of rock weighing half a ton would shoot
into the air twenty-five feet. A stream of finely ground
ore was allowed to flow from a container. When a magnet
was placed at a certain distance from the stream it would
draw the iron particles away. They would fall on one
side of a division, the waste on the other side."

This colossal enterprise (the words are used by his associates) was in full blast, with heavy investments, and at the moment of success, when, suddenly, the event occurred which was to spell its ruin. Huge deposits of rich Bessemer ore were discovered in the Mesaba mountain ranges in Minnesota. This brought large shipments at low price into the Eastern market. Edison's first great experiment had not yet gotten down the price of magnetic separation to the point where he could meet this competition. If he continued pouring money into these experiments, he could undoubtedly get the price down where no mine could compete. Debts, however, were piling up. He conferred with his associate, W. S. Mallory, and it was decided to close the plant.

Nine years of tremendous labor and daring were swept away. A fortune was lost. He had put $2,000,000 of his own money into the enterprise and was now heavily in debt. This is another instance where Edison staked all that he possessed on his own inventions.

This apparent defeat, however, was to be turned in the typical Edison manner into notable achievements. He had proved that under an emergency the country could fall back at any time on magnetic extraction of ores; that scientific and mechanical devices could be contrived to meet crises in any phase of our industrial life; that new fields were open for development in the industrial world.

The personal financial losses of Edison — $2,000,000 — in the magnetic experiments would have finished most men, but to him it was only a beginning. This is the courage and fortitude which carried him through his entire life, constantly rehabilitating lost fortunes. When the plant at Edison was closed down, he was riding back to Orange on the train, with his associate, Mallory, in deep thought.

"Mallory," he said, "we have got to make enough money to pay off our debt. No company in which I have been personally responsible has ever failed to pay its debts. I do not propose to allow this to be an exception."

Here is one of the most amazing incidents of a retreat turned into a victory in the whole history of human achievements. Edison took an inventory of his enterprises, applied the experience he had acquired in his mining venture, plunged into the manufacture of Portland cement and, with his storage battery coming to the front, paid off the entire indebtedness of the magnetic-ore venture in three years, and at the same time began the restoration of his fortunes, which were finally to reach large proportions.

Moreover, this was accomplished by the invasion of a strongly intrenched industry — Portland cement. He had watched its development for many years with the belief that it could be made to solve the problem of every man owning his own home. He believed that structures could be built that would stand as solid as the Pyramids, while wood and brick would crumble and disintegrate. The knowledge and experience which he had gained in grinding rock into iron ore would now be used in grinding rock and limestone into cement. The strong competition of the established concerns must be met by the invention of new machinery which would produce a "better cement at a lower cost."

"I have made arrangements for the financing of the cement industry," said Mallory a few days later. "I suppose you are going to hire engineers to lay out the plant."

"I am going to do that myself," replied Edison. "I have got it all laid out in my head now."

The inventor-engineer went upstairs in his laboratory and Mallory followed. With a sheet of paper on a drafting board, Edison began to draw rapidly — all day and through the night, until at the end of twenty-four hours he had laid out every detail of an immense plant, providing for every mechanical operation and reducing the movements to the highest point of efficiency and economy. This plant was erected at Stewartsville, New Jersey. It occupies nearly 800 acres of ground. It is about half a mile long and has an average capacity of 2,225,000 pounds of finished cement every twenty-four hours.

The cement industry predicted that it would be a dire failure, but it soon became the most highly developed plant of the kind in the world, with its improved automatic machinery, worked out largely through Edison's inventive genius. It is built entirely of concrete and steel and stands as a monument to the engineering skill of the great inventor.

The lessons learned in the ore-crushing plant were applied to the cement industry, and Edison designed and built a giant kiln — the first of its kind to be constructed — which, in its terrible power, could break a 5-ton rock with the ease of a nutcracker and devour like a dinosaur 15 tons of rock every four minutes. The standard kiln of the time was 60 feet long; Edison built his "giant kiln" 150 feet long; today there are kilns 250 feet long. Out of these Edison kilns came the cement that built the great Yankee Baseball Stadium in New York City — 180,000 bags of Edison Portland cement. Immense bridges, auditoriums, industrial plants, and office buildings have been erected from the Edison kilns. Edison's development of the cement industry has been of incalculable value.

INVENTOR TURNS HIS ATTENTION TO "HOMES FOR THE PEOPLE"

The genius of Edison now turned to the solution of the "home problem." He believed that this, too, lay in the cement industry. There was considerable controversy aroused when the statement appeared in the public press: "Edison solves home problem with 'poured cement houses.' He has invented sets of iron molds, through which cement may be poured and a house constructed in six hours. The molds stand in position about four days, until the concrete hardens. When they are removed, a complete house is left standing from cellar to roof, all in one solid piece, including walls, floors, stairways. The cost will be not more than $500 for a dwelling as large as ten rooms."

The basis of these statements Edison declared to be correct, with possibly some revision of figures. He found that he could build the molds for $25,000, and that a set of molds could be used five hundred times or more. This threw consternation into the building trades. The inventor announced that he had no intention of entering the construction business, but would lease the molds to the contractors. The building contractors, however, seeing their profits greatly reduced, did not take advantage of the offer, claiming that the cost of transporting the molds and setting them up would be too great; also that a $25,000 investment must be placed on the ground to produce a house that cost $500.

The inventor realized that his benefaction in this case was to meet with strong and intrenched opposition. His project, however, was practical, and in it lies one of the great developments of the future. It has been proved successful and will result eventually in fulfilling the purposes for which he invented it. Few movements could result in a larger measure of betterment and of social and economic welfare. It is said that today its adoption is being considered in Russia, in the new transition of masses of people from peasants' huts to workingmen's homes. Industrial

centers in Germany also have the matter under advise-
ment.   The future upbuilding of the vast populations of
India and China may be modeled on the Edison plan.

It was not Edison's intention to profit from this magnificent social project, but rather to give the industrial and
mining towns model communities in which to live.   Money
was a secondary consideration to the inventor.   When he
made it, he used it for the best purposes he could conceive.

While these enterprises were in successful operation,
Edison was engaged in his usual multitudinous experiments
in other lines — always reaching out.   He had worked with
the X ray, inventing the first Fluoroscope, and making
many improvements in X-ray tubes, which proved of incalculable value in the science of surgery, saving tens of
thousands of human lives; he had made many important
inventions for the improvement of the phonograph; he
had introduced the dictating machine and the universal
electric motor for operating it; he had continually labored
on improvements for the electrical industry.   He introduced the "Kinetoscope," in 1912, a combination of his
phonograph and a motion-picture projector, which resulted
in the first talking motion picture, which, as we have seen,
was the basis of that industry today.

Thomas Edison had traveled a long and arduous road
since his first invention of the "Vote Recorder" in Boston
when he was 21 years old; he had risen from poverty to
affluence and greatness; he was one of the world's leading
personalities.   Every conceivable phase of human life had
been touched by his inventions; they had entered into some
relationship with the whole human race in every part of
the globe.

CHAPTER XXI

WORLD WAR — EDISON'S SERVICE TO HIS COUNTRY

During the World War the inventor made many devices that aided in winning the war.

FOUR years of world tragedy — 1914–1918 — broke suddenly upon the nations on July 28, 1914. Epoch-making events frequently come through unknown sources; a nineteen-year-old Serbian student, named Prinzip, fired the shot that started the conflagration when, in the streets of the Bosnian city of Sarajevo, he assassinated the Archduke Francis Ferdinand and his wife, of Austria.

War was declared and the nations fell into the vortex. Sixty-five million men were mobilized; twenty-one million were wounded; and nearly nine million made the supreme sacrifice.

Throughout the world, science and invention rallied to the call of their countries. Thomas Edison, then nearing seventy years of age, answered the call to service. He was about to see a war fought with the weapons of modern invention — many of them his own. The powers of Nature which he had marshaled for the pursuits of peace were now to be employed in human slaughter. Predictions which he had made some years before were now to come true. During the Spanish-American War, in 1898, he had made the only invention in his life that was designed for purposes of destruction: the Sims-Edison submarine torpedo, operated by electricity (as coinventor with W. Scott Sims). He had further suggested an illuminating shell which could be fired for purposes of finding the enemy at night. His prophecies at this time regarding future wars created considerable consternation in Europe and America:

EDISON'S PREDICTIONS OF WARS OF THE FUTURE

"Electricity will play an important part in the wars of the future," he said. "Torpedo boats can be despatched two miles ahead of a man-of-war and kept at that distance under absolute control, ready to blow up anything within reach. I believe, too, that aërial torpedo boats will fly over the enemy's ships and drop a hundred tons of dynamite down on them. A five-million-dollar war vessel can be destroyed instantly by one of these torpedoes."

It is interesting to note that this was before the invention of the airplane by the Wrights or the airship by Zeppelin. These predictions came true in the World War with the aërial night raids on London and Paris.

"I can also conceive of dynamite guns," stated the inventor. "I have no intention of ever devising machines for annihilation, but I know what can be done with them. Nitroglycerin is one of the most dangerous substances that man can deal with. Touch a drop of it with a hammer and you will blow yourself into the hereafter. Iodide of nitrogen is even more dangerous. While experimenting with explosives in magnetic mining, I made some of them so sensitive that they would go off if shouted at. Place a drop on the table and yell at it and it will explode."

DISASTROUS FIRE BREAKS OUT IN THE EDISON PLANT

Five months after the outbreak of the World War, a disastrous fire broke out at the Edison plant in West Orange, on the night of December 9, 1914. Six buildings were burned; seven structures of concrete were gutted inside; equipment was wrecked, and supplies consumed. Firemen worked heroically, and among the mementoes saved was a framed photograph of Edison; the glass was cracked and the frame charred, but the portrait escaped. Edison picked it up and wrote these words on the photograph:

"Never touched me!"

When the firemen were clearing away the ruins on the following morning, Edison stood looking at the scene before him. Turning, to his general manager, he exclaimed:

"Well, Wilson, she's a goner, but we'll build her bigger and better than ever before!"

Within thirty-six hours after the fire, Edison had laid out plans in detail and issued orders for the construction of a new plant which would withstand the ravages of flames. He had had disastrous experiences with fire on several occasions throughout his life since the days when he was whipped in the public square for setting fire to a barn "to see what it would do." The Menlo Park laboratory had witnessed the explosion of ether on one occasion, when firemen played the hose through the smashed windows, overturning and breaking hundreds of bottles of chemicals. As they forced their way into the building, they were overcome by the fumes. When the first Edison power station had been in operation eight years, it met with a devastating conflagration, which threatened the down-town section of New York.

SECRETARY OF NAVY DANIELS SENDS FOR EDISON

The first year of the World War began to threaten to draw the United States into it. President Wilson was making every effort to keep the nation out of the holocaust, but finally decided in a Cabinet meeting that the "inventive, scientific and industrial power of the country should be mobilized." It is said that Thomas Edison was discussed at this meeting, and Josephus Daniels, Secretary of the Navy, suggested that he be impressed immediately into service. Daniels knew of Edison's humane disposition and his aversion to war, but believed he could be appealed to on matters of national defense. The entire Wilson Administration was opposed to the entrance of the United States into the European War and was pledged to peace, but it foresaw the necessity of protection in case of an emergency.

The historic letter which Secretary Daniels addressed to Thomas Edison is dated July 7, 1915. The original is in the possession of the Edison family:

Dear Mr. Edison:

I have been intending for some time to write you expressing my admiration at the splendid and patriotic attitude you have taken in refusing to devote your great inventive genius to warlike subjects except at the call of your own country . . . There is a great service you can render the Navy and the country at large . . . One of the imperative needs is machinery and facilities for utilizing the natural inventive genius of Americans to meet the new conditions of warfare as shown abroad. It is my intention . . . to establish at the earliest moment, a department of invention and development, to which all ideas and suggestions, either from the service or civilian inventors, can be referred for determination as to whether they contain practical suggestions for us to take up and perfect . . . Such a department will of course have to be eventually supported by Congress, with sufficient appropriations made for its proper development . . . I feel that our chances of getting the public interested and back of this project will be enormously increased if we can have at the start some man whose inventive genius is recognized by the whole world . . . You are recognized by all of us as the one man above all other who can turn dreams into realities, and who has at his command in addition to his own wonderful mind the finest facilities in the world for such work . . .

This is a great deal to ask and I unfortunately have nothing but the thanks of the Navy and I think of the country at large . . . to offer you by way of recompense, yet so clearly have you shown your patriotism and unselfish loyalty to your country's interests that I feel justified in making this request.

We are confronted with a new and terrible engine of warfare in the submarine . . . I feel sure that with the practical knowledge of the officers in the Navy, with a department composed of the keenest and most inventive minds . . . and with your own wonderful brain to aid us, the United States will be able as in the past to meet this new danger with new devices that will assure peace to our country with their effectiveness . . .

With you it might be well to associate a few men prominent in special lines of inventive research. And I would like also to consult with you as to who these men should be . . . I know the relief which the country would feel in these trying times at the announcement that you are aiding us in this all-important matter . . .

(Signed) JOSEPHUS DANIELS.

INVENTOR OFFERS HIS SERVICES TO HIS COUNTRY

Edison was deeply impressed by the letter, and after weighing its contents carefully, sent his chief engineer and personal representative, Dr. Miller Reese Hutchison, to Washington to discuss the problems with Secretary Daniels. The statesman and the scientist engaged in a survey of the World War situation, with various plans of action.

"I have the honor to inform you," stated Dr. Hutchison, "that Mr. Edison will consent to head such a Board as you propose.   He is willing to extend every possible service to the Government.   My services also are at the Government's disposal."

Dr. Hutchison was a recognized scientist of highest standing, a graduate engineer from a polytechnic institution, who had conducted his own laboratory in New York before joining the Edison forces.   During the Spanish-American War he had been engaged in laying submarine mines and cables in the Gulf harbors; he held several hundred patents and had received many medals in England and the United States.   His association with Edison had begun in 1910, and at the outbreak of the World War he was chief engineer of the Edison laboratories and affiliated interests.   It was through this meeting with Secretary Daniels that he arranged his affairs so that he could devote his entire time to Government service during the war.

The World's Fair at San Francisco was an important event in 1915, commemorating the opening of the Panama Canal, to commerce, August 15, 1914, and Thomas Edison was one of the distinguished guests.   With Mrs. Edison, Henry Ford and his wife, and Harvey Firestone, he traveled to the Pacific and paid a visit to Luther Burbank at Santa Rosa, California.   Here he became interested in the horticultural science which in later years he was to develop with Ford and Firestone as his colleagues.   Upon his return from the transcontinental tour, Edison prepared to enter the war service as a Government adviser.

The blowing up of the S. S. *Lusitania*, when it was sunk by a German submarine off the coast of Ireland, on May 7, 1915, had aroused the nation.   It was evident that America could not keep out of the war, as this attack was in itself a challenge; 1,198 lives were lost, of which 124 were Americans.

THE FIRST MOVING-PICTURE STUDIO

Erected by Edison in the yard of his laboratory at West Orange, built on a circular track, and popularly called "Black Maria."

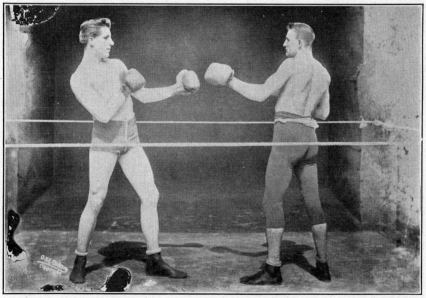

CORBETT IN ACTION FOR THE FIRST EDISON MOVIE

James J. Corbett, then Champion of the World, put on a bout with his sparring partner for Mr. Edison in the famous "Black Maria."

Photo by International News

ON THE VERGE OF WAR

An historic picture, taken in 1915, of Edison
and Josephus Daniels, then Secretary of the
Navy.

Photo by International News

EDISON : PATRIOT

In the days when war threatened, Edison offered his services in defense of his country.
He is seen here marching in the Preparedness Parade in New York, May 13, 1916.

Secretary Daniels came to "Glenmont," the home of Edison at Llewellyn Park, West Orange, New Jersey, following the conference in Washington with Doctor Hutchison. Plan of action was outlined in the Edison library, after which the cabinet member hurried back to Washington and communicated to the President the results of the conference of the eleven leading technical organizations in the country.

Two delegates from each of the technical societies, went to Washington on October 7, 1915, and assembled at the Navy Department to organize for the impending war in which the United States was to become involved. Here, at this historic conference representing the ablest scientific minds in America, the "Naval Consulting Board of the United States" was formed. Edison was elected Chairman, but urged the Board not to consume his efforts in executive duties and was therefore made President, with William L. Saunders as Chairman.

This Board later was legalized by Congress. The service it performed during the World War was of incalculable value, and the records preserved in the Government archives at Washington would fill volumes in themselves. Its first constructive task was an industrial inventory of the United States for the purpose of marshaling the entire manufacturing resources of the country to stand back of the army. Science, invention, and industry became an impregnable line of defense behind the soldiers. This survey was followed by an industrial preparedness campaign to arouse the country to its own defense.

EDISON'S LIFE THREATENED — MARCHES IN "PREPAREDNESS PARADE"

"Preparedness Day Parades" were held throughout the country on May 13, 1916. Thomas Edison had

17

received a warning that if he marched in the parade in
New York it would be at the cost of his life. Threatening
letters were received at his laboratories, and there were
even intimations that they would be "blown up." The
rumor was emphasized by the fact that a bomb was hurled
on the paraders at San Francisco, killing nine and wound-
ing forty. Throughout the cities of the country there were
disturbances and the patriotism of the people was aroused
to fever heat. This was the beginning of the celebrated
Mooney case in San Francisco, with his trial, conviction,
and sentence for life, on the charge of leading the conspiracy
in the bombing of that city.

When the great "Preparedness Parade" moved up
Fifth Avenue in New York City, Thomas Edison was at
the head of the Naval Consulting Board, leading the
engineers' section. Two Secret Service men were on each
side of him; the throngs along the Avenue cheered him
as a "conquering hero."

It was eleven weeks later that the "Black Tom"
explosion and fire shook Jersey City, killing two and
destroying property valued at $30,000,000. This was
followed by explosions and disasters in various parts of
the country. It was necessary to keep the Edison plant
under guard to protect it from "the enemies." Secretary
Daniels despatched a message to Edison, urging him to
come to Washington for an important conference. It was
now inevitable that the United States would be drawn into
the conflict.

ENTERS ACTIVE SERVICE ON "BATTLEFIELDS OF INVENTION"

"The country needs your inventive genius," said
Secretary Daniels to America's greatest inventor. "We

have serious problems before us and we believe that you will be able to solve them." He handed a document to Edison, listing the important services that he could perform for the country in this crisis.

"Whatever I can do is at your command," replied the great inventor. "I shall be glad to give my whole time to the Government without charge."

Returning to his laboratories at Orange, Edison abandoned the important researches and experiments on which he was engaged, and concentrated his entire energies on the solution of Government problems. Fifty skilled mechanics were placed on the construction of apparatus as fast as Edison drafted the designs. Working night and day according to custom, the Edison plant for the next two years was a great "invention shop" for the Government. Reinforced by technical experts from other industrial establishments, and young engineers from the universities, Edison was surrounded by technical skill unsurpassed anywhere in the world.

Attacked by submarine warfare, the United States was forced to declare war against Germany, on April 6, 1917. American industry was now speeded to its highest efficiency; American manhood rushed to the defense of the country until a force of 4,500,000 had been mobilized. During the war more than 2,000,000 American soldiers were carried to France.

"Thomas Edison practically became a Naval officer," said Secretary Daniels. "He spent long months in the Navy Department and in extended periods of deep-sea cruising that he might be in the closest touch with the problems to be solved."

Edison's secret missions on warships were closely guarded. He sailed with the naval officers and tested many inventions which he brought aboard. These have never been completely revealed as they were under guard of the Secret Service. It is known, however, that among the thousands of tests that he made were: Strategic plans (with maps) for saving cargo boats from submarines, telephone system for ships, plan for obstructing torpedoes by nets, blinding submarines and periscopes, coast patrol by submarine buoys, device for "finding" enemy airplanes, protection of merchant ships in mined harbors, detecting submarines by sound from moving vessels, locating position of guns by sound ranging, increased power for torpedoes.

Edison's war inventions further included devices for the destruction of periscopes with machine guns, plan for smudging skyline, zigzagging by ships in danger zone, turbine head for projectiles, collision mats, underwater searchlight, hydrogen detector for submarines, mirror reflection for warships, high-speed signaling shutter for searchlights, device for quick turning of ships in danger, mechanism for obtaining nitrogen from the air, and numerous other devices and formulas that came out of the Edison laboratory. Official record is made in the War Records at Washington of 39 inventions and plans. Edison's records show 45 turned over to the Government by Edison during the World War.

As the war continued through 1917–18, with the American troops on the battle lines, under command of General John J. Pershing in France, the Naval Consulting Board became the "Board of Invention" of the National Research Council, affiliated with the Council of National Defense. Its service was extended from the Navy Department to the various departments of the Government. Inventors and scientists throughout the country served with the same loyalty as the soldiers, while industry placed its entire resources back of the allied armies.

Armistice Night — November 11, 1918 — was celebrated in every town and city throughout the country.
The war was over and the troops came marching home —
119,956 American soldiers had given their lives — 193,666
were wounded — the total casualties, including prisoners
and missing, reached 318,042.   The Peace Treaty was
signed at Versailles on June 28, 1919.   The greatest conflict in the world's history was ended.

After the War—in Peace Service

A great period of expansion and prosperity followed
the end of the World War — nations fell and new nations
arose out of the ashes. Germany became a republic;
Russia, with the end of Czardom, began the building of a
new social and economic order; Austria and Hungary
and Czechoslovakia became independent states.

Science and invention entered into world reconstruction
with renewed genius and energy, blazing new paths for
human progress, opening up the new systems of transportation and communication, with aërial navigation and the
development of the radio.

Edison stood in his preëminent position as the "dean
and foremost progenitor of the new decade of expansion,"
for which, as we have seen, his inventions had helped lay
the foundations. His industries entered into this era with
the power of his vitality behind them, although he was
now mounting toward the octogenarian landmark. His
storage-battery plant, his cement industries, his wood-
products plants, his Ediphone and phonographic developments, his plants for electrical apparatus and telegraph
equipments, his new Edison Radio, and hundreds of other
products of his brain, created hives of industry.

He was fighting against time as the years advanced.

"My desire is to do everything within my power," he said, "to further free the people from drudgery, and create the largest possible measure of happiness and prosperity."

Edison's experiences in the World War and the days immediately following, convinced him that we were on the threshold of great chemical discoveries — that the economic problems of the future were to be met in the laboratory where science would find the secret of producing everything that the world needs "as and when it needs it." He believed that the method of waiting and waste and shortage of supplies necessary to the human family was antiquated and that "everything exists right at home if we will only reach out and take it."

With this conviction concerning the next great step in human progress, his intimate friends, Henry Ford and Harvey Firestone, were in complete agreement. They formed a "triumvirate" to inaugurate this new era and it was decided that rubber should be the first citadel of attack. The world had long sought for substitutes for rubber, synthetic rubber, and whatever might solve the problem of the rapidly increasing need. Firestone had engaged in large enterprises in raising rubber in Africa when the supplies in Brazil and along the jungles of the Amazon, and in the countries along the far Indian Ocean, created a crisis in American industry.

Edison started his experiments in his winter laboratory in Florida, entering upon the tireless and almost endless search with the eagerness and enthusiasm of a boy.

Making Rubber from Goldenrod

The laboratory at Fort Myers became "nature's workshop." Edison followed the general principles discovered by his old friend, Luther Burbank, and made thousand of experiments in horticultural crossbreeding. He experimented with more than 14,000 different plants and found rubber content in 1,240 of these plants. More than 600 produced in their plant juices a sufficient amount of rubber to prove potentially profitable.

"Of all this immortal six hundred," said Edison, "goldenrod is the one plant that has all of the requisite qualities. While many other plants have a somewhat higher content of rubber, they are utterly impracticable when it comes to raising large crops."

Goldenrod began to bloom all over the Edison acres. Standing in his garden, into which opened his laboratory door, he gave this information to the world through the public press:

"We have reached the point where we can say that our experiments have proved successful. My estimate at present is 100 pounds of rubber to the acre of goldenrod, with machinery invented for economical extraction. I expect to raise this to 150 pounds eventually, and then we are just beginning — for the possibilities are almost unlimited when the principle is once established."

Edison plans rebuilding as he grimly watches the burning of his plant.

The four good friends: Burroughs, Edison, Ford, and Firestone.

CHAPTER XXII

DAYS AND NIGHTS WITH EDISON IN HIS LABORATORY

The storage battery, so familiar today, was a real novelty when Edison introduced it.

EDISON'S laboratories were all industrial democracies — republics in themselves. He was the benevolent, if perpetual, president, and his men were members of the greatest inventive cabinets in the world. They worked in a highly developed brotherhood without intrigue, conspiracy, or revolt — without envy or avarice. Fires, failures, the rising and falling tides of fortune never changed their Spartan fortitude.

We are now privileged to watch Edison at work, surrounded by his men — through the scenes and events revealed in these anecdotes by the "Edison Pioneers."

Thomas Edison had six laboratories, or "invention shops," during his life. The first was in his mother's cellar at Port Huron, Michigan; the second in the baggage car on the Grand Trunk line between Detroit and Port Huron; the third in Newark, when he got his first forty thousand dollars for the stock ticker; the fourth the famous laboratories at Menlo Park; the fifth the laboratory at West Orange; the sixth and last at his winter home at Fort Myers, Florida.

His span of experiments covered more than seventy-two years, and during this time he built, leased, or entered into contract with more than a hundred factories. His workers during this period ran into the thousands, and many of them never worked for any other man during their entire lifetime. It became an axiom — "Once an Edison man, always an Edison man."

The Grand Army of the Famous Edison Legion

It was a magnificent group of men that worked in the Edison laboratories. There was Charles Batchelor, Chief Technician, who was known as "Edison's Hands," because of his skilful use of his fingers; "Honest John" Kreusi, "the best model maker in the world"; Francis R. Upton, "one of the world's greatest mathematicians," who had studied at Princeton and been a pupil of Helmholtz; Edward H. Johnson, the "most intimate personal friend and consultant of Edison"; Francis Jehl, "one of the ablest and most trusted men in the organization," who became Curator of the Edison Museum in Michigan.

There, in the old Menlo Park days, were William S. Andrews, who occupied important posts in the Edison companies and finally became a Consulting Engineer for the General Electric Company; John W. Lieb, "a great draftsman," became Vice President of the New York Edison Company; William J. Hammer went on important and confidential missions at home and abroad for Edison; Edward G. Acheson, while experimenting with an electric furnace in an attempt to make artificial diamonds, gave the world abrasive carborundum (silicon carbide) and the carborundum furnace; Charles L. Clarke, Chief Engineer, finally became one of the big men with the General Electric Company, and later helped create the electric-power industry at Niagara Falls.

Charles T. Hughes worked on the Edison electric locomotive; Martin Force helped to perfect the loud-speaking telephone; J. H. Vail had charge of the dynamos for a time; John Ott made molds for lamp filaments that measured to the ten-thousandth part of an inch; Ludwig Boehm was the glass blower who created the bulbs; Arthur E. Kennelly, head mathematician, who became President of the Institute of Electrical Engineers, was said to be "the only man in America who was ever able to interpret the intricate system of mathematics evolved by Heavy-sides, the great British electrician; Frank Sprague resigned from the navy to join the ranks of Edison and became the inventor of the Sprague Electric System; August Weber invented a new porcelain and made a fortune; H. Ward-Leonard invented an electric system for turrets on battle-ships; Philip Seubel installed the first electric plant on a warship.

Nikola Tesla began his apprenticeship, which was to lead him into science, in the Edison laboratory. He tells how he secured but forty-eight hours of sleep in the first two weeks. The roll of honor, with the Carman brothers, Dr. A. Haid, and numerous others, whom we meet with, in the "Edison Pioneers" in a later chapter, is to the industrial world a "Legion of Honor."

Samuel Insull and William Meadowcroft as "Grand Marshals"

Here again we meet Samuel Insull, who came from England and began his notable career as Edison's private secretary in 1881, and for many years ably managed the inventor's business affairs. Insull recently said that whatever he had done in the electric light and power industry he owed to these early days with Edison. It was not an easy job as private secretary, or financial manager, for Edison; he called his men together at any hour — midday or midnight. There were neither hours nor days in the week, and he seemed to be at his best at night. The best time to reach him was at midnight — even to go over his mail with him. Insull states that Edison embodied all the characteristics of the true genius.

Then there was William H. Meadowcroft, who was Edison's "right arm" for more than half a century; he remained with him as his personal secretary to the day of the inventor's death. Meadowcroft's services were of incalculable value; he was for years the great inventor's contact with the public; his diplomacy and courtesy won him the love and respect of the public press and of the many distinguished guests of the inventor. To see Edison, it was first necessary to see Meadowcroft, and when you met Meadowcroft, you met a diplomat.

If William the Conqueror had had an army like Edison's, he would not have stopped in England — he would have gone right on and conquered the world. Edison's men were out to conquer new worlds!

"What times we had together!" exclaimed Edison. "Work — work — *work!* Then we would break off and celebrate. And how we *could* celebrate!"

MIDNIGHT LUNCH WHEN THE EDISON FORCES CELEBRATED

The event at the old Edison laboratory at Menlo Park was the midnight lunch. The men crowded around the festive board at the end of the workshop, surrounding Edison at the table. Here the inventor let down on the strain of hard labor and became a genial host, laughing jovially and telling stories.

The human side of Edison was seen in these midnight revels, and it was here that "the hardest taskmaster in the world" became the most beloved. Edison had a brother-in-law, named Van Cleve, who had been incarcerated at Andersonville and Libbey prisons in the Civil War; he sat at the head of the table most of the time as the "king of story-tellers."

These "Edison Pioneers" were men of character and intellectual standing — a very superior group of men. There were scholars among them, such as Upton, the great mathematical physicist, and Clark, physicist and scientist.

Boxing gloves were brought out, and the scientists who were remaking the world entered the "ring" like gladiators fighting for the title of John L. Sullivan. Edison would stand on a chair and yell like a ring-side enthusiast when one of his scientists was knocked down. He would go over to the old organ in the corner of the laboratory and sing his favorite songs. In the midst of the joviality, his voice would boom out with "My Poor Heart Is Sad with Its Weeping." Boehm was quite a musician — he would play the zither and sing the roistering German songs. Generally, the midnight dinner closed by singing as their doxology, "Good Night, Ladies!"

Edison's father had come down from Port Huron, after the death of the inventor's mother, and was a familiar figure around the laboratory. A tall man, with a heavy beard, he was known as "Pop" Edison, and was much beloved by the workers. Quick in repartee and a good story-teller, despite his years he liked to join in the festivities whenever there was a celebration. One of the Pioneers states that he looked like "Uncle" Joe Cannon, who for so many years was Speaker of the House of Representatives.

Edison was quick at characterization. When he once learned the traits of a man, he would apply a nickname that fitted him. He called Hammer "Michael Strogoff," because of his pompadour, which resembled the courier of the Tsar in a popular play running on Broadway. One of his chemists, named Lawson, he called "Basic" Lawson because he was always working on basic principles. Some of his names were lost in mysticism, which he refused to explain, such as the man whom he dubbed "Chinese-India-Rubber-Idol-in-a-Storm."

There were two pets at the Edison laboratory — a big St. Bernard dog named "Wallace," after William Wallace, the famous pioneer in electricity, and the other was a coon, which would spend hours trying to scoop up quick-silver in his almost human hands.

The capital crime of the Edison laboratories was to go to sleep. This was a sort of disgrace, unless the boss could be caught napping, and then they all followed in line like true soldiers going to the trenches. There was an instrument in the laboratory known as the "corpse reviver." When a man had fallen into the Elysian fields of slumber-land, this diabolical instrument was rolled alongside of him and let loose like the furies of the inferno. Then there was the "resurrector of the dead" — a fluid which when placed under the sleeper caused spontaneous combus-tion. The explosion catapulted the sleeper out of his chair and he generally ran to the water tank, plunged in, and sat down to find peace and comfort.

THE GREAT NIGHT WHEN PANDEMONIUM BROKE LOOSE

The night of October 21, 1879, when the first incan-descent light had burned forty-five hours, was a great night, states one of the Pioneers, but it was not the most exciting event in the Menlo Park laboratory. The night of nights was in 1880, when the first commercial electric light was born. Tests had been made for two months. Shortly before midnight, Hammer rushed into the laboratory from the test shop, holding aloft in his hand a small lamp.

Pandemonium broke loose — an Edison lamp had actually burned for 1,589 hours — 66 days! The cheering shook the rafters of the laboratory; the men fell in line and started a triumphant procession. Edison marched beside Hammer, who held the historic lamp high in his hand, as the procession moved on like a conquering army around the laboratory table — downstairs — weaving in and out of the buildings through Menlo Park. They cheered, sang, and shouted themselves hoarse.

Major Hammer became the largest collector in the world of memorabilia relating to the history of the incandescent lamp. This collection was sold to the General Electric Company for $10,000 and is said to be worth more than $1,000,000 today.

Among the Pioneers in the Edison laboratory was James Mackenzie, the man whose son "Al" had saved when a newsboy on the Grand Trunk Railroad and who, as a reward, had taught him telegraphy in his boyhood days. Edison always retained a deep affection for the Scot, who had started him on his career, and made him a pensioned employee in his laboratory. Mackenzie was very proud of "my boy." When the inventor showed him his first sketch for a talking machine, the old Scot looked at it quizzically.

"What do you think it is for?" asked Edison.

"It looks to me like a sausage machine," said Mackenzie.

"Well," replied Edison, "I'll let you into the secret — it's going to talk!"

Mackenzie was not sure whether he was being made the victim of a practical joke, or Edison was going crazy.

The first words ever spoken over a talking machine, as we have noted, were the classic lines about Mary and her little lamb. Francis Jehl, of the Edison Museum, in Michigan, tells how Edison coughed into the funnel, then sneezed into it, and laughed into it. He then relates how the inventor recited in a deep bass voice the first verse of "Bingen-on-the-Rhine." To test the "wizardry" of the new invention, the inventor reset the needle, and in a shrill falsetto voice shouted exclamations at certain points where he had hesitated in the lines. The result, when the phonograph spoke, was this:

"A soldier of the legion lay dying in Algiers,
— Oh, shut up! —
There was lack of woman's nursing, there was dearth of woman's tears,
— Oh, give us a rest! —"

There is an anecdote told about Nick, an old man who until Edison's last illness was the only one who was allowed to bring the inventor's meals into his laboratory during the times when he was working through the night. Nick's faithful service began nearly fifty years ago, when as a boy he was first employed as a gatekeeper at the old Menlo Park laboratory. His orders were not to allow any stranger to pass the gates and to demand visiting cards.

The first day that Nick was on duty — he had never seen Edison — a man dressed shabbily, and to Nick's mind a tramp, pressed the button at the gate and demanded admittance. The man wore a long, dun-colored coat, very faded, and a wide-brimmed slouch hat came down over his face.

"What do you want?" Nick asked when he looked at the man and noticed that he was trying to pick the lock of the gate.

"What do I want?" came the answer. "I want to get in. Open the gate!"

"You can't come in," said Nick, with growing suspicion.

"Oh, I guess I can," he was told. "Don't you know who I am?"

"No, and I don't care!" was the rejoinder.

"But I own this place!"

"You can't put no such game over me," said Nick, not to be duped, and with finality in his voice, walked away.

The agitated alarm set up by the gate buzzer caused one of the laboratory men to appear to see what the commotion was about. *There stood Thomas Edison!*

Edison, impressed by the lad's faithfulness to orders, took him into his confidence and for nearly a half century following, wherever there was a mission of trust, "Nick was the man."

"These were the great days," say the "Edison Pioneers." They are the modern "Thousand-and-One Nights" in American inventive history. It was Luther Stieringer who once said: "If Edison could have chosen his birthplace, he would have located it on the planet Mars, so he could secure the advantage of a day forty minutes longer."

"I doubt if there is another man living for whom his men would do as much," said W. S. Mallory, one of his associates. "I want to say, and I know whereof I speak, for I have been with him night and day for several years, that ninety-nine per cent of the credit of all the inventions and new work is due personally to Thomas Edison."

Photos by Wide World

HIS NAME IN STONE

Edison writing his name in the wet concrete in the block that now forms the corner stone of one of the Edison memorial buildings at Dearborn, Mich. Mr. Ford is an interested watcher. The lower illustration shows the hardened slab, with Edison's footprints and Burbank's spade.

CAN RUBBER BE MADE FROM GOLDENROD?

This was the last question that Edison set out to answer. He is here seen examining a sample of giant Florida goldenrod, and watching his assistant make a rubber experiment.

CHAPTER XXIII

THE HOME LIFE OF EDISON

Mr. and Mrs. Edison view the eightieth birthday cake.

"GLENMONT," the home of the Edisons in Llewellyn Park, at West Orange, New Jersey, has been the scene of historic events for more than a half century. Here distinguished guests from all parts of the world have been entertained by the great inventor's family. It is a house of memories and mementoes, every room of which echoes the voices of famous men and women who gathered at the hospitable hearth over which presided "the most charming hostess in America," Mrs. Thomas A. Edison. To be a guest in the Edison home was a continuous feast of hospitality and intellectual and cultural discussion.

"Glenmont" is a sturdy monument to the Victorian period of architecture — a massive, rust-colored, brick and clapboard structure, with its gabled roofs, carved balconies, and richly hued stained-glass windows. It stands in a commanding position in the midst of some fourteen acres of beautiful park and gardens, with blossoming flowers and rare shrubs and picturesque stone seats.

As we pass through the portals, we enter what was known in its day as the "Grand Hall," with its winding staircase of mahogany, its huge, old-fashioned fireplace, with a log on the andirons burning in winter. It has the beauty and comfort of an old English country house, with its oak tables, cushioned window seats, and its atmosphere of hospitality. Everywhere there are flowers — flowers from the garden and hot house, in Japanese jars — until the home is filled with fragrance from the odor of blossoms.

The Edison home was created to live in, and everything invites one to relaxation and rest. The drawing-room leads from the hall, and here the Edisons entertained their guests. It has the dignity and beauty of the culture which permeates "Glenmont." This spacious living room was built with a high archway in the center, supported by huge onyx pillars. Around the grand piano, the Edison family gathered, while Mrs. Edison, who is an accomplished musician, played selections from Beethoven. Edison, sitting in his easy-chair, listened with adoration for the "great master."

"Beethoven — my favorite composer!" he would exclaim. "His Ninth Symphony is the world's greatest masterpiece. Some day I am going to preserve it on my phonograph records. When I have done that, I am willing to quit."

Mrs. Edison explains that the famous inventor especially loved the violin and at one time played it himself, developing considerable talent, until he found that his inventions required his entire time. He spent quieter hours sitting here with Mrs. Edison at the piano singing to him the songs he loved. He would lean over and place his hand to his deaf ear to catch every word and strain of the melody of "The Little Gray Home in the West":

> When the golden sun sinks in the hills,
> And the toils of a long day are o'er,
> Though the road may be long, in the lilt of a song
> I forget I was weary before.

With Edison in His World of Books

Across the Grand Hall, in the library, Edison wandered to "live with his books." Burning logs cast a soft glow from the huge fireplace, which occupied one side of the room. Books — books — books — it was a world of books in itself. Here, in the somber, half-religious glow that filtered into the library from the stained-glass window designed by Edison, one wandered through the streets of ancient Greece with Homer and Plato, along the roads of Rome with Virgil and Marcus Aurelius, along the grand boulevards of Paris with Balzac, Victor Hugo, and Dumas, entering into discussions with Voltaire, Renan, and Rousseau. Here, too, Edison lived in Scotland, the home of his maternal ancestors, with Sir Walter Scott and Robert Burns, and sat in the inns of "Merrie England" with Dickens and Thackeray, or witnessed in his imagination the dramas of Shakespeare.

Leaving his books, Edison walked up the staircase and entered his favorite room — the Den. Here he could *work*, as he spread out his drawings on the large square desk, bearing photographs of his family. Here, too, were hospitable chairs where he could recline and work out the ideas which were to help reconstruct the world.

Edison always admitted that "Glenmont" reflected the culture and character of Mrs. Edison, the former Mina Miller, whom he married in 1886, after the death of his first wife. This wedding took place at the Miller mansion in Akron, Ohio, when Lewis Miller, one of the leading men of the times, gave his beautiful and accomplished daughter in marriage to the young inventor from the East.

Lewis Miller, father of the bride, was a distinguished inventor himself, giving to the world of agriculture, reaping, binding and threshing machines; he was, moreover, a leader in the educational and philanthropic affairs of the nation, founding the famous Chautauqua, with Bishop Vincent; he was a Biblical scholar and founded the modern method of graded Sunday School lessons. His first meeting with young Edison had been at the time of the invention of the phonograph, when he had declared: "Here is one of the great inventors of the future — watch him!" From that time until the death of Miller in 1899 he was an adviser and loyal supporter of the growing Edison.

The Miller home in Akron was typical of American culture during the Victorian era. There were ten sons and four daughters. Among these sons, John V. Miller became one of the valued associates of Edison at the Orange laboratory and was one of the leading counselors and advisers with his sister and nephews in the days following Edison's death, in the settlement of his estate. The first Millers in America came from Kent, England, about 1636, from the original stock in Edinburgh, Scotland, where their progenitor, Dr. Thomas Miller, was the first rector of the University of Edinburgh. (The author of this book is descended from this line in the tenth generation in America.)

This is the background from which came the charming Mina Miller, who was to rise to even higher estate and world renown as Mrs. Thomas A. Edison. Those who know her intimately agree with Edison himself that she became a powerful influence behind his tremendous achievements. Edison was fortunate in his marriages; his first wife, Mary Stillwell, who remained with him eleven years before her death and left three children, as we have noted in previous chapters, was an important factor in shaping his destiny, while Mina Miller throughout the forty-five years at his side until the day of his death takes her place in history as the noble wife, faithful comrade and co-worker. She was to Thomas Edison what Edith Carow was to Theodore Roosevelt. The nobility of character in Mina Miller Edison is shown in the Edison home, where she treasures a painting of Mary Stillwell Edison, which hangs in a place of honor in her boudoir.

SIX CHILDREN OF THOMAS EDISON — HIS LIFE WITH THEM

The Edison family at "Glenmont" consisted of four sons and two daughters: Marion Estelle, Thomas Alva, Jr., and William Leslie Edison — the children of Mary Stillwell Edison; and Madeleine, Charles, and Theodore Miller — the children of Mina Miller Edison. The first arrivals, Marion and Thomas, were nicknamed by their father "Dot and Dash." With their grandfather, Samuel Edison, who was then living at "Glenmont," they frequently went over to the laboratory to watch their father at work. Major Hammer told them stories and cut out paper dolls for the little girl, while "Pop" Edison sat near his son's table and watched the boy whom years before he ordered to put his chemicals under lock and key. William Leslie had a corner in his father's laboratory where he was taught the rudiments of science by a great master.

Thomas has recalled his childhood in these words: "Although the world remembers my father as a man of indefatigable effort and work, perfecting and inventing the wonders of his age, there was an intensely human side to him. He was not always so engrossed in his work that he could not spend some time with his children. I remember when he was devising games and recreation for us and the children in the neighborhood . . . When we came home from school we waited anxiously for him to arrive; he never failed to bring us some surprise and usually it was alarm clocks, which he brought by the dozen. It was with keen delight that we took them apart under his supervision.

I am sure that there were no other kids on earth who gloried in such wholesale destruction.   But when the main-springs repeatedly flew across the room and smashed arti-cles that were lying on a small table, it was the end of our orgy of destruction, for no more alarm clocks entered the house."

FORTY-FIVE YEARS AS THE WIFE OF A GENIUS

Forty-five years as the wife and constant companion of a great man are treasured by Mrs. Edison.   She traveled with him, sat beside him at hundreds of banquets, was with him when he received medals and decorations, watched him at work in his laboratories, and, as his deafness in-creased, she became his interpreter during conversations with distinguished guests and at public events.   Her voice was the only one that he could distinctly hear — it seemed so perfectly attuned.

Her life was given as a guide, philisopher, and comrade to her genius husband.   Hers was the greater task of divert-ing his mind from the ever-present problems that besieged him at the workshop and laboratory.   She merged her ideals and her intelligent mind with his interest, but this not to the sacrifice of her own individuality.   She was the wife of a genius, but she was more than this — she was his jovial companion and most ardent champion.

Mrs. Edison throughout her life has been sought by magazines and the public press to tell her story of life with a genius.   Here is a transcript of what she said when pressed for information during his last illness:

> "We always try at home to give him quiet and rest after his long hours at the laboratory.   We guard him against any noise or confusion or interruption.   Sometimes he stays down at the laboratory for twenty hours at a stretch and longer

without sleep. When he does come home, he will lie down and fall asleep as easily as a child and perhaps sleep straight through for twenty hours without waking. He has no regular habits, no regular time for rising, no regular diet. He is on his feet all day, and very seldom does any walking out of doors. He loves his garden, and motoring is his favorite recreation. We have our rides together in my car every day two hours before dinner and he looks forward to them. . . .

"At home he always sits under the brilliant lamp reading as though he would devour all the books that were ever printed. He reads two or three lines at a time. Most of us read words — he reads whole sentences — more than whole sentences if they happen to be short ones. I have never seen anyone concentrate as he does. His deafness of course has something to do with it, but I think if he weren't deaf he could still do it. He is a devout believer in concentration — he thinks you can get anywhere if you know how to concentrate. He has never played bridge or cards of any kind since the children were little, and golf, never. In fact he has little interest in sports.

"Mr. Edison has always been as rebellious about consulting a doctor as a small boy with a toothache is a dentist. Two years ago we were visiting Mr. and Mrs. Ford. Between Mr. Ford and myself, we persuaded Mr. Edison to see a doctor, and have a thorough examination. The doctor discovered digestive troubles and ordered him to go on a milk diet — two glasses every two hours. Mr. Edison always detested water and would drink very little of it until it was slightly flavored with peppermint.

"His interest during the last few years has been rubber. Everything has turned to rubber in the family. We talk rubber — think rubber — dream rubber. Mr. Edison refuses to let us do anything else. It is because he feels his work is still unfinished.

"If you will think of one who is living in the highest state of exhilaration, seeing nothing, hearing nothing, thinking nothing, doing nothing except what has a vital bearing on the task in hand, then you will have a perfect photograph of Mr. Edison at such times when he is working."

CHAPTER XXIV

THE "GRAND OLD MAN" MAKES HIS LAST GREAT DISCOVERY

"Glenmont," the Edison family home in beautiful Llewellyn Park.

THE last days of Thomas Edison at "Glenmont" stand in history like the last days of Thomas Jefferson at "Monticello." Jefferson had given his country a Declaration of Independence, while Edison had given to the world of science and invention a new declaration of independence. He stood in the ranks of the octogenarians with the same indomitable will and power that had characterized the last days of Gladstone and Bismarck. His strong mentality never wavered and his physical endurance fought the encroachment of years like a true warrior.

Emil Ludwig, the noted biographer, called him "The Uncrowned King of America."

"I'm through with the past," he exclaimed, as he returned North from Florida in his eighty-fourth year. "I'm looking ahead!"

But this "looking ahead" was into the work which he had determined to accomplish in this world — not into worlds to come.

"I must work at least fifteen years longer," he said. "It's time enough to retire at one hundred. I'll have to work hard to complete all the things I have in mind before that time. You know, just now I am working on rubber. I find this an advantage, because you don't have to *hear* rubber. But I'm having more trouble with it than Gatti-Casazza has with his opera singers. Rubber is much more temperamental. There are a lot of things to be done."

When asked if he agreed on the proposed suggestion of a "Ten-Year Holiday for Science," to give mankind a chance to catch up with scientific progress, he replied that his experiences had shown him that "Science never takes a holiday — it has worked every minute for the last billion years or more and probably will continue to do so."

Patriarch of Invention Nears End of Career

"We are just beginning to scratch the surface," exclaimed the patriarch of invention. "I am interested in Einstein — but I can't understand a thing he says. I am the zero of mathematics, but I don't have to moan over it any more, since I found out through my questionnaire that professors of Harvard and Yale are as ignorant as I am. I got along with Steinmetz because he never mentioned mathematics when he talked to me. He knew I didn't know anything about it, so he forgot all about it, too, when he was with me."

The first break in the rugged constitution, the first signs of the approaching storm, came during the celebration of the fiftieth anniversary of the electric light, in 1929. The old gladiator in the arena of invention was the guest of honor at Detroit (Chapter XXVI). Surrounded by a thousand outstanding leaders of the nation, in the replica of Independence Hall at Dearborn, he listened to the tributes. His wife, sitting by his side, noticed an unusual pallor on his face. President Hoover eloquently set forth the position which Edison would occupy in history.

In response to the tremendous applause from the throng, the old inventor rose and spoke a few words of thanks — and then slumped a little in his chair. Dr. Joel T. Boone, the private physician of the President, aided by Mrs. Edison, helped him to a room in the rear of the banquet hall, where he was laid upon the sofa. Richard Jervis, Chief of the White House Secret Service, believed the great inventor was breathing his last. Dr. Boone forced between his lips a solution of adrenalin, and in a few minutes Edison stirred and sat up. The banquet was now over and President Hoover hurried to his side. Assured by Dr. Boone that the danger was past, the President went to his train and left for Cincinnati.

It was at Detroit, too, in the preceding year, that Edison left his last records for posterity. While the Edison Museum in his honor was being erected by his friend, Henry Ford, he was persuaded to walk across a square of concrete and leave his footprints for the centuries to come. He then wrote the words into the concrete — his strong signature:

"*Thomas A. Edison, Sept. 27, 1928.*"

This will stand through the ages. Then, lifting the historic spade, once used by his friend, Luther Burbank, he thrust it into the block of concrete, where it remains, at the entrance to the museum.

These last two years drew heavily upon the reserve forces of his tremendous energy, but he remained at work in his laboratories at Fort Myers and at West Orange. With the invigoration of youth, he planned and administered the National Contests for the Thomas A. Edison Scholarship Awards. Upon his return from Florida, in the first June days of 1931, the family at "Glenmont" began to realize that the days of the "Old Master" were nearing the end.

EDISON'S LAST MESSAGE: "BE COURAGEOUS"

The last message which Edison delivered to the world was on June 11, 1931, when these words from him were broadcast over the radio from the Convention of the National Electric Light Association at Atlantic City:

"My message to you is to be courageous. I have lived a long time. I have seen history repeat itself again and again. I have seen many 'depressions' in business. Always America has come out strong and more prosperous. Be as brave as your fathers were before you. Have faith —go forward."

The first collapse came on August 1, 1931 — when the news swept around the world that Thomas Edison was at the point of death. Greatly to the amazement of his family physician, Dr. Hubert S. Howe, who was in constant attendance at the bedside, the indomitable will of the aged inventor won the first skirmishes. Edison arose — sat with the sunlight streaming through the window — began his motor rides with his wife and his physician along the country lanes that he loved, and renewed his interest in the world's affairs. He refused to admit that he was even facing a crisis, and declared that he would soon be back at his work. His thoughts turned toward the music that he loved:

"If I had but twenty-four hours to live," he said, "and could hear great music, I would choose Beethoven's 'Eroica' Symphony." This was the Master's symphony dedicated "To the Life of a Great Man." Edison did not realize its significance when he made the declaration.   Five years earlier, when asked when he intended to retire, Edison had retorted:

"The day before the funeral!"

We find him again conversing with his friends, discussing his plans for the future, and exclaiming over the beauty of the autumn foliage in the rhapsody of colors that lay before him.   His discussions with his physician at this time give a true insight into his character:

"If my work is finished," he said, "I am willing to go. I would rather leave the world than keep the burden of disability and age and illness on my devoted wife and children.   It's immaterial to me — I'm willing to go."

Dr. Howe Relates Events of Last Heroic Battle

Dr. Howe testifies to these last days: "If he could not work effectively, life had no further meaning and he grasped the situation clearly, as he had always done, and fearlessly prepared to die."   His drives in the country became less frequent; he wearied as he sat in his easy-chair at the window; drowsiness overtook him and he would fall asleep in his chair by his desk, where he insisted upon sitting.   Then the coma began to deepen as the days and nights dragged along.

Mrs. Edison sat by the side of his bed and members of the family visited him.   He would slowly arouse himself, as he felt his wife's hand clasp his, or stroke his aged face, and smile or whisper a few gentle words.

These last days were hours of perfect peace.   He would gaze at times into the distance as if in deep contemplation. Dr. Howe has described these last scenes (Chapter XXV), when, arousing from a coma, Edison whispered: "It is very beautiful over there."

The beautiful October days came and went — until midnight struck the beginning of October 18, 1931. A sacred calmness rested over the halls of "Glenmont," where a great man lay dying. Slowly but peacefully his subconscious strength ebbed like waves returning to the Mother Ocean. Gently he started on his journey from which no traveler ever returns. At one o'clock the darkness grew denser around the still figure — at three o'clock there was only a faint flicker, so slight that it did not stir the light coverlet. Twenty-four minutes passed . . .

The last vigil was ended. It seemed certain that he could not survive until morning. Dr. Howe leaned over the great inventor and listened to the slow beating of the fading heart. Rising, he spoke to Mrs. Edison, and summoned the little waiting group into the chamber. Thomas A. Edison, Jr., entered — with Charles, William, and Theodore, the inventor's sons. His daughters, Mrs. John Eyre Sloane and Mrs. Marion Edison Oser, entered with Mr. Sloane. They joined Mrs. Edison at the bedside where two nurses stood.

Outside the chamber door at "Glenmont" stood John V. Miller, brother of Mrs. Edison, with his wife; and with other members of Mrs. Edison's own family: Mr. and Mrs. M. W. Nichols, brother-in-law and sister; Mrs. Robert A. Miller and Mrs. J. V. Osterhaut, with Mrs. Halberg Kellog Hitchcock, of Pittsburgh.

There was a moment of silence. Dr. Howe appeared at the door and handed a slip of paper to Arthur L. Walsh, Vice President of the Edison Industries, who had been liaison officer with the outside world, during the last few days at "Glenmont." Walsh glanced at the simple statement and hurried from the house to the waiting newspaper men on continuous guard at their headquarters.

"Well, the end has come, boys!" he said, his voice trembling as he handed over the physician's bulletin:

Thomas Alva Edison quietly passed away at twenty-four minutes after 3.00 A. M., October 18, 1931.

DR. HUBERT S. HOWE.

Instantly the message of death was flashed to the farthest corners of the earth. Across continents and seas and channels of communication which Edison had worked to perfect were now utilized to spread the news of his own death — telephone — telegraph — and radio.

"Glenmont" stood like a sentinel in the darkness and quietude of Llewellyn Park. Night shadows of the ancient elms and linden tress fell across the lawn. The news passed through the heavily guarded gates. In the chamber of death sat Mrs. Edison — lingering for a moment as the family passed out of the room. She stood and gazed into the peaceful face of one of nature's noblemen — Thomas A. Edison — aged 84 years, 8 months, 7 days.

PRESIDENT HOOVER'S PROCLAMATION ON EDISON'S DEATH

President Hoover, aboard the battleship *Arkansas* on the Chesapeake Bay — en route to the celebration of the 150th anniversary of the victorious close of the American Revolution at Yorktown, Virginia — received the news as it came by wireless from the White House at 4.00 A. M. After attending divine worship aboard the warship, he issued this historic proclamation:

"It is given to few men of any age, nation, or calling to become the benefactor of all humanity. That distinction came abundantly to Thomas Alva Edison, whose death in his eighty-fifth year has ended a life of courage and outstanding achievement. His lifelong search for truth, fructifying in more than a thousand inventions, made him the greatest inventor our nation has produced, and revolutionized civilization itself. He multiplied light and dissolved darkness; he added to the whole wealth of nations. He was great not only in his scientific creative instinct and insight, but did more than any other American to place invention on an organized basis of the utilization of raw materials of pure science and discovery. He was a rare genius. He has been a precious asset to the whole world.

"Every American owes a personal debt to him. It is not only debt for great benefactions which he has brought to every American, but also debt for the honor he brought to our country. By his own genius and effort he rose from a newsboy and telegrapher to the position of leadership amongst men. His life has been a constant stimulant to confidence that our institutions hold open the door of opportunity to those who would enter. He possessed a modesty, kindliness, a stanchness of character rare among men.

"His death leaves thousands bereft of a friend, the nation bereft of one of its notable citizens, and the world bereft of one of its greatest benefactors. I mourn his passing as a personal friend over a quarter of a century."

Gloom was cast over the nation. When the first rays of the morning sun glistened on the gables of "Glenmont," endless streams of messengers began to arrive — bringing telegrams and cables from all the nations of the world, from rulers, diplomats, statesmen, scientists.

The "Grand Old Man" had gone on his last great discovery — he had solved the last and greatest of all mysteries — now he knew the meaning of life and the infinite forces which create it — the realms of the universe in their vastness were his for new conquests. And the world he left behind was paying him tribute.

It was on Wednesday, October 21, 1931 — the fiftieth anniversary of Edison's invention of the incandescent electric light — that the final memorial services were held, at his home, "Glenmont." A eulogy formed part of the service — a tribute written by an old associate, Arthur J. Palmer, on the occasion of the jubilee celebration of the electric light at Detroit. This beautiful expression of admiration and devotion was read by Dr. Lewis Perry, Head Master of Phillips Exeter Academy, a member of the Edison Scholarship Committee:

"He has led no armies into battle — he has conquered no countries — he has enslaved no peoples — yet he wields a power the magnitude of which no warrior ever dreamed. He commands a devotion more sweeping in scope, more world-wide than any other living man — a devotion rooted deep in human gratitude, and untinged by bias of race, color, religion, or politics.

"This democratic, kindly, modest being has bestowed upon the human race blessings instead of bondage, service instead of serfdom, construction instead of conquest.

"Possessed of an immeasurable breadth of vision, his world aspect comprehends peoples rather than people, masses rather than men. That great restless, surging tide of creatures — that mighty human glacier pressing irresistibly toward an ever-widening horizon of civilization.

"They call him the 'Wizard of Menlo Park.' They call him a 'genius' — but he dismisses such adulation with a wave of the hand. Once, when pressed for a definition of genius, he coined the adage, 'Genius is one per cent inspiration and ninety-nine per cent perspiration.'

"Though he disdains the hero worship of a grateful world, less exalted beings must ever sense him as a peculiar force of nature in human form, a phenomenon quite beyond the comprehension of ordinary mortals.

"Picture an electric-lightless, an electric-powerless, a telephoneless, a motion-pictureless, a phonographless world and a faint realization of his greatness dawns upon us. By taking Edison and his works *out* of the world we engender the keenest appreciation of Edison *in* the world.

AMERICA'S "BRIGHTEST BOYS"

Two fortunate winners of the Thomas A. Edison Scholarship: Arthur Williams, Jr., of Rhode Island (left); Wilbur Ruston, of Seattle, Wash. (right).

LINDBERGH AND THE EDISON QUESTIONNAIRE

Judges of contestants in the interesting quiz prepared by Edison. Left to right are: Lewis Perry, of Phillips Exeter Academy; George Eastman; Col. Lindbergh; Edison; Henry Ford; and S. W. Stratton, of Mass. Inst. of Technology.

TO TAKE A LAST LOOK AT EDISON
The long lines of mourners outside the Edison laboratory at West Orange, waiting to pay their last respects to the memory of the inventor.

"On the worth of his own works he is inarticulate. They must speak for themselves; they must earn the world's approbation on their merits or be consigned to oblivion with Spartan fortitude.

"Though humanity owes him an unpayable debt, he seeks no recompense beyond the means to experiment to his heart's content; beyond the joy of living and toiling in behalf of a debtor world.

"In the passionate pursuit of material truths and their conversion into practical, usable, beneficent forms, civilization has never seen his equal.

"And of this man, this super being who defies classification, what more can be said; what greater tribute paid than this — He is humanity's friend."

At the request of Mrs. Edison, the poem by Alice Marston Seaman was read by Dr. Perry, commemorating the passing of the great inventor:

THEY DO NOT DIE

They do not die, those dauntless ones who go
    Into the silence of that narrow room;
Great spirits are not conquered by the tomb;
    Ever the onward march of man shall know
Their presence; nor shall torch of time consume
    Their soul's achievement. They who gave overflow
Of consecration, that new truths might bloom
    On rugged heights, where we go faint and slow —
They are immortals.

So has one passed the day
    From life's full years of service grand and high;
Out — from the confines of his house of clay —
    One with the winds, the waves, the earth, the sky;
One — in the work he loved, to live alway —
    He is not dead — such men can never die.

CHAPTER XXV

EDISON'S VIEWS ON LIFE—HIS PHILOSOPHY AND RELIGION

Even in early days Edison was fond of dipping into books of all sorts.

THOMAS EDISON stands with Benjamin Franklin and Lincoln among the most notable examples of the self-educated man. We have seen how as a boy he gained his rudimentary knowledge under his mother's tutorship and then undertook to read every book in the Detroit Public Library. He estimated that he read during his life more than ten thousand books and his remarkable memory retained an unbelievable mastery of their essentials to the end of his life. He mastered science and history and was erudite in the classics. It was his habit for years to "absorb three books a day during stolen minutes from my work."

Edison created his own philosophy of life by practical demonstration, for he was always a practical man who reduced ideas, theories, and even visionary speculations into material forms which could be utilized for the benefit of mankind — a great utilitarian. And yet he realized that everything that exists is based on what we call spiritual laws, believing that these in themselves are discoverable and usable as man's natural contact with the infinite forces which have created and operate the universe.

Einstein, in whose theories Edison was deeply interested, called him "an inventive spirit"; Freud classes him as a "prolific genius"; Sir Oliver Lodge places him among "the greatest beings of the world"; Sir James Jeans classes him with "imaginative science"; H. G. Wells speaks of his power as "divine creativeness." These estimates would perplex Edison, as he considered that he merely "did whatever he found to do, to the best of his ability" — he laid no claims to genius and resented the word. "My philosophy of life is work," he constantly proclaimed. "Bringing out the secrets of Nature and applying them for the happiness of man — I know of no better service to render during the short time we are in this world."

Discussions with his intimate friends and family reveal the true Edison, a man who loved simplicity and honesty. With strength of character, a high sense of honor and integrity, he set up his own standard of ethics, which was based largely on love for his fellow man. He had a nobility of mind and soul which gave him tolerance and humility for everything except sham and pretense. These, with disloyalty, intrigue, and injustice, he would not tolerate. He hated deception and hypocrisy.

"All I ask of a man is that he have honest convictions and principles and live by them," he once said to a friend. He frequently quoted the words of Thomas Paine: "My country is the world and my religion is to do good." And yet he believed that man's first duty was to home and country. His constructive mind demanded law and order. There has been much discussion regarding the religion of Thomas Edison; he had a practical religion, based on the Golden Rule and the Ten Commandments. His nature was intensely spiritual, but he had neither time nor inclination toward creed or dogma, although he had profound respect for every institution which set up and lived by wholesome rules of conduct.

"I know this world is ruled by Infinite Intelligence," he said. "It required Infinite Intelligence to create it and it requires Infinite Intelligence to keep it on its course. Everything that surrounds us — everything that exists — proves that there are Infinite Laws behind it. There can be no denying this fact — it is mathematical in its precision."

His Scientific Mind Set Up a Mathematical Universe

Edison's scientific mind could not conceive of a universe so mathematically accurate without a guiding force or "captain on the bridge of the ship." The planets on their courses through the millions of years — the wonders of the earth with its multitudinous forms of life — the marvels of botany, geology, biology, all proved to him there was a supreme and ruling intelligence behind it.

In a discussion with George Parsons Lathrop, he said: "To me it seems that every atom is possessed by a certain amount of primitive intelligence. Look at the thousand ways in which atoms of hydrogen combine with those of other elements to form the most diverse substances. Do you mean to say that they do this without intelligence?"

"Where does this intelligence come from?" asked Lathrop.

"From some power greater than ourselves," replied Edison.

"Do you believe then in an Intelligent Creator — a personal God?"

"Certainly! The existence of such a God can, to my mind, almost be proved from chemistry."

Edison had a well-defined religion, which conformed to the strictest tenets of principles and ethics. He was familiar with all the philosophies of religions and believed that they all set up postulates that were provable in fact, although he did not conform with all the physical concepts of these spiritual realities. He was familiar with the Bible and with the scriptural teachings of other religions, and considered them "the greatest rules of human conduct ever set up for man." He did not see how man could live without them, as he required these guideposts to direct his way; therefore he confirmed the necessity of the church and the great work it has accomplished.

His family made this statement: "Although he subscribed to no orthodox creed, no one who knew him could have doubted his belief in, and reverence for, a Supreme Intelligence, and in his whole life the ideal of honest, loving service to his fellow men was predominant." There is a letter in existence which he wrote on the stationery of his laboratory at Orange, in which he states: "I believe in the existence of a Supreme Intelligence pervading the universe."

During his camping parties with his intimate friends, John Burroughs, Henry Ford, and Harvey Firestone, he frequently revealed himself on these matters relating to his philosophy of life and death. This statement is made by Harvey Firestone: "Mr. Edison was recovering from a severe illness and this led us to a discussion of the philosophy of the Hereafter. I asked him what he thought the controlling power of the universe to be, and he expressed himself along the same lines as he had in previous discussions, especially on the camping trip we made after attending President Harding's funeral, when he said: 'I believe in the teachings of our Lord and Master. There is a great directing head of people and things — a Supreme Being who looks after the destinies of the world.'

"'I am convinced that the body is made up of entities that are intelligent and are directed by this Higher Power,' continued Edison. 'When one cuts his finger, I believe it is the intelligence of these entities which heals the wound. When one is sick, it is the intelligence of these entities which brings convalescence. You know that there are living cells in the body so tiny that the microscope cannot find them at all. The entities that give life and soul to the human body are finer still and lie infinitely beyond the reach of our finest scientific instruments. When these entities leave the body, the body is like a ship without a rudder — deserted, motionless and dead.'"

When Henry Ford Bade His Old Friend Good-By

Henry Ford bade good-by to his old friend a few weeks before the end: "Mr. Edison believed in the Hereafter," declares Ford. "He thought there were more and weightier reasons in favor of it than there were against it. At one period of his life he gave no thought to the Hereafter, but when the years increased and he began to think of the natural end of this stage of life, he turned his thoughts to the great question. He then reached the independent conclusion that individual life continues through the change which we call death. He felt there was a central progressing core of life that went on and on. That was his conclusion. We talked of it many times together. . . . Call it religion or what you like, Mr. Edison believed that the universe was alive and that it was responsive to man's deep necessity. It was an intelligent and hopeful religion if there ever was one. Mr. Edison went away expecting light, not darkness."

Edison found that this question of God and Immortality was always confronting him in letters and interviews.

"We really haven't got any great amount of data on the subject," he said at one time, "and without data how can we reach definite conclusions? All we have — everything — favors the idea of what religionists call the 'Hereafter.' Science, if it ever learns the facts, probably will find another and more definitely descriptive term."

FAMILY PHYSICIAN TELLS OF EDISON'S LAST DAYS

This testimony of Dr. Hubert S. Howe, personal physician to Thomas Edison during his last illness and present at his deathbed, was given to the Associated Press to meet the great demand throughout the world in regard to the great inventor's beliefs:

"His last conscious hours were cheerful, and at intervals his mind turned to thoughts of the hereafter. On one occasion, after remaining for some time in an attitude of deep contemplation, he said: 'If there is a life hereafter or if there is none, it does not matter.' When asked if he believed in immortality, he answered briefly, 'No one knows.'

"A few days before he passed away," continues Dr. Howe, "he was sitting in his chair, apparently enjoying a pleasant dream. Suddenly opening his eyes and gazing upward into space, his face illuminated with a smile as he said:

"*It is very beautiful over there!*'"

Dr. Howe then asks the question: "Had the great inventor climbed the heights which lead into Eternity and caught a glimpse beyond the veil which obstructs our earthly vision? Who will answer? Must this question always remain hidden in the mystery of death?"

CHAPTER XXVI

A VISIT TO THE FAMOUS EDISON MUSEUM

Henry Ford, who reconstructed "Menlo Park" at Dearborn, greets Mr. Edison.

HENRY FORD, who has declared Edison to be "the greatest man in constructive achievement that the world has ever known," has laid the foundations for a *real* Edison "Valhalla" — the reconstruction of an American country village in the days when Edison was a boy, and the preservation of the famous laboratory where he began his work. The great industrialist has made an endowment of $5,000,000 for the preservation of old-time country life in America. This village is located at Greenfield, on the borders of Detroit — not far from where Edison lived and worked as a boy at Port Huron, when trying to read "all the books in the Detroit public library."

Ford discussed his plan with Edison and it met with the inventor's enthusiastic approval.

"That's a great idea," exclaimed Edison. "That's the true American 'Westminster Abbey' — a country village."

The Invalides of Napoleon, in Paris, or the palaces of Versailles and Fontainebleau, did not appeal to the American spirit of Edison. The country village met with his heart's desire. The rehabilitation of the little village of

Greenfield was one of the delights of his last years. The village occupies 200 acres at Dearborn, and is incorporated under the name of "The Edison Institute of Technology" — a school and a museum — under the laws of Michigan.

Here, in the setting of a country village, stands the edifice which holds the Edison Museum exhibits, with groups of buildings containing workshops, libraries, class-rooms, and an auditorium. And here again is a stroke of genius — these structures are architectural replicas of the historic Independence Hall, Congress Hall, and the old City Hall of Philadelphia. Near by is the old Rittenhouse Observatory of Philadelphia, and the old tool house used on George Washington's estate at Mount Vernon. The Edison Institute is "a museum which is really a living textbook of human and technical history."

The President and Edison Visit Historic Shrine

Thomas Edison lived to see this magnificent shrine erected. With President Hoover, Mrs. Hoover, and Mrs. Edison, the great inventor, at eighty-two years of age, went to Michigan to the dedication of this greatest of American memorials, on October 21, 1929, the fiftieth anniversary of Edison's invention of his electric light. The eulogies failed to impress him; President Hoover spoke eloquently of his great achievements, but Edison's mind wandered through the country roads of Greenfield village; he relived his boyhood and was supremely happy. There he saw his old laboratory at Menlo Park reconstructed exactly as it had been in the old days, with the same old historic mechanisms, chemical apparatus, and tools with which he had worked in his youth. He stood, with President Hoover and Mr. Ford, and "recreated the electric light" in the old laboratory on this anniversary.

Let us take a walk through the historic village of Greenfield today (the birthplace of Mrs. Henry Ford) and visit its quaint landmarks. Stroll through the old Colonial community, with its buildings arranged around the "commons," or "green," as we start on our visit to the reconstructed Menlo Park. Here is an old Colonial chapel, with its spire modeled after a church in Bradford, Massachusetts, and a bell cast by Paul Revere's son.

This is historic ground, where the pilgrim treads softly to sacred shrines. Here, before us, is the building in which the famous horticulturist, Luther Burbank, intimate friend of Edison and Ford, worked and studied on his experimental farm in Santa Rosa, California. It is a little structure but 14 by 20 feet, and in it we find original record books kept by the genius, Burbank. Now we come to the Edison Laboratory, which has been brought from Fort Myers in Florida, in which the inventor worked during his winter sojourns and perfected the wax record phonograph from its tin-foil predecessor. This quaint house, near by, is the old Sarah Jordan "Boarding House," from Menlo Park, New Jersey.

We enter the gate in the white picket fence and walk into the scenes of Thomas Edison's achievements during the years 1876 to 1886 — with the buildings reconstructed, or replicas erected exactly as they were on the historic ground back in New Jersey. Even the streets have been named after those at Menlo Park. Here is the old two-story brick library and office; here is the brickyard; and here is the two-story laboratory where the phonograph was invented, the electric light, the microphone, the telephone transmitter, and the hundreds of other inventions that made Edison the "Wizard of Menlo Park." Here, too, we meet Francis Jehl, of the "Edison Pioneers," who worked by his side during the invention of the light.

Step out of the historic laboratory into the carpenter shed where the woodwork, models, and old patterns were constructed. Near by stands the little "carbon shed," where the night watchman collected the soot from the kerosene lamps for the experiments of Edison on the telephone. The scenes are so accurately re-created that there is even a "pit" in the yard, where the broken material was thrown. The wild-cherry tree and elm were too old to transplant and new trees stand in their positions. This building in front of us is the old "Glass House," where the first successful lamp bulb was blown; and there is the old one-story brick Machine Shop, erected in 1878, the first central station for incandescent lighting in the world.

Here, too, are an historic inn, a log house, a blacksmith shop, an old Toll House shoe shop from Massachusetts, the courthouse where Lincoln practiced law, a carding mill of a century ago; and Smith's Creek depot (near Mt. Clemens), where Edison as a boy was put off the train.

This is the shrine which pilgrims will visit for generations to come — a greater memorial to Edison than the Pantheon. Students from all sections of the country will follow in his footsteps at the Edison Institute of Technology. Henry Ford, in immortalizing Edison and in "keeping alive the spirit of the village days in America when great men were born," has performed a service to his country which has no parallel in the world's landmarks. We linger here for a moment as an old record is placed on one of the first Edison phonographs. We stand reverently, and raise our hand in salute:

It is the voice of Edison speaking — from the record he left behind.

CHAPTER XXVII

ACHIEVEMENTS OF THOMAS EDISON—WHAT THE "EDISON PIONEERS" GAVE TO THE WORLD

The memorial boulder at Menlo Park, dedicated by Edison Pioneers

THE achievements of Thomas A. Edison — his accomplishments in invention, discovery, and science, in the release and control of new forces for the betterment of mankind, and in laying the foundations for great industries which were to increase the world's wealth, are probably greater than that of any one man in the world's history.

Exclusively for this memorial book, the leading statisticians of the country have worked out their estimates based on values existing at the time of Edison's death in 1931. These figures reach the stupendous sum of $25,683,544,343 — with gross revenues reaching nearly $7,000,000,000 every year — employing more than a million workers and paying wages exceeding a billion dollars a year. The tabulations are given at the end of this chapter.

How this was accomplished, with the loyalty of the men who surrounded him, is an epic story in itself.

Edison created the first organized laboratories, gathering about him skilled men in every phase of technological investigation — mathematicians, physicists, engineers, mechanics — and coördinating their efforts under his own masterful generalship.

A strong individualist and at all times in full control — his creative mind conceived and executed every invention — he was a supreme leader of men. To these men, he always gave the fullest measure of credit and they are known today throughout the world as the "Edison Pioneers." They worked at the side of the great inventor through the years, growing old with him, but retaining his spirit and enthusiasm. Edison never "let a man go because he was getting old."

Thus it is that around Edison there has been created the only organization of its kind in the world: "Edison Pioneers" — the men who worked with Edison in laying the foundations for this industrial empire valued at more than twenty-five billions of dollars. It is the only guild ever formed for the purpose of perpetuating the name of an inventor with whom men labored, and to bequeath the honor to their descendants in perpetuity.

The "Edison Pioneers" is an hereditary organization founded on the plan of the officers of General George Washington's staff at the close of the American Revolution and the establishment of the United States of America, when they formed the "Society of the Cincinnati," in 1783. When the first meeting for organization of the "Edison Pioneers" was held in New York, on January 24, 1918, there gathered men who had become famous throughout the world in the development of the New Age. Every one of them had worked with Edison during or before 1885.

This historic organization then provided for election of its officers, its management, and the preservation of historic records. Its members meet each year at the banquet table to "stand at attention in honor of the distinguished Thomas

A. Edison" — and so it will go on through the centuries, until descendants will consider it as great a distinction to bear 'the Legion of Honor of the "Edison Pioneers" as if their progenitors had been on the ship with Columbus in the Discovery of America — for Thomas Edison, too, discovered new worlds of conquest which forged human progress and remade civilization.

Wealth Created from Inventions, Nearly $26,000,000,000

Let us now survey the records of the statisticians setting forth the industrial wealth created by Edison with his "Edison Pioneers." Official figures of the Edison patents have been checked by his firm of patent attorneys from the records of thirty-one years and by the Patent Office at Washington for the purposes of accuracy in this book.

"All statements heretofore made are found to be inaccurate," is the official report. "It is apparent that errors have been made through duplication in books and records. The exact number of Edison patents granted in the United States is 1098 up to the time of his death, with one patent granted since his death which brings the total to 1099. The number of patent applications, designs, trade-marks, etc., bring the figures up in excess of 1,500. Foreign patents in thirty-four countries it is estimated will exceed this number as the same invention was patented in many countries. Edison's patents throughout the world for the sixty-four years from his first patent (large numbers of which have expired) probably reach somewhere around 3,000."

Thomas Edison. lived to see his incandescent electric light grow until 86,500,000 people in the United States (70 per cent of the population) were living in electrically lighted houses, with 644,421 American farms using electric current supplied by electric light and power companies.

His first power station had grown to 3,873 central plants furnishing power for 24,701,972 buildings in which occupants were using 19,600,000 electric irons, 17,313,000 radio sets,

7,360,000 clothes washers, 7,420,000 toasters, 5,750,000 fans, 5,750,000 percolators, 3,220,000 space heaters, 1,860,000 electric refrigerators, 880,000 electric ranges.

Edison witnessed the growth of the telephone from the time of his invention of the transmitter (in the development of Bell's invention) to 28,100,000,000 phone calls a year, over 34,526,629 telephones in the United States alone. He saw 127,779,255 miles of telephone wire in operation — enough to reach around the world more than five thousand times.

Edison saw the telegraph develop from the time of his invention of the quadruplex (developing Morse's invention) until it reached 235,000,000 telegraphic messages a year over 7,105,076 miles of wire in the United States. Wireless and radio messages were developing to large proportions.

From the first Edison motion-picture studio at Menlo Park, and the first nickleodeons as theaters, he saw this industry reach out to audiences of more than 12,000,000 people a day in over 21,000 theaters in the United States. These figures when developed on a world basis, with the tremendous growth of industries, based on nearly 3,000 patents in thirty-four countries and the United States, give us an estimate of the achievements of Thomas Edison.

THE MEN WHO STOOD BEHIND EDISON IN HIS LIFE WORK

Let us further record for posterity the names of the men who worked with Edison in laying the foundations for these stupendous enterprises, as recorded in the archives of the "Edison Pioneers":

"Four Principal Assistants of Thomas A. Edison
CHARLES BATCHELOR
Born at London, England, December 21, 1845
Died at New York City, January 1, 1910
JOHN KRUESI
Born at Heiden, Switzerland, May 15, 1843
Died at Schenectady, N. Y., February 22, 1899
FRANCIS R. UPTON
Born at Peabody, Mass., July 26, 1852
Died at E. Orange, N. J., March 10, 1921

EDWARD H. JOHNSON
Born at Malvern, Chester Co., Pa., January 4, 1846
Died at New York City, September 9, 1917"

DISTINGUISHED HONORARY MEMBERS OF "EDISON PIO-NEERS" — Members of the Edison family, with children and grandchildren:

THE PIONEER — THOMAS ALVA EDISON

Mrs. Thomas A. Edison (née Mina Miller), Edison's sons and daughters in the order of their birth: Mrs. Marion Edison Oser, Thomas A. Edison, II, William Leslie Edison, Charles Edison, Mrs. John E. Sloane (née Madelyn Edison), Theodore M. Edison, and the Edison grandchildren: John Edison Sloane, Thomas Edison Sloane, Peter Edison Sloane.

FOUNDERS OF THE "EDISON PIONEERS": Arthur S. Beves, Chas. A. Benton, Chas. S. Bradley, Wm. M. Brock, Wm. Carman, Philip S. Dyer, Geo. G. Grower, Wilson S. Howell, Edwin W. Hammer, Wm. J. Hammer, Alfred W. Kiddle, L. H. Latimer, Robt. T. Lozier, T. C. Martin, H. A. MacLean, Samuel D. Mott, F. D. Potter, Samuel L. Mitchell, Alex S. Campbell, Christian Rach, Fredk. A. Scheffler, F. S. Smithers, Francis R. Upton, Peter Weber, Schuyler S. Wheeler, Fremont Wilson, Frank A. Wardlaw, Sidney B. Paine.

EDISON'S COWORKERS — MEMBERS OF "EDISON PIO-NEERS" (associated with Thomas Edison on or before year 1885): Edw. G. Acheson, Edw. D. Adams, Daniel M. Althouse, Hugo Anderson, Wm. H. Atkins, Chas. G. Barfoot, Edw. A. Barnes, S. E. Bateman, C. A. Benton, Ernest J. Berggren, A. S. Beves, Frank Bourne, Wm. H. Brenner, Wm. M. Brock, T. J. Brown, Dennis Callahan, H. A. Campbell, Rob. A. Carter, Chas. L. Clarke, John Diehl, Wm. I. Donshea, H. M. Doubleday, D. E. Drake, John Dwyer, Chas. L. Edgar, Chas. L. Eidlitz, Chas. E. Estabrook, John C. Fagan, R. D. Fine, W. H. Francis, Wm. J. Hammer, Edwin W. Hammer, Wm. Hand, Matthew J. Hankins, E. A. Harley, Albert B. Herrick, David K. Hickman, J. Parker Hickman, John W. Howell, Wilson S. Howell, Samuel Insull, Chas. W. Jefferson, John J. Jeffries, Francis Jehl, Alfred W. Kiddle, Chas. G. Y. King, Arthur S. Knight, Philip A. Lang, Jos. Lee, Herman Lemp, Robt.

INVENTORY OF INDUSTRIES IN UNITED STATES DIRECTLY FOUNDED UPON OR AFFECTED BY INVENTIONS OF THOMAS A. EDISON

This Tabulation has been made exclusively for this book by the Statisticians of the Corporations from most accurate data obtainable at time of Thomas Edison's death — October 18, 1931.

Class of Industry	Investment	Annual Gross Revenue	Number of Employees	Annual Payrolls
Electric light and power (Oct. 31, 1931)	$12,500,000,000	$2,155,000,000	285,000	no data
Electric railways (Jan. 1, 1931)	4,700,000,000	980,000,000	....	no data
Telephone and telegraph (Jan. 1, 1931)	4,620,000,000	1,000,000,000 (approx.)	....	$486,597,070
Total number of employees for three utility groups, 1,092,000				
Electrical machinery, apparatus and supplies (Jan. 1, 1931)	2,150,000,000	1,925,000,000	329,361 (1929)	425,294,638
Phonographs (1919)	105,241,000	61,057,000 (1925)	23,000	19,000,000
Motion pictures (1928)	1,500,000,000	750,000,000	350,000	no data
Thomas A. Edison, Inc. (1930) — (incl. Portland cement)	13,853,000	21,000,000	5,000	no data
Typewriters (1926)	85,798,942	64,262,413	14,969	19,000,000
Dictaphones (1926)	1,706,000	....	......	no data
Mimeographs (1927)	6,945,401	....	......	no data
Stock tickers (included in telephone and telegraph.)				
Total	$25,683,544,343	$6,956,319,413	......	......

Sources of Data: N. E. L. A. Statistical Department; U. S. Census of Manufacturers; Poor's and Moody's *Manuals* —*Industrials, Utilities; Electrical World; Film Daily Year Book,* 1928; *World Almanac; Wall Street Journal.*

Lindsay, A. D. Lundy, James Lyman, Wm. H. Mackay, H. A. MacLean, Wm. D. MacQuesten, John F. McClain, Jos. F. McCoy, J. F. Madgett, Wm. H. Meadowcroft, Geo. F. Melick, James F. Middleton, Sidney Z. Mitchell, M. F. Moore, Geo. F. Morrison, Samuel D. Mott, Alex. Mungle, L. E. Myers, S. D. Nesmith, Edw. L. Nichols, E. C. Noe, John F. Ott, Fredk. P. Ott, S. B. Paine, Henry V. A. Parsell, Geo. Foster Peabody, Wm. Pelzer, Chas. F. Peterson, Eugene H. Philips, Jos. F. Porter, Fredk. D. Potter, Chas. R. Price, Christian Rach, Fredk. A. Scheffler, J. W. Schroeder, Jas. M. Seymour, Samuel J. Shaw, P. B. Shaw, Chas. A. Simmen, Thomas Spencer, Henry Stephenson, Chas. F. Stillwell, Alfred O. Tate, Montgomery Waddell, Frank A. Wardlaw, Edwin R. Weeks, Anton R. Westerdahl, Axel K. Westerdahl, Frank H. Whiting, Arthur Williams, Fremont Wilson.

ASSOCIATE "EDISON PIONEERS" (associated with Thomas Edison between years 1886–1900): Herbert F. Avery, Albert D. Babson, Geo. A. Baker, Henry Price Ball, H. L. Baltozer, Wm. Slocum Barstow, Theo. Beran, Jas. Birnholz, Jas. W. Bishop, Samuel A. Blan, Louis Denton Bliss, Warren H. Bogart, R. R. Bowker, Frank N. Boyer, Herbert N Brooks, Jas. Burke, Douglass Burnett, Daniel C. Campbell, Cloyd M. Chapman, Francis G. Daniell, David Darlington, Geo. V. Delaney, Wm. T. Dempsey, John T. H. Dempster, J. V. N. Dorr, Wm. F. Drees, J. W. Dunbar, Nelson C. Durand, Arnold Stuart Durrant, Frank L. Dyer, Harry Thomas Edgar, W. L. R. Emmet, H. F. T. Erben, Fred. W. Erickson, Frank L. Fenn, Henry Ford, John E. Franzen, E. W. Frazar, W. W. Freeman, E. E. Ganter, Chas. S. Gardner, N. M. Garland, Henry Geisenhöner, John F. Gilchrist, Philip G. Gossler, Chas. T. Gwynne, Chas. S. Hadaway, Robt. S. Hale, Howard W. Haskins, Chas. J. Hatch, Fred G. Havlin, Adolph Hertz, Wm. H. Hill, Chas. H. Hodskinson, A. L. Holme, Oren S. Hussey, Jos. Insull, Martin J. Insull, W. F. Irish, K. Iwadare, F. Moreton Jack, Fredk. W. Jesser, Walter H. Johnson, Oscar Junggren, P. Junkersfeld, Jos. J. Kennedy, A. E. Kennelly, Fred M. Kimball, Chas. F. King, Peter Kirsch, M. B. Kitt, A. F. Knight, Edw. H. Kocher, Paul J. Kruesi, Chas. R. Lehmann, Chas. W. Luhr, John MacHaffie, Augustus L. MacPadden,

Wm. M. Madigan, Walter S. Mallory, Edw. S. Mansfield, Chas. W. Marcley, Synan M. McGrath, J. P. McKeown, Mrs. M. H. Middelton, David Miller, Harry F. Miller, John V. Miller, Walter H. Miller, D. MacFarlan Moore, Brice E. Morrow, Irving E. Moultrop, Peter J. Mulvey, August P. Munning, H. Whiteway Nelson, W. J. Newton, Lars G. Nilson, John H. O'Brien, F. J. Odell, A. D. Page, Albert O. Petit, A. N. Pierman, Edwin Place, Herman Plaut, Albert Arthur Pope, Geo. C. Reilly, Henry B. Rogers, Rudolph Romeling, Harry C. Schlegel, T. G. Seixas, I. H. Silverman, Eugene A. Skehan, Elmer A. Sperry, Robt. L. Smith, Theo. Stebbins, Geo. F. Steel, Walter Stevens, Edw. A. Stevenson, F. M. Tait, August F. Tinnerholm, Ernest Van Duyne, Wm. J. Vega, Louis R. Wallis, Alfred K. Warren, Albert D. Watermann, J. Weber, Walter F. Wells, Samuel N. Whitehead, Samuel L. Whitestone, Carl H. Wilson, F. P. Wilson, Edw. E. Winters.

DESCENDANT MEMBERS OF "EDISON PIONEERS": Edw. G. Acheson, Jr., Kempton Adams, Mrs. T. C. Assheton, Fredk. D. Barstow, Miss E. E. Batchelor, Geo. E. Beves, W. J. Brown, Harry Stout Campbell, W. Henry L. Casho, Mrs. Naomi M. Chaffee, Mrs. M. R. Clifford, Mrs. F. E. Demarest, Robt. F. Dwyer, Leavitt L. Edgar, Chas. E. Estabrook, Jr., Mrs. H. D. Geisler, Philip Gossler, Jr., Wesley T. Hammer, Conrad Holloway, Miss S. M. Holzer, Mrs. W. R. Hoyt, Jr., W. R. Huntley, Samuel Insull, Jr., Wm. Insull, Barton M. P. Jones, Alfred M. Kiddle, Bernard A. Klein, Addis Edward Kocher, Walter Edison Kruesi, Adolph Wm. Lieb, Mrs. Robt. T. Lozier, Oliver B. Lyman, Kingsley Gould Martin, W. Myron Meadowcroft, Jas. A. Mungle, Alva Edison Ott, Sidney S. Paine, Mrs. Mae C. Peck, Clyde H. Porter, E. C. Rowland, Jr., Ralph Sargent, R. T. Tinnerholm, Miss Lucy Upton, Mrs. Shirlie McCarty Van Riper, Francis A. Wardlaw, Jr., Mrs. Allene W. Willson, Arthur B. Wilson, Herbert D. Winchester.

INTIMATE ASSOCIATES OF THOMAS EDISON (men who worked with the great inventor but passed away before the organization of the "Edison Pioneers," from records in archives of the organization): Pardon Armington, J. W. Alysworth, J. F. Bailey, Jas. H. Banker, Chas. Batchelor, Ludwig K.

Boehm, Wm. L. Breath, Chas. Burnham, W. Henry Burnett,
Theo. F. Carman, Chas. E. Chinnock, Edw. J. Clark, Wm. J.
Clark, Dr. Herman Claudius, Major Clowbridge, Prof. A.
Colombo, Thomas Conant, Chas. E. Coster, Eugene Crowell,
David Cunningham, Robt. L. Cutting, Robt. L. Cutting, Jr.,
Jas. DeWolf Cutting, Chas. Dean, Daniel Dodd, Thos. Dooling,
Richard N. Dyer, Major Sherburne B. Eaton, Samuel Edison,
Ernesto Fabbri, Chas. Flammer, Martin Force, Jas. M. Gallo-
way, Wm. Lloyd Garrison, Edw. T. Gilliland, Calvin Goddard,
Col. Geo. E. Gouraud, S. Dana Green, Norvin Green, Stockton
L. Griffin, Dr. A. Haid, Chas. F. Hannington, J. C. Henderson,
Geo. Hickman Hidden, Geo. Hill, Jas. Hipple, Col. W. Preston
Hix, Wm. Holzer, John Hood, Julius L. Hornig, Wm. Hortsek,
Chas. T. Hughes, Jas. S. Humbird, Francis Jackson, Edw. H.
Johnson, Patrick Kenny, N. S. Keith, Chas. J. Klein, John
Kruesi Lawrence, H. Ward Leonard, Eugene H. Lewis, Thomas
Logan, Grosvenor P. Lowrey, Alick G. MacAndrew, Jas. U.
MacKenzie, Jas. Mahoney, Arnold Marcus, Prof. Wm. D.
Marks, John T. Marshall, Frank McGowan McIntyre, Major
Frank McLaughlin, J. C. Melick Metzger, Wm. H. Moore,
J. Pierpont Morgan, A. W. Morton, Dr. Otto A. Moses, Chas.
Mott, Wm. D. Mottram, José F. de Navarro, Jos. P. Ord,
H. C. Patterson, Chas. T. Porter, M. Puskas, John F. Ran-
dolph, Dr. Emil Rathenau, Geo. F. Sandt, K. Sawai, F.
Saxelby, Sigmund Schuckert, John Seguadore, Miss Selden
(Mrs. McCall), Phillip Seubel, Chas. D. Shain, Alex. Shaw,
Gardiner C. Sims, Harrison J. Smith, Gustav Soldan, Geo. C.
Sonn, Wm. F. Sonn, Wm. A. Stern, W. N. Stewart, C. D.
Stickney, Wm. Stickney, Luther Stieringer, Alfred Swanson
Tracy (bookkeeper at 65 Fifth Avenue), Spencer Trask, Henry
Villard, G. W. Waters, August Weber, Alex. Welch, Thomas
C. Whittemore, J. Hood Wright.

While monuments and memorials will be erected to
Thomas A. Edison and he will eventually take his place
with distinguished Americans in the "Hall of Fame," the
"Edison Pioneers" will carry the records of his labors as
the "Benefactor of Mankind" down through the ages.

APPENDIX

EDISON SCHOLARSHIP AWARD—OFFICIAL EXAMINATIONS IN NATIONAL CONTESTS

The purpose of this Scholarship Contest is to stimulate the interest of the youth of America in mental development, with particular emphasis on scientific matters; and, more generally, in the high ideals that make for the finest types of American manhood.

THE Official Examination Papers in the National Contests for the Thomas A. Edison Scholarship Award are given historical record for the first time herewith. These original documents have been held in the Edison Historical Collection, but owing to the method of examination were considered "private papers." Fragmentary transcripts appeared in the public press, but heretofore the official questions, complete, have not been given public record. They are now released for the benefit of the school children throughout the country, as standard tests of general information and intelligence.

The Thomas A. Edison Scholarship Award was announced in 1929—a national contest in which the winners would be awarded scholarships in American institutions for the development of scientific knowledge. The spirit of American youth was aroused, and in every village and city the contest began. In the forty-eight states and the District of Columbia, candidates were chosen through competitive examination or on the basis of their school work.

The first Edison examination took place August 1, 1929. Forty-nine contestants were given the examination papers (on which space was left to write the answers).

Two hours and fifteen minutes were allowed to fill out the famous questionnaire. The examination papers were then returned to the Board of Judges — passed upon — and sealed in secret archives for a period of "ten years." This method was devised to protect the boys by not allowing the questions or their answers to become public.

The winner of the First Edison Award was Wilber B. Huston, of Seattle, Washington, a high-school student sixteen years of age; he scored 92 in the test. The contest was so close that additional scholarships were awarded to Ivan A. Getting, of Pittsburgh; James Seth, of Santa Fe, New Mexico; Bernard Sturgis, of Butler, Indiana. Huston received a four-year scholarship at the Massachusetts Institute of Technology, with all his expenses paid.

The Second Edison National Contest was held on July 31, 1930. The winner was Arthur O. Williams, Jr., of Providence, R. I., a seventeen-year-old boy who had just graduated from high school. During the summer he was a bank messenger and had worked every summer to earn money to enter Brown University. Young Williams is a direct descendant of Roger Williams in the early American Colonies. He was given a four-year scholarship "at any college," but chose the Massachusetts Institute of Technology, where he joined Wilber Huston the first Edison winner.

The examinations were divided into parts, with the technical questions appearing first, but for general service with the public-at-large, we have organized the examinations of both years into two groups: "Intelligence Tests," followed by "The Scientific Examinations:"

GENERAL INTELLIGENCE TEST — FIRST EDISON EXAMINATION

1. Outside of the field of religion, what three men, not now living, do you think particularly deserve your respect and admiration? What qualities do you admire in each?
2. What do you consider four of the most important qualifications necessary to success in any pursuit?
3. Which classes of books listed below do you most enjoy reading? Number them 1, 2, 3, et cetera, in the order of preference: Adventure — Biography — History — Mystery Stories — Fiction — Economics — Travel — Invention — Science.
4. If you could only read regularly four periodical publications (any kind), which four would you choose?

5. If you were marooned alone on a tropical island in the South Pacific, without tools, how would you move a three-ton weight, such as a boulder, 100 feet horizontally and 15 feet vertically?

6. If you had been given a certain experiment to perform and had been informed that it could be done successfully, but you had failed ten times, what would you do?

7. What new discovery or invention do you believe would be the greatest benefit to mankind? Why?

8. If you were to inherit $1,000,000 within the next year, what would you do with it?

9. What place in our daily lives do you think the automobile will have one hundred years from now?

10. If some acquaintance of yours unfairly accused you of cheating, what would you do?

11. What, if anything, does music mean to you beyond the usual reaction which most persons have to rhythm and melody?

12. When do you consider a lie permissible?

13. Two towns, on opposite sides of a river one mile wide, are cut off from communication with each other by any electrical means, due to a calamity. How would you attempt to establish communication between the two cities without the use of electricity? The river cannot be crossed by human beings.

14. Which one of the following would you be willing to sacrifice for the sake of being successful? Happiness — Comfort — Reputation — Pride — Honor — Health — Money — Love.

15. If there is a boy at your school whom you consider to be superior to you in intelligence and character, please write his name and address down here.

16. If you were on the verge of an important discovery and found the one missing link in another worker's laboratory, what would you do? Why?

17. Is the present relation of capital to labor reasonably fair?

18. Will you act as spokesman for the candidates when we meet Mayor Walker in New York City or would you prefer to let someone else do it? Why?

19. Why do you think you were chosen to represent your State in this competition?

20. Give a brief statement of what you hope will be a typical day for you when you are fifty years of age.

21. Assuming that you have just graduated from high school and are anxious to land a job — write a letter such as you would send to the chief engineer or to the president of the concern with which you would like to become connected. Assume that this letter is the only means open to you of securing the desired employment.

22. What are the principal United States cities on the Atlantic Coast?

23. Who invented the cotton gin?

24. What did James Watt do?

25. Who wrote Treasure Island?

26. (a) Of what elements is common salt composed?
    (b) What is the principal salt producing locality in the United States?

27. Why does this country honor Admiral Farragut?

28. What three very low forms of life can you name?

29. What is a mammoth?

30. Who was Jenny Lind?

31. What is a tourniquet?

32. (a) At what point on the Fahrenheit thermometer does water boil?
    (b) On the Centigrade thermometer?

33. On what physiological phenomenon is the success of motion-picture projection dependent?

34. What is a meteor?

35. Name the use of the following: Galvanometer — Vernier — Oscillograph — Pantograph — Micrometer — Pyrometer.

36. What is the underlying principle of an internal combustion engine?

37. What is the function of the antenna in Radio?
38. What, in your opinion, should be done to improve the airplane?
39. Do invention and industry promote international agreement?

(NOTE.—Science Examination of 1929 is given under classification following record of Intelligence Tests.)

GENERAL INTELLIGENCE TEST — SECOND EDISON EXAMINATION

These are the Questions asked in the 1930 National Competition for Edison Scholarships.

1. If you owned the following items, set down the approximate price in dollars and cents for which you would sell them, and the sort of purchaser you would select:
   (a) Ford coupe which has run 5000 miles.
   (b) Basic patent which will reduce cost of manufacturing shoes twenty cents a pair.
   (c) Secret process of manufacturing a drug which will definitely cure cancer.
   (d) Ten acres of land in a good farming section of Iowa.
   (e) Trade information which will enable one competitive firm to take $1,000,000 worth of net profits a year away from another.
   (f) The secret of a new poison gas which will make any nation supreme in war.
   (g) Definite proof that the dishonesty of an employee is costing a multimillionaire $200,000 a year.
2. When you look back on your life from your deathbed, by what facts will you determine whether you have succeeded or failed?
3. What qualifications do you think a man should have to be on the Board of Judges of the Edison Scholarship?
4. You are the head of an expedition which has come to grief in the desert. There is enough food and water left to enable three people to get to the nearest outpost of civilization. The rest must perish. Your companions are:
   1. A brilliant scientist 60 years old.
   2. Two half-breed guides, ages 58 and 32.
   3. The scientist's wife — interested mainly in society matters — age 39.
   4. Her little son, age 6.
   5. The girl you are engaged to marry.
   6. Your best friend, a young man of your own age who has shown great promise in the field of science.
   7. Yourself.
   Which would you choose to live and which to die? Give your reasons.
5. In the year 1900 how would you have gotten the first cable of a suspension bridge across an impassable gorge ½ mile wide?
6. If you could prescribe and enforce a system of education for the whole population of the world, on what essentials would you place the greatest emphasis?
7. If you had a brother who wanted to be an artist or a poet, would you encourage him or attempt to dissuade him? Why?
8. Assuming it were an engineering and financial possibility, and you were given the opportunity of devoting twenty years of your life to be in sole charge of digging a hole thirty miles into the earth's interior, would you accept it or turn it down? Give your reasons.
9. Suppose your best friend came to you and admitted regretfully that he had deliberately wrecked your chances of winning the Edison Scholarship by writing a letter designed to hurt your standing with the Judges; what would you do?
10. Briefly state how you think Communistic propaganda should be dealt with.
11. Answer the following letter:

Office of the Dean,
XYZ University.
DEAR MR. ———
    A visiting professor has made a study of Manchurian life and manners. He has volunteered to give three lectures on Manchurian cooking.
    Before advising the professor whether or not the university would sponsor such a course of lectures I desire to get the reaction of the student body. Please write me frankly.

JOHN ADAMS,
Dean.

12. (a) Briefly identify the following: Jane Addams — Leonardo da Vinci — Charlemagne — John Ericsson — John Hay — Colonel T. H. Lawrence — Pasteur — Marco Polo — Phidias — Tamerlane.
    (b) Give the approximate dates of the following: Fall of Troy — Battle of Gettysburg — First successful aëroplane flight — Solomon — Birth of the earth — Michelangelo — Discovery of America by Europeans — Formation of the League of Nations — Pithecanthropus erectus — Norman conquest of England.
13. (a) Name the planets in the solar system.
    (b) What is a light year?
    (c) What causes the seasons of the year?
    (d) Name 4 anthropoid (manlike) apes.
    (e) What is the function of leucocytes?
    (f) What are chromosomes?
    (g) How is the bubonic plague transmitted?
14. (a) What did Lewis and Clark do?
    (b) How many great civilizations can you name which flourished before the year one, A.D.?
    (c) What races have invaded the British Isles?
    (d) What was the Holy Roman Empire?
15. (a) In what countries are the following located: Taj Mahal — Johannesburg — Mandalay — Lake Titicaca — Monte Carlo — Oslo — Khyber Pass — Danzig?
    (b) What authors created the following characters: Tom Sawyer — Desdemona — Mulvaney — Dauber — Nicholas Nickleby — D'Artagnan?
    (c) Who were: Thor — Apollo — Tristram — Siegfried — Oberon — Robin Hood?
16. (a) From what source or sources are the following commodities derived: Aluminum — Ambergris — Asbestos — Bakelite — Brass — Chocolate — Felt— Glass — Rayon — Turpentine?
    (b) Name the five largest cities in the United States.
    (c) What connection has salt with the present revolutionary movement in India?
    (d) Who are: Joseph Stalin — Aristide Briand — Primo de Rivera?
    (e) What was the purpose of the recent international conference in London?

FIRST SCIENCE EXAMINATION IN EDISON NATIONAL TEST

These Questions in Chemistry, Mathematics, and Physics are from the Examination Papers of 1929.

PHYSICS — ANSWER FIVE QUESTIONS

1. Define Work, Energy, and Power, and give an illustration of each. How does weight differ from mass? How does force differ from energy? Would a body weigh more or less on the moon than on the earth? Why? Where would bodies weigh nothing?

2. The specific heat of water is 1.0 and of mercury 0.033; the specific gravity of water is 1.0 and of mercury 13.6. For a foot warmer state which you would choose and why — a two-quart hot-water bottle filled with water at 100° C. or a two-quart flask of mercury at 100° C.

3. The specific resistance of an alloy is four times as great as that of copper. A copper wire 1000 feet long has the resistance of 40 ohms. How long a wire of the alloy having the same diameter as the copper wire would have the same resistance as the copper wire? Compared to the diameter of the copper wire what diameter of alloy 1000 feet long would have the same resistance as the copper wire?

4. The index of refraction of a glass is 1.5 and of another glass 1.7. If a biconvex lens of the same geometrical design was made of each of the two glasses, how would they differ optically? If they were placed in a transparent liquid of index of refraction 1.6 what effect would each have on a beam of light parallel to its principal axis?

5. The captain of a boat when passing a certain cliff on a summer night heard the echo of his whistle four seconds after blowing. How far away was the cliff? If he repeated this observation from the same point on a day in January would he notice any change in the time? If so, what and why?

6. The volume of an automobile tire is approximately 900 cubic inches and it is pumped up to a gage pressure of 60 pounds per square inch. Its temperature is 20° C. Left in the sun its temperature increased to 35° C., and it exploded. What was the volume of the expanded air directly after the explosion? Could the pressure just prior to the explosion be computed from the above data?

CHEMISTRY — ANSWER FIVE QUESTIONS

1. When you read the names of the following persons, what fact is immediately associated with them in your mind? Answer in one or two words in each case. Mendeleef — Davy — Perkin — Faraday — Curie — Priestley — Gay-Lussac — Dalton — Solvay — Ramsay — Lavoisier.

2. How would you prepare and collect in a reasonably pure state the following gases: (a) Nitrogen, (b) Ammonia, (c) Chlorine?

3. A set of bottles was known to contain the following powdered substances: Blue vitriol, ultramarine, manganese dioxide, carbon, potassium chloride and potassium chlorate, but the labels on the bottles have been destroyed. What tests would you apply, mental as well as physical, which would enable you to correctly and quickly relabel the bottles?

4. If you were nailing a copper sheathing on an exposed surface, what kind of nails would you use, and why?

5. Steel producing companies often have large quantities of ammonium sulphate for sale. How does the production of this substance happen to be connected with the iron industry?

6. Balance the following equation by inserting the proper coefficients:

$$AgNO_3 + Na2HPO_4 \longrightarrow Ag_3PO_4 + NaNO_3 + HNO_3.$$

MATHEMATICS — ANSWER FIVE QUESTIONS

1. Simplify: $\dfrac{1}{\dfrac{\sqrt{x+1}-1}{\sqrt{x+1}+1}} \left[\dfrac{(\sqrt{x+1}+1)\frac{1}{2}(x+1)^{-\frac{1}{2}} - (\sqrt{x+1}-1)\frac{1}{2}(x+1)^{-\frac{1}{2}}}{(\sqrt{x+1}+1)^2} \right]$

2. Solve: $\begin{cases} x^2 + y^2 = 8 \\ xy = 4 \end{cases}$

3. Assume the increase in any colony of mice to be such that the number doubles every three months. How large will the colony be at the end of three years if we start with a pair?

4. The acceleration of a body outside the surface of the earth is known to be inversely proportional to the square of the distance from the center of the earth. At the surface of the earth the acceleration is 32. What will the acceleration be fifty miles above the surface? The radius of the earth is 4000 miles. (Write answer in form of equation but need not simplify results).

5. Without expanding, write the term containing x^{11} in the expansion of $(\sqrt{x} - 2\,x)^{18}$.

6. A triangle each of whose sides is 6 is divided into three equal areas by drawing two lines parallel to the base. Where will these lines intersect the altitude?

SECOND SCIENCE EXAMINATION IN EDISON NATIONAL TEST

These Questions were asked in the Examination of 1930.

CHEMISTRY — ANSWER FIVE QUESTIONS

1. What container would you select for storing each of the following substances? State what special precautions should be observed in each case: (a) Sodium, (b) White phosphorus, (c) Hydrogen, (d) Hydrogen peroxide, (e) Hydrofluoric acid.

2. State Avogadro's hypothesis and show how it is used by Chemists in the determination of molecular weights.

3. Mention by name and formula the substances required for a laboratory preparation of each of the following: (a) Nitric acid, (b) Ammonia, (c) Chlorine. Describe briefly the procedure in the laboratory preparation and collection of *one* of the foregoing substances.

4. (a) When MnO_2 is heated strongly it evolves oxygen, forming Mn_3O_4. Write a balanced equation for the change.
   (b) and (c). Why is alcohol used in the radiator of an automobile in winter? Which is more effective, a pound of alcohol, C_2H_5OH, or a pound of sugar $C_{12}H_{22}O_{11}$? Why?

5. Suggest a method which might be used for producing pure silver from a silver coin.

6. Make a brief statement defining the meaning of each of the following terms: (a) Combining weight, (b) Density, (c) Atom, (d) Heat of reaction, (e) Valence.

MATHEMATICS — ANSWER FIVE QUESTIONS

1. Solve and check by a graph,
$$xy = 9$$
$$3\,x - 4\,y = 12$$

2. (a) An elastic ball bounces to ¾ of the height from which it falls. If it is thrown up from the ground to a height of 15 feet, find the total distance traveled before it comes to rest.
   (b) Find the fourth term in the expansion of $(x\sqrt{2} - \sqrt[3]{3})^6$.

3. A man has two solutions of a certain chemical in water, one containing 50 per cent of the chemical by weight and the other 10 per cent. He wishes to obtain 80 grams of solution containing 25 per cent of the chemical. How much should he take of each of the solutions he has?

4. The base of a pyramid is a square each side of which is 12 inches, each of the other four edges is 20 inches. Find the altitude and the volume of the pyramid.

5. (a) A triangle is divided into three parts by lines drawn parallel to the base and trisecting the altitude. Find the ratio of the area of each part to the area of the triangle.
   (b) From a point P at a distance of 4 feet from the center of a circle of radius 2 feet, tangents are drawn. Find the area bounded by the tangent lines and the convex portion of the circle. (The result need not be simplified.)

6. (a) Simplify: $(r^{\frac{1}{3}} + s^{\frac{1}{3}})(r^{\frac{2}{3}} - r^{\frac{1}{3}}s^{\frac{1}{3}} + s^{\frac{2}{3}})$

(b) and (c) A, B or C could complete a piece of work in 10, 12, or 14 days, respectively, working alone. They work on the task together for two days when A stops and at the end of the third day B stops. How long will it take C to finish?

PHYSICS — ANSWER FIVE QUESTIONS

1. (a) Why is the energy of a rifle bullet greater than that of the gun from which it is fired?
   (b) Under what conditions may a force act continuously on a moving body and still do no work?
   (c) Distinguish clearly between work and power.
   (d) Explain how the water line of a boat would be affected if its lead keel were taken off the outside and placed inside the boat.

2. Two wires, having a resistance of 2 and 4 ohms, respectively, are connected in parallel across the terminals of a 6 volt battery having an internal resistance of $\frac{1}{6}$ ohm.
   (a) What is the current through the battery?
   (b) What is the potential difference between the battery terminals?
   (c) At what rate is energy being dissipated by the 4 ohm wire? (Give answer in watts).

3. (a) Why does a magnifying glass of short focus give greater magnification than one of longer focus?
   (b) Why is greater magnification obtained in a telescope whose objective lens has a focus of 2 feet than in one with an objective of 1 foot focus?

4. (a) What is the difference between noise and musical sounds?
   (b) If a church organ is not provided with some sort of heating arrangement it will play out of tune when the church is cold. Explain.
   (c) What is the smallest height mirror standing vertically in which a man 6 feet tall and standing erect can see his entire length?

5. (a) Define coefficient of friction; dyne; microfarad.
   (b) Aluminum is claimed to be a very superior substance for cooking utensils. What are the physical properties which are in favor of or against such use?

6. (a) What is heat?
   (b) What is meant by absolute zero?
   (c) Define coefficient of expansion.
   (d) If a hole in a metal plate is 3 inches in diameter at a temperature of 20° C., what will be its diameter at a temperature of 30° C., if the linear coefficient of expansion of the metal is 0.00001?

This Self-Examination is now bequeathed to the youth of the world for generations to come. It stands as a standard test devised by Thomas A. Edison to ascertain the general qualifications of the young men of America for self-development and future service to humanity. Thomas Edison stands as one of the great characters and personalities in the world's history — a self-educated man who mastered great domains of human knowledge and became the "Benefactor of Mankind."

INDEX